FAIR & SQUARE

FAIR & SQUARE

A Collection of Stories
From a
Lifetime Among Friends

BY

JOHN BURTON TIGRETT

SPIRIDON PRESS, INC.
NASHVILLE, TENNESSEE

Published in Nashville, Tennessee,
by Spiridon Press, Inc.

Publisher's Cataloging-in-Publication
(Provided by Quality Books, Inc.)

Tigrett, John Burton
    Fair & square : a collection of stories from a lifetime among friends / by John
    Burton Tigrett. -- 1st ed.
    p. cm.
    ISBN: 1-889709-03-4

    1. Tigrett, John Burton. 2. Financial planners--Biography. 3. Investment
    advisors--Biography.   I. Title. II. Title: Fair and square

HG172.T54A3 1998   332'.092 [B]
                                    QBI97-41299

Editor and Publisher: Randall Bedwell
Contributing Writer: Robert Kerr
Managing Editor: Carol Boker
Contributing Editors: Palmer Jones, Trent Booker, Beverly Cruthirds

Jacket Design: Pat Patterson, Patterson Graham Design
Page Layout and Design: Beverly Cruthirds, Cruthirds Design

published in the United States by

Spiridon Press, Inc.
Post Office Box 120969
Nashville, Tennessee 37212

First Edition
10 9 8 7 6 5 4 3 2 1

For my precious Pat,
whose encouragement created this book

Table of Contents

PART TWO: THE INTERNATIONAL CITIZEN

Chapter IV: Postwar Adventures

Chapter V: Fun and Games

Chapter VI: A Few Good Con Men

Preface

BY ROBERT KERR

TAKING A RIDE ON THE TIGRETT EXPRESS

This book is a collection of stories of the experiences of one man — John Tigrett. I first met him in Memphis in the spring of 1992. I was writing a newspaper feature on Car 50, the historic private railroad coach that once belonged to John's uncle, Isaac Tigrett, head of the Gulf, Mobile & Ohio Railroad for some four decades until his death in 1954.

Car 50 had been lost for many years but then tracked down and restored by John's son, Isaac, founder of the Hard Rock Cafe. Instead of flying, Isaac used the beautifully appointed railroad car whenever possible as a more comfortable way to travel around the country. At the time, he was just launching plans for his House of Blues clubs.

Though we were born with the same last name, John's wife, the famous designer Pat Kerr, and I are of no known relation. But from the time I moved to Memphis in 1990, she has treated me like a long-lost cousin. More than once, when I was assigned stories involving fashion and society, Pat provided me with invaluable assistance and saved me from exposing, in print, my ignorance on such topics.

On the Car 50 story, Pat helped me arrange the interviews with Isaac and John. Isaac was visiting Memphis that day and had Car 50 parked overnight on a rail siding in front of John and Pat's downtown penthouse. John, Isaac and Augusta (Isaac's daughter, then 5) spent the afternoon showing me and a photographer around the elaborately refurbished 83-foot home on wheels.

After that, whenever I would see John around town, he would always visit with me amiably and leisurely. Most businessmen anywhere near his rank talk to reporters only when they need something from them. John seemed to just like being friendly and talking, often about writing.

On one of those occasions, he told me a story (which is included in this book) about how *Saturday Evening Post* Editor Ben Hibbs once explained to him the "Gypsy Rose Lee Theory" of writing. At the time, however, John told me he had experienced little success in his efforts as a writer. Only later did I learn he earned more from his freelance magazine articles in the 1940s than do most writers working today.

That modesty is characteristic of John. Why else would he wait until he reached his 80s to publish an account of his ventures and adventures—when practically any decade of his life could provide more than enough material to justify a book of its own.

John is not only a man who has walked with kings, but he has also horse-traded with them. He learned the art of diplomacy and negotiation early in life and made those skills the work of his life.

When we first sat down to talk about his book, I referred to it as his autobiography. He replied, "Oh, it's not an autobiography. It's just a hundred or so stories of mine. If that's not enough, I'll give you a hundred more."

In some of the sessions that followed, he did just that. The result is this book—the best of John's endless stories. Together they form an up-close portrait of a remarkable life.

Readers will discover the lessons John learned from a loving mother, who taught him to greet every new day as the opportunity of a lifetime. How, without ever finishing college, he taught himself to become a successful investment banker based in Jackson, Tennessee, in the heart of the Great Depression. How he made his way around the globe in World War II, personally encountering practically every major figure of the war—Sir Winston Churchill, General Dwight Eisenhower, General Douglas MacArthur, Secretary of the Navy James Forrestal and General George Marshall, to name a few—along the way. How he came home and immediately set about putting together the American Trailways national bus network, then switched to the toy business, in which he made a small fortune and attracted the national spotlight with such gadgets as the Drinking Duck and the Yogi Bird.

In the 1960s, John responded to crushing family tragedy by leaving Tennessee to build a new life in Europe. Starting over from scratch, he went on to work a mind-boggling string of deals worth millions and often billions of dollars with the likes of Sir James Goldsmith, Armand Hammer, Lord Roy Thomson, J. Paul Getty and Bunker Hunt.

At the same time, John began his determined courtship of Pat. A few years after their marriage and the birth of their son, Kerr, she launched Pat Kerr, Inc., a lace fashion house. By picking up the phone and calling a buyer at Neiman-Marcus, she launched a career as one of the top designers in the world.

The first Hard Rock Cafe was born in a converted Rolls-Royce show-room on London's Hyde Park Corner in the mid-1970s. John tells the inside story of how Isaac parlayed a youthful hunch into a fabulously successful global enterprise, and how Isaac has since followed an intuitive, spiritual quest into other earth-shaking ventures.

The saga of John Tigrett and his remarkable clan includes such a dizzying array of the famous faces and places of the 20th century that some readers may even mistake it for a novel. But every word is true.

Just consider it a literary version of Private Car 50. The "whistle" is blowing and it's "All Aboard." Climb on and enjoy a fabulous ride with John, the Tigretts and their unforgettable collection of friends.

PART ONE:

The Self-Taught
Entrepreneur

Part One

In Part One of this collection of stories, we see how the young John Tigrett learns to meet challenges very early in life. When his father leaves the child and his mother on their own two years after John is born, they go to live at an orphanage in Jackson, Mississippi. "A born survivor," his mother, Anita, looks after the children by day and attends nursing school at night. And John learns more survival skills in seven years of living in an orphanage than most people learn in a lifetime.

"My mother was a woman who had to make her own way in times that were not very easy for a career woman," John writes. "She had a special way of showing her kindness and love, and I am indebted to her for not only giving me life, but also for blessing me with the ability to live a life full of great happiness and love."

Later, Anita goes to work as the public-health nurse for Bolivar County in the heart of the Mississippi Delta and its grand cotton plantations. There, John begins to grasp the forces of nature and economics that shape planter society, narrowly escapes with his life in the great Mississippi River Flood of 1927, and helps a mother-to-be trapped by the floodwaters bring her child into the world.

When John goes to live with his Uncle Isaac and Aunt Mary in Jackson, Tennessee, during the school year, his social skills are sharpened by "two of the greatest charmers the South has ever produced . . . . Whatever good qualities I have that I didn't inherit from my mother came from living with them. They were the guiding force for a great part of my formative life," John reflects.

Isaac B. Tigrett was one of America's great railroad men, building the

Gulf, Mobile and Ohio into more than 3,000 miles of line spanning the South and Midwest. It is in downtown Jackson that John begins developing his entrepreneurial skills every Saturday morning by selling *Saturday Evening Post* magazines and coconut candy made by a friend of his grandmother. He learns how to sell a product that has plenty of repeat customers (the magazines)—and a product that doesn't (the candy). Both lessons will serve him well in the years to come.

Becoming a young man, John discovers the grown-up delights of Memphis, Tennessee, particularly those to be found at the Peabody Hotel in the golden age of the big bands. At 18, he experiences the ways of the world by shipping off to Europe as a seaman on a tramp steamer.

Returning home, John tries college, but the devastation of the Great Depression motivates him to get out and earn his own living. "I realized that it all involved money and credit. If I could find some way to strike a compromise between financially estranged parties, that would be a service . . . there were so many debtors who couldn't meet their payments and so many creditors who weren't being paid, that they would have to get together on some new basis . . . . It was a very rough and uneducated idea, but to me it made practical sense."

On that gut instinct, John starts his Tennessee Securities Company, then begins picking the brains of county clerks and small-town bankers until he tracks down a situation that offers the perfect opportunity to test his hunch: the Hatchie Bottom Drainage District Number 1. Moving quickly and quietly, he brokers a deal with the district's bondholders that breaks a stalemate and earns John $50,000—more cash than almost anyone in Jackson. A master financier and dealmaker is on his way.

A few years later, World War II interrupts John's thriving business and life with his young family, but introduces him to some of the most powerful men and most beautiful women in the world. As he seems to do everywhere he goes, John refuses to be a pawn of fate, even with the world turned upside down by the most sweeping war in history.

— ROBERT KERR

1

Early Years

THE BEGINNING

S hed no tears for orphans. An orphans home is a great place to start life. I personally recommend it.

The children in an orphanage have a standing start over any child in an average home. Disciplined with love and dealing with the competitions of life from day one, orphans learn how to meet challenges at a very early and formative age. In a typical American home, a child is well-protected until he is 16. By that time, any orphan can run rings around him.

My mother, Anita Massengill, of Henderson, Tennessee, was a beautiful Southern belle who had just graduated from the Mississippi State College for Women when she was swept off her feet by Augustus "Gus" King Tigrett of Jackson, Tennessee. He was a recent graduate of Harvard University—in fact, the *only* graduate of Harvard in West Tennessee at the time. Exceptionally handsome, he wore stiff, three-inch collars and acted, as you might expect, like the only Harvard graduate in the area.

Anita and Gus were married in the summer of 1912 and moved into a small house in Jackson. He managed Southern Seating Company, which made church pews. It was an appropriate calling for the son of a "circuit rider," the late Samuel King Tigrett, who had served as pastor of

Augustus King Tigrett

three small Baptist churches—Friendship, Maury Junction and Tigrett. He rode horseback between the churches each week and, at his passing, left his two sons Isaac and Augustus the strong heritage of having been "a man among men."

I was born on September 29, 1913, at 127 Division Street in Jackson. About two years later, in Monteagle, Tennessee, where my family had rented a small vacation home, Gus told Anita that he was leaving her. From that moment on, as far as I was ever able to determine, he never gave her a penny. In spite of him leaving her stranded, however, my mother never spoke one ill word of him or uttered a single criticism of my father. In this, she gave me my first important lesson: Always keep a good heart.

Anita—who was called "Nita" by most everyone who knew her—was, in many ways, typical of Southern women of the time; she had been protected from birth to maturity by her parents, the church and the society of that era. Suddenly, though, she was left on her own with a 2-year-old boy and not even enough money to close the little vacation house and get us back home.

John Burton with his mother, Anita Massengill Tigrett

However, Anita—strikingly beautiful, of limitless charm, forever friendly and helpful to everyone—was also a born survivor. She made it back to Jackson and started looking for work. A friend from college worked as head supervisor at the Baptist Orphans Home in Jackson, Mississippi. Within two weeks Anita was placed in charge of more than 40 children there, including me. She went to nursing school three nights a week, training to become a public-health nurse.

I can remember nothing from our seven years in that orphans home but happiness. Everyone was equal. We had wonderful things to play with—marbles, tin cans, rocks and sticks. We turned cardboard boxes into palaces. And the place was run with a kind discipline we understood and loved.

The "home" was a simple, two-story brick building on the outskirts of town. Boys slept in one dormitory, girls in the other, with the supervisors' rooms and the nursery between.

We were up every weekday morning at 6 a.m., took our baths, had breakfast and were ready for school by 7 a.m. Children under age 5 were taught in a make-shift kindergarten next to the nursery. Above age 5, we walked more than two miles to the public school. We all wore second-hand clothing that had been donated by members of the various Baptist churches. I was particularly proud of a bright-yellow jacket with worn-out elbows that my mother had sewn together with purple thread. You could see me coming a mile away.

Several of the larger boys at school who came from regular homes always made fun of the way we were dressed. After school one day, all the orphans, led by a 12-year-old, took them on. At 8, I was in my first wrestling, kicking fistfight. We licked the bullies good, and thereafter very few remarks were ever made about us.

Though I realize you can't go back, I look around today and know that less is more. In my son's closets today are box upon box of everything from G.I. Joe's Complete War Equipment to the latest Sony personal recorder and computer—all assembled for him. He never experienced the kind of thrill and pride I had one Christmas when Mother gave me my first "aggie" marble, so beautifully round with hundreds of reflections in the sunlight. I was the envy of every orphan. I kept it in a soft little pouch and carefully placed it under my pillow every night.

At the ripe age of 6, I definitely saw Santa Claus. I saw him clearly as he landed on our roof with his well-packed sleigh and eight reindeer. I saw him get out for a moment, put some packages down the chimney and then with a mighty "Ho, Ho, Ho," quickly take off into the beautiful moonlit night. Sometimes, even now, if the moonlight is just right on Christmas Eve, I think I can still see this wonderful little man busy at his happy work.

John Burton in 1921
"Is it not a thing Divine to have a smile which none knows how has the power
to lighten the weight of that enormous chain which all the living in common
drag behind them." — Victor Hugo

THE MISSISSIPPI DELTA

After graduation from nursing school, my mother secured a position as the public-health nurse for Bolivar County in Cleveland, Mississippi. She took a room for us at the home of Watt Bishop, the deputy sheriff, and we started a new life together. I was 10 years old.

In 1923, the Mississippi Delta was like no other world that ever existed. Life was a great roll of the dice for Mississippi plantation owners. They had to fight for favorable market prices for their cotton while battling the weather, the boll weevils, brown leaf and the many new crop diseases that came along each year to test them. They were entirely dependent upon black workers to tend the crops and, with very few exceptions, treated them as family. The soil, the crops, the insects and the vagaries of the weather served to bind them and make them one.

Cleveland lies in the heart of the Mississippi Delta, situated between Rosedale, Greenville and Clarksdale. All of the big plantations were within 50 miles of Cleveland. If prices were favorable and the crop plentiful, the planters, their friends and their families would celebrate endlessly. Cadillacs would roar down the gravel and dirt roads, and driving a hundred miles for a date with a "Delta Queen" was routine. It was a fantastic time, and I couldn't wait to grow up.

I had just turned 12 when my Uncle Isaac came to Cleveland to visit us. He had been upset by my father's treatment of Anita, and he came to offer to take me to Jackson, Tennessee, to live with him, Aunt Mary, and my grandmother, "Mammy," during the school year. The summer and holidays I would spend in Cleveland. My mother cried for a week before she decided what was best for me and finally put me on the Yazoo and Mississippi Valley train bound for Memphis. I spent many long nights crying myself to sleep waiting to spend holidays in the Delta with her.

John Burton, the Volunteer

SUMMERTIME, SUMMERTIME

Summer in the Delta with my mother was pure heaven. She was always planning picnics or having friends like Watt Bishop or Lena Sillers take me fishing. Mother was great at making light doughnuts, and she let me shake on the powdered sugar. She also made a fabulous chocolate filling, which she put between two vanilla wafers. I can still taste them.

I was 13 when I had my first real love affair. It was with an older woman—a beautiful blonde named Pearl White. We met every Saturday at 11 a.m. in the Plaza Theater. I paid my dime and sat on the edge of a front-row seat nervously watching the silver screen as my love escaped from every disaster known to man. What a life! What a love affair! I could hardly wait for the next Saturday.

When the show was over, I would head for the public-health office on the second floor of a small brick building opposite the Bolivar County courthouse. It had a room with a barber's chair in the center and a big light hanging down from overhead. Here, my mother helped Doctor Dedwilder remove the infected tonsils from black plantation workers. Following this operation, the patients recuperated for a few hours on one of the cots in a back storeroom where three electric fans stirred up the unbearably hot air. My responsibility in the operation was to run across the Y&MV railroad tracks to Williams' Drug Store every hour or so for ice cream to help soothe the patients' throats. I always had to race back as fast as I could to get the ice cream to the patients before it melted.

On Fridays, my mother and I traveled out to the plantations to inoculate the black workers against typhoid fever. Our "clinics" were usually held in a country store or a church, where the needles and serum were neatly laid out on a card table that we carried in the back seat of her old Buick. Fearfully, the workers would step up to the table one by one, always under the watchful eye of the plantation owner or manager, who made sure none of them slipped away.

As I gained experience, my mother allowed me to clean their arms

---

with alcohol before she vaccinated them. Later, I was allowed to vaccinate the children. It went surprisingly well. The children were not as frightened as the adults. Many of the adults had skin as tough as leather from working long hours in the hot sun. Sometimes, a patient would jerk his arm, causing the needle to break off. My mother would have to calm everyone while I fished out the end of the needle with a pair of tweezers.

At the end of these sessions, my mother would be exhausted, her arm and hand almost numb from administering so many vaccinations in succession. I always had to rub her hands and arm for a half-hour or more before we were able to start the drive home. While working with Mother in those days, I began to understand the struggle of life in the deep South in the 1920s.

Our life changed dramatically when my mother married Charles Clark Sr., a most unusual, remarkable and famous man. The only son of a two-term governor of Mississippi, he was extremely handsome, a crack shot, scratch golfer and master fly-fisherman. In my eyes, he could do everything important superbly—like a real-life Secret Agent 007. He was acknowledged as the best trial lawyer in the South. His law firm of Sillers, Clark and Sillers represented nearly every large corporation and plantation owner in Mississippi and Arkansas. With his partner, Walter Sillers, Charles Clark controlled politics in Mississippi.

Mother and Charlie bought a large white frame house on LeFlore Street in Cleveland and entertained the world. They were invited to hunting and fishing trips and parties at the great plantation houses, and they traveled constantly, even to visit friends in Europe. It was a grand life in a grand age, and they lived it with style

"Gonna Name Dis Baby John"

Charlie Clark taught me to shoot a .410-gauge shotgun and to catch bream and crappie. He also taught me how to keep a 20-horsepower Johnson outboard motor running when I became the proud owner of a Sea Sled, a small, flat-bottom boat. In fact, Charlie taught me most of the important things in life.

The great Mississippi River was a part of everyone's life in the Delta, and every spring all who lived along "Old Man River" feared for their lives. Although millions of dollars had been spent building massive levees to control this giant, everyone always knew that someday it would run wild.

In the spring of 1927, I was living with Uncle Isaac in Jackson when Charlie asked me down for a weekend. I was allowed to travel alone, so I rode the Nashville, Chattanooga & St. Louis to Memphis. Then I walked the two blocks to the Illinois Central station, where I waited a couple of hours and caught the Y&MV to Cleveland.

About 9:30 that night, Charlie drove us straight down to a great bend in the river just above Greenville called Mounds Landing. What a sight! Under giant floodlights, hundreds of men were stripped to the waist, covered in dirt and sweat. They were filling large sacks with sand under the eerie glow of portable floodlights. Then men dragged the sacks to that part of the levee that was bleeding the worst from the Mississippi's muddy waters.

We stayed most of the night on the levee, helping wherever we could. Dawn was just breaking when suddenly the floodlights went dark. There was a boiling of the earth and the beginning of a rumble that quickly turned into a deafening roar. Charlie grabbed my wrist tightly, whirled me around and screamed, "Run, run, run, Johnny Boy! Run for your life! The levee's breaking!"

His strong grip galvanized me to him. We ran up near the top of the levee through the weeds, water, mud and muck faster than any two humans in rubber boots had run before. Knee-high rubber boots are

Charles Clark

not exactly suited for sprinting, but they did not slow us down one bit
that night.

As we ran and ran, we could see the lights in the far distance. Behind
us we heard bloodcurdling screams, passionate cries for help, everyone
yelling and the sound of great chunks of the levee being ripped away by
the Mississippi. Old Man River was free at last!!

We finally fell in a mudhole, exhausted and gasping for breath, but
in relative safety for the moment. Charlie leaned over me and said,
"Johnny Boy, you will have a lot of close calls in your life, but none closer than you've had tonight. Remember it, and be as careful with your life
as Fate will let you."

Two hours later, we walked into the City Hall of Greenville. In the
mass confusion, Charlie and Will Percy, as heads of the local Red Cross,
took charge and focused on rescue plans. I sat in a corner and went
to sleep.

When Charlie awakened me, it was bright daylight, and he said,
"Johnny Boy, I called your Uncle Isaac, and he agreed to let you stay on

a few days. I'm having your boat and motor brought down from Cleveland, and you are going to run one of our rescue units."

One of the greatest thrills of all my life was that moment when I knew I would be a Red Cross rescue captain in the Great Mississippi Flood of 1927.

Our rescue base was located on a high gravel road just outside of Leland, Mississippi, where ambulances could get to nearby hospitals, and supplies could remain protected. Down the road, a truck was used as a temporary morgue for victims of the Mississippi's rage.

As the river, streams and bayous overflowed with water, survivors were found in trees, on rooftops, and in barns, cotton houses and churches. We were assigned to specific areas where our boats would rescue survivors throughout the day. As the boats approached a rescue site, we would be greeted with yells of relief and thanks. I never heard so many cries of "Praise the Lord" in my life.

This was, and still is, the greatest natural disaster America has ever known. Almost a million people were forced out of their homes. The death toll was in the thousands, and the Red Cross fed nearly 700,000 refugees for months. The flood finally stretched from Illinois and Missouri to the Gulf of Mexico. More than a million acres were flooded, leaving water as deep as 30 feet on the land.

During one of my rescue efforts, I spotted a large black woman and two small children bundled together on the roof of what looked like an outhouse or small cotton-storage house. As the boat approached them, I cut the motor and helped the children climb aboard. The oldest child held the front end of the boat while his mother squeezed her way into the middle. At first glance, I thought she was just very fat, but I soon realized she was actually quite pregnant.

The woman sat down, and I turned to start the motor. Suddenly she screamed, "Fo' God, my baby's comin' now." Despite my early experiences assisting my mother with medical matters, I said, "Ma'am, could you hold it for 45 minutes 'til we get to the camp?" As a nurse, my mother had talked to me about a number of womanly things, but I was certainly not a midwife. I could see the pregnant woman wanted to say, "I'll try." But all she could manage was, "This baby's comin' now."

I quickly tied the back of the boat to a large branch and, with the help of her oldest child, moved her off the seat and sat her in the dirty water on the bottom of the boat. Then I removed the seat and put my jacket over a gas can to serve as a pillow. Although she was in great pain, she said calmly, "Don' worry none, young man, I's gonna tell yo' all what's to do."

My hands and arms were covered with gasoline, oil and dirty water. I quickly rinsed them off as best I could in the river and wiped them dry with an old rag that hung on the motor handle. When I turned around, I couldn't believe what I saw—a little, fuzzy-haired black head beginning to come into the world.

"Let me git him a mite further," the woman said, "then you can take his head, and you pull him while I pushes. Jus' be gentle with him though."

I don't know how long it all took, and I never imagined there could be so much blood and flesh lost during a birth. However, the woman told me exactly what to do. I used my pocketknife to cut the umbilical cord. I washed the baby off in the river, and after I spanked his bottom a few times, he started bellowing immediately. The mother was still lying in the water in the bottom of the boat when I gave her the baby to hold to her massive breasts.

Thirty or forty minutes later, we reached the rescue base. There was great excitement and joy as the Red Cross ladies held the baby and the medics tended to his mother. As she was being lifted out of the boat, the woman looked at me and said, "I thanks y'all. What's yo' name?"

"John," I said.

"Well," she replied with a wide smile, "you know I's gonna name dis baby John."

F A R E W E L L ,   C H A R L I E   C L A R K

In my mind, any boy would have been lucky to have Charlie Clark for a father. Whatever he did in sports, the courtroom or any other aspect of his life, he did with unique skills. Fortunately for me, one of his main interests was passing on his abilities to young people, and he spent countless hours of his life doing just that.

He was every lawyer's dream, and whether he was defending a poor black man for free or representing the Mississippi Power and Light Company, he gave both equal attention. Whenever Charlie Clark was supposed to appear in a courtroom, you could count on a full house. Lawyers, in particular, would come to watch his creative courtroom strategies. He was a gentleman to all. People of every walk of life extended their friendship to him, and he always returned it double.

During the flood of 1927, he was on the front lines 20 hours a day. On one of the last days of rescue work, Charlie was returning in a rainstorm with 10 people in his large boat, when he spotted three survivors stranded on the tin roof of a large barn. Despite the heavy winds and unfavorable conditions, he headed toward them. As he was trying to secure the boat along the barn's roof, a sudden blast of strong wind jammed the tin corner into his right side, puncturing his abdomen and spleen.

Despite the efforts of those on board, he lost massive amounts of blood and was rushed to Greenville Hospital and then to Baptist Hospital in Memphis for endless transfusions. My mother was already with him when I went to see him a few hours later. He tried to smile at me, but he was too weak even to hold my hand. My mother—the great source of strength that she was—stood by his bedside tearfully all through the night. Every specialist in the Baptist Hospital was summoned to help.

Even so, Charles Clark died early the next morning. No amount of tears shed by his beloved state of Mississippi could bring him back.

THE STRENGTH OF MY MOTHER

When Charles Clark died, he left my mother some life insurance, the house on LeFlore Street and two Buick automobiles. She was also left with three children: Kate Foote Clark, Charlie's daughter by his former wife; Charles Clark Jr.; and during the summertime and holidays, me.

I made the sad trip back to Cleveland with my mother to bury Charlie. Ever the strong one, she greeted the endless visitors and thanked them personally for their bountiful food and flowers. I was in charge of opening the door, and she told me, "Johnny, give everyone that comes at least one of those wonderful smiles. Our friends in kindness will try to drag us down with sorrow, but Charles was in every way a happy man. Remember we are representing him."

When all the pomp and circumstance that followed a death in the Old South was finished . . . when the last drink and toast had been made by Charlie's many friends . . . when neighbors and others who had helped over the three days had gone and the door of our home closed for the last time . . . then my mother and I put our arms around each other. She went and poured herself a half-glass of Jack Daniels, and we spent that night in tears, remembering Charlie and how lucky we were to have had him.

During the night, we heard someone sobbing. I went to the back porch, and there was "Shorty" sitting on the edge of his bed.

Shorty Stark was barely five feet tall. He was very black and had a broad smile that exposed two front teeth of shiny gold. Insofar as I

remember, that smile never left Shorty's face. He had killed a black man in a dispute over a woman and had been serving a life sentence at Parchman Prison when Charles Clark had Shorty paroled to him personally. He was our driver, occasional cook, errand man, fishing guide, duck and goose picker man, dog handler, baby-sitter, caddie and general repair man. We loved him, and he loved us.

Shorty "Gold Tooth" Stark

18

That night, mother gave him some whiskey, and the three of us cried, laughed and told story after story of the great champion who had unexpectedly come into all our lives and tied us tightly to him with undying adoration.

The next afternoon, I caught the Y&MV to Memphis. My mother applied for her old job as public-health nurse of Bolivar County and opened the house on LeFlore Street to boarders.

It is only through the years that I have realized the heritage my mother gave me and how lucky I am to have it. The most important thing she blessed me with was a high quality of happiness. Like her, I have never rolled out of bed any day of my life, anywhere in the world, when I did not believe it was going to be one of the greatest days I've had.

Dr. Norman Vincent "Doc" Peale flattered me once when he said, "Johnny Boy, you could well be the mold for my *Power of Positive Thinking*." Some days were heartbreaking, but the next morning I always awakened with a belief that the new day was going to be a great one.

I owe this gift to my mother, a woman who had to make her own way in times that were not very easy for a career woman. She was often criticized for her warmth and desire to help all people. Nonetheless, I never heard her say one critical word about anyone, nor did she ever gossip or show the slightest prejudice against anyone of any race. She was always smiling and always thinking about how she could help others.

When Anita Massengill Clark died of cancer in 1947, hundreds of friends, many of them black, came from all over the Delta to her funeral. She had a special way of showing her kindness and love. I am indebted to her not only for giving me life but also for blessing me with the ability to live with great love and happiness.

She was the most beautiful woman of my life, not just because she was my mother. She was a unique breed of woman. I can never forget her smiling with love in her eyes, always on a mission from God.

2

The Young Entrepreneur

LIVING IN JACKSON, TENNESSEE

U ncle Isaac and Aunt Mary Sue were two of the greatest charmers the South has ever produced.

Isaac Burton Tigrett was the eldest son of the Reverend S. K. Tigrett, a Baptist circuit rider who died at the age of 50. Uncle Isaac inherited a small house in the little Tennessee town of Friendship, $200 and 60 acres of land. He had to look after his mother, whom everyone called "Mammy," and his younger brother, Augustus King Tigrett (my father).

Uncle Isaac sold the farm and the house and moved the family to Halls, Tennessee. There he found an empty building and painted the word "Bank" on the windows. Inside, he installed a counter built out of two-by-fours and chicken wire, which separated him from his customers. He knew nothing about banking, but his bank was the only one in town. His greatest asset was the fact that everyone always trusted him implicitly.

The Bank of Halls was successful then and remains so today. Uncle Isaac sold part of it and moved the family to Jackson, where he became cashier of the Union Bank and Trust Company.

He was made "temporary" president of the Birmingham and

Uncle Isaac and Aunt Mary Sue

Northwestern, a tiny railroad that ran 49 miles from Jackson to Dyersburg. From that base, Uncle Isaac built the Gulf, Mobile & Ohio, a great railroad of more than 3,000 miles of line running from Chicago to St. Louis, Mobile, New Orleans and Kansas City. So much has been written about his career that I can add little.

But I can tell you what it was like to live with him, Mary Sue and "Mammy." Whatever good qualities I have that I didn't inherit from my mother came from living with them. They were the guiding force for a great part of my formative life.

Mary Sue Kennedy Tigrett was from Tuscaloosa, Alabama. She was tall, distinguished, very pretty and the greatest storyteller who ever lived. She had a million stories, and no one ever left her without laughing. Aunt Mary was head of the Red Cross and every charity in Jackson, and was also an enormous help to Uncle Isaac.

When I was between 12 and 15 years old, Aunt Mary had a large paddle on the wall in the kitchen with a big "9" printed on it. Whenever

I began to get out of line, she would get my immediate attention by simply saying, "Don't forget Number 9, Johnny Boy."

Uncle Isaac had the most open, unbiased mind that I think I have ever known. He was chairman of the Board of Trustees at the University of Tennessee, Union University and Lane College, Jackson's large college for black students. He was also on the Catholic Board and head of the Jewish and Christian drives. I never heard him express any prejudice about any race or any person. He loved them all, and they loved him.

* * *

When my Uncle Isaac first took me to Jackson for schooling, we lived in a wooden barn of a house at 607 Highland Avenue. A bit later, we moved into a beautiful new brick house in the fanciest neighborhood in town. There, I shared a connecting bath with my grandmother and her companion, Miss Lutie Carpenter.

I was enrolled in the Alexander School under Miss Montague. It was the public school located closest to us, and I walked there every morning. Ada was our cook and William Nicholson the houseman and driver to church. Rex Curry, who had once been Uncle Isaac's caddie, cleaned the office and drove Uncle Isaac to the golf course every day. Ada's husband, Joe, was our part-time yard man—that is, when he wasn't spending time in the local jail for drunkenness. As Aunt Mary used to say, "Joe is sure strong for that Green River Tea."

One day I asked, "Ada, why do you stay married to that no-good Joe?" Smiling at me she said, "Well, sonny boy, I figures it this way: I makes de livin', and he makes de livin' worthwhile." That was my family in Jackson.

I am convinced that Mammy Tigrett was the strictest white woman who ever lived. She dominated the household and permitted no card playing, or "bad cards" as she called them, no Coca-Cola (because she had heard it contained cocaine) and no smoking of any kind. When my Uncle Isaac died and we gave his suits away to old friends, every coat had

John with his grandmother, "Mammy" Tigrett

a burn hole on the right side where he had stashed his pipe after being caught unexpectedly by Mammy.

She also had me at the First Baptist Church every time the doors were open. This meant two services on Sunday, the BYPU on Monday, Boy Scouts on Tuesday, prayer meeting on Wednesday and youth choir on Thursday.

Friday night we usually made coconut candy (with a red devil on top) or fudge. My job was to break the coconuts, get the meat out and grate it for the candy. My hands were a mass of scratches because Miss Lutie wanted me to use every piece of coconut down to the very last little bit.

Every Saturday morning, I took the streetcar to town, or William drove me, with my stack of *Saturday Evening Post* magazines and a basket of little brown bags full of Miss Lutie's coconut candy. I had a sign on my candy basket that read: "Candy—10 cents and 20 cents." I would work the downtown area until I sold all my magazines and candy. Usually I would finish up around 3 p.m. and would ride the streetcar home. The *Saturday Evening Post* was an easy sale, but Miss Lutie's candy was a bit more difficult—particularly with anyone who had tried it before. Her recipe was heavy on sugar and light on coconut.

One of my favorite regulars was Hugh Hicks, president of the First National Bank. He would always take a *Post* and then give me 25 cents for a 10-cent bag of candy. One day Mr. Hicks said, "Johnny, let me make a trade with you. From now on, let me pay you a quarter for the candy, but you keep it or give it away. It's probably the worst candy that was ever made."

I agreed with him entirely, but I could never get up the nerve to tell Miss Lutie.

THE PEABODY SKYWAY

As I grew older, I began visiting Memphis regularly and discovering the grown-up delights of that truly marvelous old Southern city, which was about an hour west of Jackson.

It has been said that the Mississippi Delta begins in the lobby of Memphis' famous Peabody Hotel. In my youth, which was the golden age of the big bands, the Peabody was known all over the South for the name bands that played on its roof, called the Skyway. In the summertime, that was the wonderful place to go.

Alonzo, the charming black headwaiter, was a close friend of mine in those days. He delivered the notes I wrote that helped me get acquainted with every female singer who came to the Peabody to perform. I dated them all, from Dorothy Lamour—who was then singing with Horace Heidt—to Virginia Rousseau, who was featured with Smith Ballew's orchestra.

I first saw Virginia on the roof of the Peabody when I was 18. As fate would have it, it was only a week before I was due to ship off to Europe. (In a moment of youthful fancy, I had signed with the Waterman Steamship Company of Mobile, Alabama, to work as a student seaman on a tramp steamer, the S.S. *Wacosta*.)

Alonzo handed Virginia my note, asking that she come over to my table for a drink during the band's next break. I could see him "building me up" as he gave her the invitation. When she came over, we were attracted to each other immediately.

She was an absolutely gorgeous redhead with a marvelous figure and a great voice. Within two hours, I was completely infatuated, and she returned my feelings with warmth and enchantment. It was as if we were both bewitched. We spent the following three or four days and nights together and had an exciting and happy time.

Before she ever met me, Virginia had married Ted Rousseau, then a sophomore at Yale and the son of the head of Morgan Guaranty Bank in Paris. When they were married, she was a showgirl working in New

York. She had started out in one of the title roles in *Three Little Girls in Blue* with Ruby Keeler and Barbara Stanwyck. When Ted's father found out about the marriage, he literally kidnapped the young man in New York and brought him back to Paris.

After Ted disappeared, Virginia took a job singing with Smith Ballew's orchestra. Tall and handsome, Smith had a Rudy Vallee voice but—as Virginia put it—"no sense." She explained that Glenn Miller, the trombone player, was the smart one who ran the band.

Virginia intrigued me with all kinds of stories about life in the big bands and her experiences as a singer. She also showed me that there is nothing that makes one's heart beat faster than having a beautiful redhead singing to you alone in a crowded room.

Naturally, I was downhearted beyond belief that I had obligated myself to head out to sea. But somehow I went through with it, kicking myself for making such a foolish commitment.

About six days out of Mobile on the S.S. *Wacosta*, I was overwhelmed by Virginia all over again. She had found a way to send me a two-page cablegram expressing her love. I was in ecstasy for the balance of the 14-day voyage across the Atlantic.

THE S.S. WACOSTA—A REAL TRAMP

Why I ever decided that working as a seaman on a tramp steamer would be a romantic adventure, I'll never know. And why Mammy, Uncle Isaac, my mother and Aunt Mary Sue actually let me do such a thing remains even more of a mystery to me.

I think a major factor in convincing my family to okay my scheme was that I had also persuaded Dan, my 21-year-old friend, to go with me. Dan was the son of the famous Vanderbilt football coach, Dan McGugin, and Mammy, in particular, was very trusting of him. As it turned out, I was the one who had to look after Dan!

We were assigned to the S.S. *Wacosta* and told to report to Mobile to ship out. Mammy went along with us on Uncle Isaac's private railroad car, Number 50, and the next morning at 6, we drove to the docks. After signing in, we stored our things and went back out to wave goodbye.

As Mammy and the chauffeur stood on the docks, she shouted, "I want you two to sing 'Yield Not to Temptation' with me."

The scene was more than comical—it was surreal. There was Mammy leading us in a hymn from the dock, with Dan and me singing from the ship's rail at the top of our voices, while 25 or 30 of the toughest looking guys you could ever assemble looked on in complete awe.

From the first time we tied up at the London East India docks through every port that followed, Dan never failed to send Mammy a postcard reporting, "Yielded a little here" or "Yielded a lot here" or "Didn't yield a bit here." How I wish I had saved those cards.

The S.S. *Wacosta* usually worked the English Channel. London, Newcastle, Bremerhaven, Rotterdam, and Le Havre all became places that I knew well—not the tourist sights, but the dock areas. At 18, I was in the toughest part of a very tough world. Our crew had dock fights at least once a week with Chinese, Italians, Africans and Arabs. My head still has scars from broken beer bottles.

London's East India docks housed at least 10 opium dens. Everything known in any underworld was available there, including the ugliest, toughest looking women who ever lived. At the same time, we worked like dogs. In every port at dawn, every hold on the ship was as hot as hell, and every load had some special handling problems.

I had moved from a warm bed in Jackson, Tennessee, to a bunk with a worn mattress and a permanent sag. If we slept out on the deck, the rats nibbled at our toenails all night. As I look back on it now, I'm amazed by what you can adjust to when nothing else is available.

Dan and I finally decided we had had enough and we were going to skip ship. At that time, there was an international law against breaking a seaman's contract. The first thing any captain would do was notify the nearest police department, which would then alert the border points. So if we were going to skip, we would have to get across the nearest border before anyone knew we were gone.

We finally decided to make the try in Rotterdam, where ships dock out in the harbor. Dan and I made a deal with a man who had a rowboat. He would come at midnight to pick us up from the bow of the *Wacosta*, where we would slide down a rope to his boat.

At midnight, we slipped out of our bunks and picked up our belongings, which we had stored under a lifeboat. Our escape boat showed up on time, and Dan and I quietly dropped the rope down to it. Dan shinnied down the rope first with no problem. I went next, but just as I reached the rowboat, a gust of wind swept it from under me. I landed in the coldest water I have ever felt in my life.

It was all I could do to keep from screaming while they fished me out. We rowed ashore, and I sat by a fire in a nearby bar. As soon as I was warm, we ran a few blocks to the taxi company where we had earlier arranged for our escape across the Dutch border into Belgium.

For once, everything worked. Nevertheless, it was hardly the norm for two young Americans and a Dutch taxi driver to arrive at the border station at 3 a.m. We suffered through what seemed like an endless wait before the immigration officers finally stamped our passports.

A few hours later, we caught a train from the little Belgium border town to our final destination: Paris.

P A R I S — C I T Y   O F   L I G H T   A N D   R O M A N C E

Spectacular, romantic Paris! Dan and I had never been more excited than that afternoon when we arrived, but we had to settle down and find a place to stay. We tried two or three hotels near the railroad station, but they were too expensive for our now very limited funds. It was getting late when I saw a very pretty, blonde French girl sitting alone at a table in front of a bar on the Left Bank.

She smiled when I asked, "Do you speak English?"

"Yes," she replied, "a bit."

"Do you have any idea where two tired Americans might find a cheap room for the night?" I asked.

She looked us over very, very carefully. Finally she smiled and said, "If one of you can sleep on a sofa and the other on the floor, I can put you up for the night. Tomorrow I will help you get a room." This was our introduction to Marie, who was as kind a person as the world ever made.

We walked six or eight blocks to her apartment, which was located above a bar and consisted of two small rooms. In one was a table and a sofa on which Dan slept. I slept on the floor in front of the fireplace. The bedroom was just large enough to hold a double bed, a small chair and a wash basin. The bath and toilet were a few doors down the hall.

The next morning, Marie took us up and down her neighborhood. We finally found a small room with two short, French single beds above a bar with a name that translated into "The Dead Rat." We found out later that years before it had been the famous hangout for the Impressionist painters. For us, it was just Paris—our Paris home.

Marie was a figure model who worked at two of the better art schools. From the start, she became our companion and our greatest friend, as well as our helpmate, advisor and protector. She made Paris come alive for us. We could hardly wait for the day to end so we could all be together. We laughed our way through everything. Naturally, Dan and I both fell in love with her, and once we told her, she returned it four-fold. How lucky we were.

Now that we had a base, Dan and I started to look for a way to make a few dollars. Our money was dwindling quickly, so we decided to give tours to gullible Americans. We checked out the American Express, Harry's Bar at the Ritz and one or two other bars that Americans frequented. We finally decided that our best bet was American Express because middle-class Americans came there, and they would be an easier mark for our "guide" service.

We invested in a detailed map of Paris, and that night Marie drilled us for hours. Dan studied all the sights including the Arc de Triomphe, Eiffel Tower, Maxim's and so forth. I specialized in the shopping tour: Hermes, Galeria LaFayette, Printemps and others. Both of us pronounced ourselves as experts on the Paris night life, from the Lido to the Sphinx Club.

Dan was a constant and convincing talker. He had only a smattering of actual knowledge about the various sights (mostly what Marie had told us), but he started with that and then made up the rest. Dan's double-talk act was so audacious that I had to watch myself to keep from laughing out loud.

Our first strike couldn't have been luckier—a brother and sister from St. Louis, Bill and Mary Stock. They were in their early 20s, were traveling in a convertible and were looking for a guide for three days. I first approached them, and when they mentioned they were from St. Louis, I quickly took them to Dan, hoping he might know someone there. I also was well aware that if he didn't know anyone, he would make up some fictitious person and talk about what great friends they were.

As it turned out, Dan actually did know a couple of fellows from St. Louis who had recently finished college at Vanderbilt, and Bill and Mary knew them too. From that point on, we were in. They paid us daily and kept us for 10 days.

About the end of the second day, Dan and I had a case of conscience and decided to gamble by confessing our actual lack of guide experience. When we told Bill and Mary, they just laughed and laughed.

"From the start, we knew you were not guides," said Bill. "We had studied the tour books enough to know that what Dan was saying had only a passing relation to the facts. We were just enjoying his made-up stories."

We introduced Bill and Mary to Marie, and soon the foursome became a fivesome. They were most generous and paid for everything until the last night, when Dan, Marie and I gave them a delightful Paris farewell party.

We picked up several other short guide jobs after that, but nothing approached the fun we had with our friends from St. Louis. Toward the end of our third week in Paris, Dan and I decided we should finally look homeward. We tried several steamship offices in Paris, but they all told us that if we wanted seaman's jobs, we would have to go to Le Havre, Cherbourg or another of the French ports. We finally settled on Le Havre, and the next morning Marie came to the station with us. We had one of the saddest and most tearful farewells of our lives.

* * *

We tried every ship with an American destination, but there were no jobs available. We were getting pretty discouraged when on the third day a great passenger liner, the S.S. *France*, came into port. We hit up the first mate immediately. He wanted to be helpful, but when he asked the captain to take us on, he refused.

As the first mate gave us the bad news, he said, "If you have a little money, there is an old arrangement we have to take home stranded American veterans from World War I. Ask your consulate about it."

We hurried to the consulate and encountered an unbelievable stroke of fortune. The assistant consul had gone to Vanderbilt and knew Dan well. He located the necessary papers and agreed to certify us as World War I veterans. The cost for steerage passage was $44 for each of us. When Dan and I added up our funds we had exactly $85 dollars and three postage stamps.

We went back to our little room to regroup and plan. My only assets were a fairly new pair of tennis shoes and a sweater that I was taking to Uncle Isaac. It took me 10 minutes to sell them to our French landlady for $10. An hour later, we were happily ensconced in a tiny inside room with two bunks next to the engine room of the S.S. *France*.

When passenger ships are in port, "freedom of the ship" allows passengers to visit any public area, regardless of ticket class. Dan and I immediately went up to first class to see if we could make acquaintances there. He found a gray-haired lawyer who worked for the Pennsylvania Railroad, but I took the prize with a very pretty, blonde 23-year-old Jewish girl named Jo Osborne. Luckily for us, her family had a charge account with the French line. She was intrigued by our stories, especially Dan's mostly fictitious concoctions. Before we left, she arranged permission for us to come up each day from steerage to first class. A day or so later, she had us moved to an unoccupied second-class room at no cost to us. Jo was a lifesaver. With her marvelous help each day, we spent virtually the entire voyage in first class.

After arriving in New York, Dan and I took a taxi to the Biltmore Hotel, where Uncle Isaac always stayed when he was there. I had the assistant manager call him in Jackson, and he arranged room and board for us, plus $300 in cash. That night, we gave Jo a grand farewell dinner and danced the night away to the music of the Paul Whiteman Orchestra.

The next day, I was on the train heading back to Jackson.

Virginia Rousseau and Glenn Miller

When I returned to Jackson in the fall of 1931, I made two moves. Uncle Isaac was chairman of the Board of Trustees of the University of Tennessee, and he was anxious that I go to school there. I agreed to try it for a year, and it turned out I had just barely enough credits from high school to enter.

The other thing I did was try to locate Virginia Rousseau. However, I knew so little about the music world at that time, I could not find a trace. At the university I was forever busy, either trying to keep up my grades, or running a cleaning-and-laundry service I started for the fraternity and sorority houses.

About a week before the end of the school year, I picked up a copy of the *Knoxville Journal* and saw an advertisement for one of the local night spots. It announced: May 30th for One Night Only—The Famous Smith Ballew Orchestra Direct from the Villa Vallee.

When May 30th arrived, I waited outside the club for an hour before the doors opened, and then another hour inside until the band began to set up. I was so nervous I could hardly speak. Finally, the band began to play and the dancers took the floor, but still there was no Virginia. My disappointment began to mount. And then the band swung into my favorite, Hogie Carmichael's *Stormy Weather*. From behind the curtains, beautiful Virginia walked to the microphone.

I moved slowly through the dancers toward the stage to a spot where I could look right up at her. My thoughts raced: Had she forgotten? Could she possibly remember me? Finally she looked down and saw me standing there. Big tears started rolling down her face, and I started crying as well. At the first break in the song, she stepped to the edge of the stage, leaned down and kissed me softly and said simply, "Love of my life—where have you been?"

Then she said, "Wait for me out front. I'll be there in five minutes. All the singing I'm going to do tonight is to you!"

Smith Ballew, Glenn Miller, Ray McKinley and the others in the band were on their way to New Orleans for a six-week engagement playing at the famous Broadwater gambling club across the river. But now that Virginia and I were together again, I was not about to let her out of my sight. So I was New Orleans bound as well.

We had a fabulous romantic time at the Pontchartrain Hotel. I still have great memories from the time we spent in New Orleans. While I was there, I also came to know Glenn Miller quite well. He would soon become world renowned with his own band, but at that time he was still playing trombone for the Smith Ballew Orchestra.

Glenn was a taskmaster beyond belief. While Smith was out drunk, which happened quite often, Glenn would have the other musicians in constant rehearsal. He was always building for the future. We became friends, and Glenn, Virginia and I spent many late nights together. I asked him if the band could return to Memphis when the New Orleans gig was finished, and Glenn said they could.

After I returned to Jackson, I went to Memphis to see my friend Frank Schutt, manager of the Peabody. He agreed to book the band for another stand there. About six weeks later, they arrived in Memphis, and Virginia and I grew very attached.

We both wanted marriage, but there were two complications. I had just started the Tennessee Securities Company. As a young, self-employed banking entrepreneur in the midst of the Great Depression, I was not confident I could support a wife. More importantly, Virginia was still a married woman, at least on paper. She and Ted had never divorced, and Ted's recent letters indicated he was still very much in love and wanted to come back to her.

During this time, Glenn and I became even closer friends. He told me how anxious he was to get away from Smith's band, but that he didn't quite have the nerve to try to make it on his own.

From Memphis, the band headed for the Cosmopolitan Hotel in Denver. I did my Tennessee Securities work from place to place during the day, and then spent most of my money on long-distance telephone calls to Virginia every night after she finished work. I was in St. Louis trying to make a bond deal with General American Life Insurance Company when I received a call from Glenn in Denver.

"I'm distressed to tell you, Johnny," he said, "but Virginia was quite upset about leaving you and not having any plans for marriage. She tried to commit suicide tonight before she went on, and she almost made it. We have her in the hospital here, and the doctor says he feels she's going to be all right. They pumped her stomach out, but she still is in bad shape. We all agree you are not to come here."

The news shocked me and broke my heart when I thought of being responsible for Virginia's distress.

"Something else has developed as well, John," Glenn said. "Smith has just closed a contract today to make some western movies. When we finish here, I want to take Ray McKinley and part of the band to the West Coast and start over on my own. I wondered if you would consider coming out and being our manager. I'll split my part with you 50-50."

"Glenn, that's a flattering offer," I said. "I have great confidence in your making it to the top. First of all, though, let's see what tomorrow brings with Virginia's progress. That's the only thing on my mind now.

"If I don't conclude my negotiations tomorrow morning, I'll join you and take over the management of the band. If I do conclude them, I'll be involved for another six or eight weeks, and I'll have to pass."

"That's a deal," he replied.

I went to General American the next morning and fortunately, or perhaps unfortunately, was able to negotiate the contract. I called Glenn and told him that I wouldn't be able to manage his band, but that I was coming out immediately to see Virginia.

"Please don't under any circumstances," he said. "I think if you did, there is no telling what would happen with her in her present state. I just left her, and it's still touch-and-go. I want you to leave her in the hospital for another week with me, and if she recovers, I will send her back to her family in Long Island. Just believe me, Johnny, I'm on the ground and I know what's best."

I argued with him at length, but finally said, "All right, but keep me fully informed. Tell the nurse I will call every few hours until she is out of danger."

Things worked out the way Glenn had planned. Virginia recovered and returned to her family, and I sent her what money I had saved. Fate is strange. Though Virginia and I talked by phone innumerable times, I did not see her again for three or four years. By then, both our lives had taken different paths, not to be joined again.

While I went on with my career, Glenn also went his own way. And what a success story he made with his music. In an era when big bands were the equivalent of today's rock bands, Glenn Miller became the greatest band leader both in terms of celebrity and financial rewards.

Whenever he saw me walk in the Pennsylvania Hotel in New York, or any other ballroom he was playing, he immediately had the band swing into *Stormy Weather*. He knew how much I loved that song.

And he never failed to remind me, "You dumb son-of-a-bitch! You wouldn't join up with me, and now look. You could have been right here with me—a millionaire and on top of the music world!"

Investment Banking, Self-Taught

The worst years economically that America has ever known were probably 1932 and 1933. The Great Depression wrecked countless fortunes and lives. Uncle Isaac went bankrupt and was just barely able to keep afloat the Gulf, Mobile and Northern Railroad, of which he was president and later chairman. His investment house, I.B. Tigrett and Company, also faced serious trouble.

Uncle Isaac went to see his major creditors and told them if they would stick with him, he would see that everyone was paid. It took him six years, but he did just that—paid them all, with interest. He was held in such great respect by everyone, that not one single person ever sued him. I thought the least I could do was go to work and try to help. That was why I had left the University of Tennessee.

Returning to Jackson, my only thoughts—other than that of Virginia—were focused on how I could help Uncle Isaac and my mother. Yet, there were no jobs available in Jackson, and it was tough for anyone to make a living anywhere. One or two older people that I knew were even selling apples on the street. It was a desperate situation.

I realized, however, that it all involved money and credit. If I could find some way to strike a compromise between financially estranged parties, that would be a service. I didn't have any specific plan. All I knew was that there were so many debtors who couldn't meet their payments and so many creditors who weren't being paid, they would have to get together on some new basis—because the original one on which the debts were established was not workable anymore. It was a very rough and uneducated idea, but to me it made practical sense.

I had organized the Tennessee Securities Company for a $13 application fee to the Secretary of State. The address and phone number of my office were actually those of my uncle's office in a building over the Sample Shoe Store. Uncle Isaac had most of the second floor, and he gave me a little office at the far end of it.

I had sent Virginia my small "stake" that I had saved from the cleaning and laundry business, and I certainly knew nothing about investment banking. So I went to the public library and picked up a book titled *Investment Banking Today*. Some said later that I didn't even open the book. However, I think I did read the first couple of chapters.

My basic idea remained fixed in my mind, though, and I was determined to pursue it. The best help I found was the county clerk of Madison County. I asked him to explain municipal bonds to me. He told me how the county bonds were issued and for what purpose. Most municipal bond issues were behind on making interest payments to bondholders because revenue was coming in so slowly to the cities and counties that issued the bonds. Some 8- and 10-percent bonds had fallen into default in this manner. The clerk suggested I visit nearby counties to see what bond issues I might find that were in default, but on which the issuers had the ability to pay at least a part of the interest due.

I liked the idea, but I didn't have any way of carrying it out. I didn't even have any transportation. However, I did know the best loan shark in town: Lib Birmingham. Lib had a "personal" loan operation in the back of a paint store in Jackson. We talked one day for half the afternoon, and he finally loaned me $350 for three months. He charged me 10 percent interest and took it out in advance. I was impressed with myself. But when I thought back later, I realized Lib had only made the loan because he knew Uncle Isaac would get it paid if I didn't.

I took the first $100 and bought an old Ford. It was beat-up and looked awful, but it ran and had four reasonably good tires. I was now in the investment banking business.

The next morning I struck out to make my first attempt at putting my debt-compromise theory into practice. I went to Alamo, Tennessee, and walked into the county clerk's office. We reviewed the entire county debt and talked about all their bonds. Every one was in default.

"We are still collecting some money," said the clerk. "As a matter of fact, we could be paying these bondholders something—but we can't pay them the 6 or 8 percent that is due, so we don't pay them anything."

I knew then I was on the right track.

As I started out the door I turned and said, "By the way, do any of these bond issues have funds available to pay any part of the principal?"

"No, they don't," he replied.

But then he added, "Now wait a minute. It isn't a regular bond issue, but the Hatchie Bottom Drainage District Number 1 has $100,000 in the bank over there. Nobody's ever shown up to collect it, and we've never located the bondholders.

"Are you sure that money's there?"

"Yes, it's at the Bank of Alamo."

"Would you mind calling and confirming it for me?" I asked.

The clerk called the bank, and the cashier said they indeed had $100,000 in the name of Hatchie Bottom Drainage District Number 1.

"Thank you so very much," I replied, doing my best to contain my excitement.

I hurried back to Jackson and went to the First National Bank to see Hugh Hicks, my best candy customer from years before.

"Hugh," I said, "how do you find the addresses of bondholders?"

"You can't—unless they have written in and there's some record in the clerk's office or maybe with the broker that sold them," he replied. "There's not really any easy way to locate them. However, if they are held by an insurance company, a book is put out listing their holdings each year."

"Do you have such a book?"

"The one we have is probably two or three years old. If you'll wait a minute, I'll get someone to find it for you."

Hugh left his desk and had the book located. I began going over the holdings of the many different insurance companies. I went down the seemingly endless list page by page, looking for Hatchie Bottom Drainage District Number 1. Just when I was ready to give up, I came across the St. Paul Fire and Marine Insurance Company of St. Paul, Minnesota.

There my eyes lit up, for I saw a listing that read: "Hatchie Bottom Drainage District Number 1—$100,000." I didn't say anything to anyone. I thanked Hugh for letting me look at the book, then walked straight to the Illinois Central Railroad Station and bought a ticket on the Seminole Limited to Chicago.

From Chicago I went on to St. Paul. There, I called the St. Paul Fire and Marine Insurance Co. and asked for the bond department. When a man came on the phone, I told him I represented the Tennessee Securities Company and that I would like to come by and talk to him about his Tennessee holdings, if it was convenient for him. He told me to come by any time, and the minute I was able to catch a taxi, I was on my way to his office.

We talked about many different things, and finally I said, "By the way, do you have any holdings down our way—Memphis, Jackson or Nashville?"

"Yes, we have some Memphis bonds," he told me. "We have some good maturities. Wait a minute, and I'll get a list of what we have in Tennessee."

It turned out they had quite an investment in bonds of the State of Tennessee. He went down the list and finally came to Hatchie Bottom Drainage District No. 1.

"What do you know about Hatchie Bottom?" I asked.

"That's a drainage district that's been in default forever. It's just another one of those drainage districts gone bad down South. Nearly all of them have."

"You know, I have a client who's been buying drainage bonds for the land. Would you want to sell yours?"

"Sure, we'd like to get rid of them."

"What's a fair price?" I asked.

"I expect $75,000 or maybe even $70,000," he replied.

"He wouldn't pay that much for bonds of that type. But I might get you 50. I might be able to get him that high."

"Well, we might sell them at 50—if you can find a buyer in the next 10 days."

"All right, I'll keep that in mind and I'll call you if there's any interest," I said. "You'll have to send them down to the First National Bank of Jackson, Tennessee, and I'll take them over to my friend and see if I can make a trade."

"Sure, I'll be glad to work with you," he replied.

I returned to Jackson and went to see Hugh Hicks again.

"I'm going to get some bonds sent in," I explained, but didn't tell him which ones. "I want to be able to take them out for half a day to see if I can collect them."

"I'll trust you, Johnny," Hugh said. "Don't worry about that."

I called my new friend at the insurance company and told him I thought there was some interest. I also asked him to send the bonds of the Hatchie Bottom's to the First National Bank in Jackson, attention Hugh Hicks, president.

Between that time and the time the bonds finally arrived a week later, I called at least three times a day to check on their arrival. I was one nervous wreck. When at last they reached the bank, I took the bonds in my $100 Ford over to Alamo and presented them to the county clerk.

He called the Bank of Alamo and told them that he had the bonds in hand and was going to issue a check for $100,000 payable to the First National Bank of Jackson. I took the check to Hugh, and he sent $50,000 to the St. Paul Fire and Marine Insurance Company and then deposited in my account the other $50,000.

Fifty thousand dollars!

Just like that, I had more cash money to my name than anyone in Jackson, except perhaps Lib Birmingham. I sent my mother $20,000, Virginia $10,000 and tried hard to give my Uncle Isaac the balance, but he wouldn't take it. In fact, he would never take a single penny I tried to give him.

I went and paid Lib the $350 I had borrowed from him and didn't even ask for any of my interest back. I must say that my credit was so good at that moment that whenever I saw him from then on, Lib would always say, "I would have loaned you anything you wanted."

I never had to go back to him again.

CULVER "RED" WHITE

My next step in developing the idea of being a financial arbiter came in the form of a contract in Sheffield, Alabama. I was able to get it only with the help of Culver "Red" White, the city attorney there.

I was to receive $15,000 plus expenses to reorganize the town's outstanding debt on five bond issues. Culver had all the qualities I needed in these transactions. He was a very good attorney and had a financial mind that was absolutely marvelous. It was not long before we became partners and worked together until his death.

We scheduled a meeting with the Sheffield bondholders at the Mayfair Hotel in St. Louis and had about 80 to 90 percent of them in attendance. The town had bonds outstanding, with interest due as high as 8 percent. At best, they could only pay about 2 to 3 percent interest. We finally convinced the bondholders to agree to reduce the rate to 3 percent for three years, then go to 4 for three years, 5 for two years and thereafter 6 percent as the top.

What surprised me was that none of the bondholders were angry. In nearly every one of my dealings in such matters, we reached a happy solution between debtors and creditors. The Depression was so severe that the creditors were delighted to get anything they could. From the start, it was a solid and successful idea.

Culver White had a small law business in Sheffield and was the city attorney, but he was barely getting by. When I asked him how he was doing financially, he said, "Well, you see this suit? I still owe the fellow down the street for the suit before this suit."

I moved Culver and his family to Jackson, and we became 50-50 partners. He was a man of character of the first order, and it proved to be a happy and profitable relationship. We went from Sheffield to Tuscumbia to Florence to Homewood, and all sorts of other little towns, where we employed the same system with bondholders and bond issuers in each place.

It was during these times that I learned an odd but significant fact about communication. We had always typed our reorganization plans and run them off on a mimeograph machine for the bondholders. At one of our bondholder meetings in St. Louis, a man from Topeka, Kansas, representing one of the insurance companies there, had a printed plan of his own. In effect, it raised the amount of money that the city had to pay by roughly 1 percent more than in our plan. To my amazement, however, the city chose his plan (which the bondholders naturally preferred) over the one that we had developed—even though ours would have cost the city less money.

Afterward I said to the fellow from Topeka, "How did you manage to get your plan accepted over ours?"

"It's very simple," he replied. "My plan was printed, and yours was typed. The human mind can change typed words or handwritten words easily, but it hesitates very much to change the printed word."

From then on, Culver and I had the McCowat Press print all of our reorganization plans, and they went through almost every time without difficulty.

* * *

Those early days in business were some of the happiest days of my life. Uncle Isaac was running the railroad from his small office above the funeral home and the Sample Shoe Store. He had a secretary and an accountant, Arnold Lindseth. The headquarters of the line were housed in the largest building in Mobile, but Uncle Isaac ran the railroad by telephone from Jackson. He usually went to Mobile only two days a month.

He once told me, "Johnny Boy, if you can't get your work done by 1 or 2 o'clock in the afternoon, you're in the wrong business." I must say, he followed that rule to the letter.

I had the Tennessee Securities Company in one room with a secretary; Culver White had the middle room. Down the hallway in the same set of offices was Uncle Isaac. Every afternoon at 1, Rex Curry would show up and tell us it was time to get to the golf course. We would first stop at Diffee's Drug Store for a sandwich with a glass of milk, then head off to the Jackson Golf and Country Club.

This was our routine every single day of the week—except Sunday—in rain, sunshine, snow or sleet. If it was raining, we would wait until it slacked up and play in rain gear for two holes or five or 18 or whatever we could. I am sure Uncle Isaac is following the same routine now in Heaven.

While working only a half-day, Uncle Isaac built one of the finest rail systems in America. He was first to eliminate steam engines and completely replace them with diesels. He was the first to have streamlined trains—the sleek machines called the Rebels—in the South. He was also the first to have hostesses on the trains, and was responsible for many, many other innovations.

He also had the personal strength and determination of a truly remarkable man. He was playing golf in Hot Springs, Arkansas, when on the ninth tee he had a stroke. At the time, he was more than 60 years old. His left arm and side were partially paralyzed, and he could not speak a word.

An ambulance arrived quickly, but Uncle Isaac insisted on finishing the round. Playing with only his right arm for the last 10 holes, he shot a round of 85. The ambulance took him to the local hospital, where the doctor told Uncle Isaac that he should not be moved. Nevertheless, he left the bed and had himself driven to his private car and then taken to the Missouri Pacific Hospital in St. Louis.

Mary Sue and I arrived in St. Louis about the same time he did. He could write notes, and he gave me one as soon as he saw me. It read, "Johnny Boy, go to town and buy some English books for the first, second and third grades."

From that day forward, he spent one hour each morning and afternoon and later two hours twice a day learning basic English again. He would never give up until he had a word back in his memory pattern. The first weeks were so painful that every time I left him, I went out in the hospital yard and had a good cry.

Ike Tigrett demonstrates his personal cure for the headaches that come from building a major rail system: Swallow the latest remedy, read a western, smoke a pipe. By 3 A.M. the headache is gone.

The Hesitant Hero of Jackson

By ARTHUR W. BAUM

They made Ike Tigrett temporary president of a rusty Tennessee railroad until a "competent person" should turn up. While waiting, Tigrett transformed the 408-mile rust streak into a 3000-mile empire worth $175,000,000.

Within one year from the date of the stroke, however, Uncle Isaac was able to fight off a group that tried to take over the railroad. A little later, I stood in the wings watching him deliver a speech on courage to 5,000 members of the Newcomen Society in Jackson, Mississippi. He never mentioned his own problem.

The doctors all said that it was a miracle. But I knew that it was only my Uncle Isaac.

Fair and Square

William Nicholson was a tall, thin, very black man who was an important part of the Tigrett family for 30 years. He was dearly loved. He never married, though he ran one of the largest accounts at Vineyard's, the local florist. Flowers were sent on a regular basis to his "lady friends." He was also the head deacon at the Macedonia Baptist Church.

At the age of 71, while walking across the back yard of 34 Northwood in Jackson, William dropped dead. Uncle Isaac and Mary Sue were away, so it was my job to arrange the funeral. After selecting a burial plot, giving notice of his death to the Jackson *Sun*, naming 12 pall bearers (with the help of his pastor) and agreeing to "testify" at the funeral in the Macedonia Baptist Church, I went by Richardson Funeral Parlor to select a casket.

Mr. Richardson greeted me with tears. "I just don' knows what we gonna do, Mister John, with William gone. He was our leader."

"Well, all the Tigretts are going to miss him very much, Mr. Richardson," I said. "He was an important part of our family."

"Such a fine man, Mister John, such a fine man. I knows you wants to bury him with da bes'. Now, Mister John, dis here casket I personally picked fo' William. It's outa dat heavy bronze steel. Waterproof—not a drap can git in it. Satin lined—here's da satin. Jus' feel it, ain't it soft? Jus' as sof' as dis pillow fo' his haid. And the han' holds, dey's gold-plated, 18-karat gold."

"How much is that one, Mr. Richardson?" I asked.

"Now, I knows you wants da bes' fo' William, Mister John, so I's goin' to give you de wholesale price." He lowered his voice. "Dis one fo' William is $7,500."

"Well, I like it Mr. Richardson, but let me see what else you have," I said. "How much is this next one? Would that be suitable for William?"

"Dat wouldn't be suitable fo' William, Mister John. Dat casket's $3,800—but it ain't got that soft satin! And da silver box in de corner, dat's $2,500, but it ain't waterproof—it leaks!"

I priced about 15 caskets and said, "This is a very impressive display, Mr. Richardson. But I'm wondering if this is your complete line?"

"Well, Mister John, we do has some boxes 'cross da alley, but nuthin' you'd think 'bout fo' William. He was such a fine man."

"Well, I'm sure if you say so, Mr. Richardson. We won't even consider them for William, but I'm intrigued with your business. I'd like to see your complete line."

With that we walked across the alley to an old tin building with a dirt floor and a 100-watt bulb hanging down from the ceiling on a cord. There were about six wooden caskets on stands.

"Now dese here wooden boxes, Mister John, dey's from $500 to $200, depending on da finish."

In the darkest corner, I saw a wooden casket of a different shape that was extremely narrow. I went over to it and said, "Mr. Richardson, what is this one?"

"Oh, Mister John, you jus' couldn't possibly think 'bout anything like dat fo' William. Dat's jus' $75."

"Well, it certainly is unusually narrow in its construction, Mr. Richardson."

"We calls it da 'Fair and Square,' Mr. John. Course, it has one little problem: You has to slide him in dere sideways."

I smile whenever I think of that $75 casket. In fact, I have written in my will that I would be very happy when I pass if they would just ease me sideways into a "Fair and Square."

I can't think of a better way to slide into heaven.

3

The War Years

In 1939, fighting had begun in Europe, and the whole world moved toward war. But as the decade began, I was riding high. There I was, 27 years old, driving a white Packard convertible and never without plenty of spending money. I was still living at 34 Northwood and was courting pretty girls all over the South.

At the time, I wasn't dating any Jackson girls. I suppose I thought they were not as sophisticated as those in bigger cities. I was always bringing them down from Memphis, Nashville, New York, Chicago or somewhere else to visit for the weekend. Aunt Mary was always helpful and charming, so it was a delight to have people come see us.

One day, I had a broker friend coming down from Chicago to spend the weekend with us. I had arranged a date for him with a girl from Memphis, but she fell ill at the last moment.

Hurrying to look for a replacement, I discovered that the Tomlins across the street had a very pretty daughter, Frances, who had just graduated from Sarah Lawrence. In fact, she was only dating boys from New York, Memphis, etc. I hadn't paid any attention to her before, but with my friend coming and no date lined up, I rushed over to become better acquainted. She accepted my invitation to date him.

Then, as luck would have it, my friend couldn't make it to Jackson. Meanwhile, Frances had broken a date with some Memphis boy to accompany my friend. We laughed, and I invited Frances to be my date.

I thought I was so sophisticated at that time. I don't know how she put up with me, but she did. I found her to have a great sense of humor and true beauty. The first thing I knew, we were dating steadily. After a courtship that lasted about three or four months, we married in The First Methodist Church in Jackson.

Frances was a perfect wife. She was interested in doing exactly what I wanted to do, and was helpful in every way. She had exceptional abilities and was as charming as she was beautiful. And she gave me three wonderful sons.

When the double tragedy of losing two sons struck us some years later, we both went off track. I think anyone would have. Our marriage was at an end, but my high opinion of Frances has never wavered. Today she is still a remarkable person and a woman of great ability.

PROSPERITY AND SADNESS

Our Tennessee Securities Company prospered, and Culver White went on to become vice president of finance of the Gulf, Mobile & Ohio Railroad, though he remained my partner as well. He proved his merit when different banking houses, including Morgan in New York and a large house in Chicago, offered him all sorts of partnerships.

One day, when we were bird hunting, a dog bit Culver on the hand. The dog ran off, and we searched for him unsuccessfully for three days. Culver's doctor said the terribly painful rabies shots were necessary.

Culver, however, had an odd blood structure that would not accept the shots. The second injection paralyzed him from the waist down. For a couple of weeks, it was touch-and-go as to whether he would live, but he finally pulled through. The doctors recommended that we move him to a warmer climate. We flew to Tucson, Arizona, and found a home for him and his family.

I knew Culver needed to keep his wonderful mind active, so I looked around Tucson. We were sitting on a bench one day waiting for a bus to come by when I said to him, "I wonder who owns the bus line around here?" We decided to find out and then try to buy it.

A conglomerate owned the Tucson Rapid Transit Co., but a divest order had already been entered on the property. Within a month, we had bought control of the company, and Culver became president.

In spite of everything we tried and every specialist we found to help Culver, his physical condition continued to decline. He died in 1941. I miss him deeply to this day. Culver White was a great and true partner—and my friend forever. It was a sad day when I had to take over for him as president of the bus company, as well as try to run Tennessee Securities Company alone.

A D U C K ' S B E S T F R I E N D I S J A C K M I N E R

In the early 1940s, I went on a hunting trip to Cairo, Illinois. I killed a big Canada goose. As it fell, I noticed a small band on its leg that glinted in the sunlight. When I reached the goose, I removed the band to discover "God is love" written on one side and "Write Jack Miner, Kingsville, Ontario" on the other.

Three days later, I was on a houseboat shooting geese in the marsh at the end of the Mississippi River below New Orleans. The first goose I dropped had another small band on its leg. This band had a Bible quote printed on it, along with the message: "Write Jack Miner, Kingsville, Ontario." It was too great a coincidence for me.

I had the guide take me up to the Pilottown Bar, which was built over the water on stilts, and I put in a call for Jack Miner. I found that he had been banding ducks and geese for a number of years and was studying their flyways. I told him I would see him in a couple of days. Then I flew up to Detroit and drove over to Kingsville.

Jack Miner and his wife were both around 80 years old. He had a very small pond in what had been part of a brickyard. Years before, his pond first had five duck visitors; now it had about 60,000 ducks and geese that came annually. Miner had some support from the state wildlife association, but the increased cost of feeding the huge numbers of ducks and geese had pushed him into considerable debt. I stayed a day and a half talking with him, then returned to Jackson.

In the late 1930s, I had begun writing articles for magazines, just as a hobby. I wrote a number for *The Saturday Evening Post*, *Reader's Digest* and *Esquire*, and had finally reached the point where they assigned me stories that I suggested. I was getting paid $3,500 per story, when I heard that the *Post* had paid $5,000 for a two-part article on a new invention— the lie detector. I knew the Jack Miner story was a winner.

I finished writing it, then sent it to my old friend, Ben Hibbs, editor of *The Saturday Evening Post*. I told him I wanted $5,000 for it. I had previously sold the *Post* two or three articles.

Mrs. Jack Miner is fond of reading the Bible, often finds a text of which she says: "This should go on the geese next spring."

Jack Miner stamping leg bands with his name, address and a biblical quotation which differs each day and thus dates the band.

A Duck's Best Friend is Jack Miner

By JOHN BURTON TIGRETT

Nearly 100,000 ducks and geese have been dined and repaired at this Ontario preserve, and have carried away gospel verses on their leg bands.

A LITTLE Indian hunter named Justo Montero was poling his homemade boat through the water hyacinths in the Magdalena River, in Colombia, one day not long ago, when he spotted five teal ducks bobbing in an open patch just ahead. The ducks heard him and started up. Montero quickly raised a long-barreled hammer gun and fired, and one of the ducks fell. Attached to one of its legs was a peculiar silvery band bearing an inscription: "Write Jack Miner, Kingsville, Ont., Canada. Let us consider one another. Heb. 10:24."

Fortunately, Montero did not understand English, or he might have thought he was having a hallucination. Instead, inhaling the thick aroma of Colombian coffee from the fields, he made haste to consult a lawyer in Barranquilla who spoke English.

Paternally, in the manner of his calling, the lawyer explained to his visitor that the band had been placed on the duck's leg by a man who lived about 3000 miles from Barranquilla and who was simultaneously engaged in the scientific study of bird migration and in spreading Biblical texts.

"Come," the lawyer told Montero, "sit down, and let us write this Jack Miner."

This story of Justo Montero and the teal duck is only one of about 30,000 that have been written to Jack Miner since 1909, when he first scratched his address on a small piece of metal and wrapped it around the leg of a black duck named Katie. In 1910, a hunter killed Katie near Anderson, South Carolina, and established Miner as the pioneer bird bander of the North American continent.

In their basement workshop, where they operate a bird hospital, Mr. and Mrs. Miner put a splint on a goose's broken leg.

During the migrating season Miner traps, bands and releases about three hundred birds daily. Here he sends a banded goose on its way.

MARCH 18, 1944   10¢

Hibbs was a tall, lanky taciturn Vermont native who was considered to be the best magazine editor of the era. He had previously taught me a lot about writing. In fact, one day when I was at Curtis Publishing in Philadelphia, which published the *Post*, he called me into his office.

"John," he asked me, "have you ever seen Gypsy Rose Lee?"

I was puzzled. "You mean the famous strip-tease gal?"

"Yes. That's the one," he answered. "She's appearing in a burlesque show now on 42nd Street in New York. The next time you're there, I want you to go down and see her, for she'll give you the best lesson you'll ever get on how to write articles that sell."

"Could you elaborate on that a little, Ben?" I asked, still puzzled.

"When she comes out in that sparkling tight dress, long gloves, tits about to jump out—she stops you cold. That is the first paragraph of your article. You've got to firmly get their attention right there or you'll lose your audience," Ben began.

"From there on, Rose very slowly takes off the gloves and the stockings. She then bends down toward the audience a few times, and the tits jump out, but they're covered with a tiny bra. Then she unzips the dress—that part of her show represent the main part of your story. Then as she begins to close up her act, she moves over toward the curtain, and suddenly she drops the dress and steps out of it. She stands there for just one closing 'paragraph' in a jeweled bra and diamond G-string, smiles and winks at you, and goes behind the curtain. You haven't seen a damn thing, but she's kept you on the edge of your seat every single moment."

I went to see her, and Ben was right. She was some article!

So by the time I wrote "A Duck's Best Friend Is Jack Miner," I felt I had mastered the literary techniques of Gypsy Rose Lee. When Ben called me, he said he liked the piece, but the best he could pay me was $4,000. I replied, "Ben, send it back. I'll sell it to someone else. It's $5,000 or nothing."

The next morning, he gave me the $5,000. A month or so later, Stanley High, the editor of *Reader's Digest*, paid me the same amount for it. "A Duck's Best Friend Is Jack Miner" went on to be printed in the school books of 21 countries, and Jack Miner had more than $50,000 sent to him to feed his ducks and geese.

As for me, I never wrote another story until now. I had reached my journalistic goal.

Lt. John Burton Tigrett, U.S. Navy, World War II

THE DAY THE WORLD CHANGED

Frances and I had a happy, easy life in our early years of marriage. My days were spent hunting, playing golf, working now and then, building a new house and raising a family. It was comfortable, but not too exciting. But, with such pleasurable living, I don't know that I yearned for much excitement.

However, on December 7, 1941, the Japanese struck Pearl Harbor, and the whole world changed. I waited for a while, trying to decide what to do, and then I guess they waved the flag once too often for me. Without saying anything to anyone, I went down to the post office in Jackson. That's where the volunteers were lined up outside the recruiting offices.

There were three offices: Army, Marines and Navy. I knew nothing about any of them, but I saw the shortest line was in front of the Navy office, so I joined that branch of the service. Within about 30 minutes, I was signed up to become a member of the United States Navy.

Being in the Navy was an experience of endlessly remarkable events.

Even now, I cannot recall a dull period or one in which I wanted to change anything. There were several narrow escapes with my life during that time, but fate smiled on me, and I never looked back.

When I finally received my orders in Jackson, I was instructed to report to the Hollywood, Florida, Officer Training School for six weeks. On arrival, I found that the Navy had taken over the Hollywood Beach Hotel, where the accommodations were certainly not a hardship.

Drills started immediately for 1,500 of us in small platoons. When I was finally given a platoon to drill, I shouted the orders out in a very loud voice. By chance, the Navy captain in charge of the training school passed by one day and stopped for a moment to watch our drill.

Unbelievably, three days later—entirely as a result of that chance encounter—I was made the student commandant of the school. I knew nothing whatsoever about the Navy or its rules and regulations, or about what I was supposed to do as student commandant.

But there I was every day at 6:30 a.m., calling to order 1,500 better qualified men, some with U.S. Navy experience, and giving the orders for the day. I also had the responsibility of assessing discipline for some who had been AWOL or had committed other transgressions. On Sundays, everyone wore dress whites, and I called out the orders for the parade.

As it turned out, that first break shaped everything I did in the Navy from then on. Time after time, I was selected for important jobs about which I knew nothing. Somehow, I always managed to keep a straight face and scramble just quickly enough to learn the ropes in time.

N A V Y   O R D E R S

I once sold a story to *Esquire* titled "Transportation Tomorrow." Among those I interviewed was a regular Navy captain named "Dutch" Schildauer, the developer of the famous Mars seaplane that operated in the Pacific.

When I volunteered for the Navy, I wrote Dutch a note. Without replying to me, he had me assigned, after training, to the Naval Air Transport Service. After my graduation as a lieutenant junior grade, my orders sent me to VR3 at Norfolk, Virginia. There, together with a wonderful Navy chief, I was placed in charge of handling the new officers reporting daily to Norfolk. My friend, the chief, was without doubt the best double-talk man who ever lived. I would let him explain the base and barracks to the newcomers, a daily event that he conducted like a circus.

We soon had to move our operation to a larger receiving room to accommodate the captains, commanders and many others who came every morning to secretly listen to him while they pretended to be doing something else. Every morning, he gave a hilarious performance. After the war, the chief took his act to television, where it became the basis for the classic show *Candid Camera*.

* * *

Navy orders puzzled me. How did they select me for these different jobs? I was determined to get control of my fate in the U.S. Navy.

Two weeks after I had been stationed at Norfolk, I took one day's leave and flew to Washington, where I headed for the Navy Bureau of Personnel in Arlington with a copy of my orders. In the right-hand corner of those orders were five rows of numbers and letters that held the key. I asked one of the information clerks to direct me to the person who had actually issued them.

Two hours later, I was sitting at the desk of a young ensign who admitted he had made the selection to send me to VR3 simply by spinning his Rolodex and picking a name at random. I took him to lunch at a fancy restaurant, and he casually explained to me how "the order business" worked. That afternoon, I sent a case of bourbon whiskey to his home and kept in close contact with him for a number of months.

From that moment on, I had control of my future. That ensign would never again issue me a change order without calling me first. And whenever he had a good assignment available, he would call to see if I would like to take it.

Ultimately, I obtained a pad of the necessary forms, and for the last 18 months of the war I wrote my own orders.

SHOWBOAT'S NATS

One day, my ensign friend called me and asked if I would like the number-two job in Washington in the Naval Air Priorities Division. He explained that Naval Air Priorities controlled the traffic that was allowed to ride on the Navy Air Transport planes (mostly DC3s or PBYs), and that they also had charge of Pan American and American Export Airlines seaplane service to Europe. It sounded interesting, so I took it.

I had an office at Gravelly Point next to the Washington National Airport, and my job was to load the planes operating on the East Coast. One day I had a call from a regular Navy captain named Smith who needed a favor. I arranged it for him, and thereafter he called me every week to request additional favors. They always consisted of raising the priority status of friends so they could get on a plane when they wanted.

He called one day and asked me to join him for lunch at the Mayflower Hotel, where I met an unbelievable character. Later in the war, when he had an aircraft carrier under his command, he would become known as the famous Captain "Showboat" Smith.

We spent two or three hours drinking and sizing each other up, and then he said, "John, I've just been ordered to be director of the Naval Air Transport Service. How would you like to be assistant director?"

"I would like it," I replied, as quickly as I could.

No one in their wildest imagination could possibly have guessed where that remark would lead.

Two weeks later, I moved into the office next to Captain Smith in a downtown Washington building where the Naval Air Transport Service occupied several floors. The captain and I worked together closely for a week, and then one evening he asked me to have dinner with him. After several drinks he said, "I want to tell you how we're going to operate NATS," and then he delivered an astounding set of instructions.

"I'm married to a very wealthy woman, and we have a lovely home out on the Chesapeake," he said. "You can reach me there from Friday night until Sunday night. Here's the phone number. On Monday mornings at 8 a.m., I will be at the regular weekly meetings held by the chief of Naval Operations."

He continued: "Every day, Monday through Friday, you are to meet me at my regular table at the restaurant Louis XVI. Bring all my phone messages and any bulletins or orders you want to put out, and I will sign them there. If there is anything pressing, I may go back with you to the office for an hour or so."

I was growing more amazed by the moment.

"If Secretary Forrestal's office or the chief of the Naval Operations calls, stall them and call me at this room number in the Shoreham Hotel. Or, if I'm not there, then at this room at the Mayflower Hotel. If you get in any kind of a jam, don't call me with anyone around you. Go out to the public telephone in the lobby downstairs. All the office staff are to be told that I am working on a secret project. You handle them."

The reality finally sunk in on me: I was apparently mixed up with a wealthy semi-alcoholic who kept two mistresses and a wife. More frightening was the idea that I was evidently going to be almost solely in charge of the Naval Air Transport Service, with 385 airplanes running all over the world carrying thousands of Naval personnel.

For three nights, I never slept a wink trying to decide whether to see this thing through or to run as fast as I could. The thing that worried me the most was that I knew nothing about airplanes and had no experience or competence in air transport. Besides that, there was no one I could even talk to about the crazy situation, except my wife. And I knew if I did, with her background, Frances would never understand such a thing or approve of it, and she might even "spill the beans."

One evening, I sat drinking in a little restaurant near the office for several hours before I finally decided that I had no choice. There was too much at stake, and if anything ever came out, the regular Navy boys would always stay true to their own. I would be the victim, and the captain would be the most innocent man alive.

I went back to the office, called in the four division heads and began to plan for the future of NATS.

BOTWOOD, NEWFOUNDLAND

In the 18 months that I worked with Captain Don "Showboat" Smith, so far as I know, no one ever uncovered the true story of his activities. When word came that Captain Jack Whitney, hero of the Pacific, was coming in to replace him, I was greatly relieved. For the first time, Captain Smith stayed in the office all week, and I caught him up on most of the things we had done so he could make a reasonable transition.

Jack Whitney was as different from Don Smith as anyone could possibly be. He was a hero of the Battle of the Coral Sea, serious about his work and a top-flight officer in every respect. We hit it off from the start and became warm and lasting friends. He knew a bit about Don Smith, but I never gave him the facts until we were finally parting company. The odd thing was that he did not seem even slightly surprised.

I stayed with Jack for six months and then told him I would like to move on. He put me in charge of installing the new operational air stations as the war progressed. In this job I worked jointly for Jack, the chief of Naval Operations and the State Department. I had progressed to where I had a pad of orders, and from then on I wrote my own: Port Lyauty, Africa; Northwest River, Labrador; Brisbane, Australia; Cairo, Egypt; and the line all the way to Calcutta, India; Belem, Brazil; Bluie West One, Greenland; Reykjavik, Iceland; Foynes, Ireland; and many, many other spots. I suddenly knew the world, and in my game, that was essential.

The chief of Naval Operations sent me to India to explore an operation similar to the Army's Hump Operation between Calcutta and Kunming, China, and sent me jointly with the State Department to Lisbon to get some air rights, which later became part of TWA.

I literally lived in an airplane for months before I grew completely exhausted. One day I got up my nerve to talk to the CNO and Jack. They gave me two weeks leave and a berth for the summer at Botwood, Newfoundland, on the Atlantic Coast above New England.

Pan American and American Export Lines were under contract to the

Navy to inaugurate a summer service from Baltimore to Botwood to Foynes, Ireland. It was the fastest and most direct route between the U.S. and Europe. Convoys of ships were not popular at the time, for the German submarines were a real threat, and no high-placed military member or civilian wanted to risk an encounter.

The Atlantic Ocean is a "bitch" to fly at low altitudes, even in the summer. It was my job to check operational weather. If both my people and operations agreed it was okay, we then talked to the pilots by radio as they flew out of Botwood across the Atlantic to what was called the "Point of No Return." From there on, they became Foynes' responsibility.

At Botwood I had a contingent of about 100 Canadian Air Force personnel, a representative of each of the two airlines and a small mechanical repair base. Pan Am was operating the short-wing Boeing B14 seaplane and American Export the smaller and less dependable Sikorsky seaplane. The planes would come in between 6:30 and 7:30 almost every evening. We would feed the passengers, and they would take off again about 9:30 p.m.

We always served the same thing for dinner: the very best lobster in the world. I had made a deal with the three fishermen with the greatest number of lobster traps, so we had a daily supply. Fresh out of that very cold water, our lobsters had a marvelous flavor. Every passenger who had one always remembered it.

During that summer, I think almost every famous person in the world came through Botwood and had dinner with me—including perhaps the most famous individual in the entire war effort.

WINSTON CHURCHILL
AND ONE CLOSE CALL

One afternoon, the Botwood cable man came to my quarters with a coded, super-secret dispatch. When we completed translation, it simply said: "Important personages on flight tonight. Exert extreme care before sending them across." I made many guesses as to whom it might be, but they were all wrong.

About 6:30 p.m., I walked down to the dock and waited. Finally the Pan American B14 seaplane came across, then turned and landed in the lake. As it taxied toward the little dock, a square figure who looked solid as a rock stepped out and stood on the short wing. When the plane moved closer in the dusk, I saw the man on the wing had a large cigar in his mouth and his left hand extended upward in a victory sign. It could only be one person: Sir Winston Churchill—prime minister of the British Empire and Europe's staunchest leader against Hitler.

I grew even more flabbergasted as the plane began unloading up the gangplank. To meet my salute, handshake and greetings came not only Churchill but also General George Marshall, Lieutenant General Hastings Ismay and General Alsobrooke.

Besides President Roosevelt and General Eisenhower, these four made up the group of six who were running our side of World War II. I could not help but wonder in amazement about who had made the unbelievable decision to put all four of these leaders on the same aircraft during a critical time of the war.

As we walked up the short rocky road to the base, Churchill said, "Lieutenant, what is your name?"

"John Tigrett, sir, and I come from Tennessee."

"John, have you any Scotch on hand?

"Yes, sir."

"Well, get me a double with a little water, and I want to take a bath."

"Sir," I replied, "I have the only private bath on this base, and it's a shower. If you don't mind a shower, though, I will take you to my quarters."

"Fine," he said. "Let's go."

My quarters consisted of a small room with a desk and two chairs, and an even smaller bedroom with an adjoining bathroom and metal shower cabinet. I sat at my desk while Churchill showered and meanwhile asked for three more doubles. From the time he arrived until I bid him and his party farewell, he had 13 double Scotches and some wine. However, he never showed the slightest sign of intoxication.

During dinner, he talked constantly in his low, guttural English accent, and though I was sitting between him and General Marshall, I could understand very little. He asked me a number of questions, and almost every time, I had to ask him to repeat what he said.

At one point, the chief pilot of the Pan Am plane came up to the dining room and asked me to step outside. He said, "Lieutenant, this flight is so secret that I did not know until I opened my orders that we were to go from Botwood to Lisbon. I have just been studying the weather, and it looks as though there is a major North Atlantic storm right on that route. I can't see any way of getting around it."

"You're right," I said. "That's the same storm that hit us with part of its tail last night. It's big, deep and heavy. You can't go to Lisbon tonight with this cargo. Only Foynes. And we may decide even that is too much of a gamble."

"Who's going to tell the Prime Minister and General Marshall?"

"Go get me a weather map showing that storm and your route plotted through it," I replied. "I'll tell them."

That was one of the remarkable things about this little post in the Newfoundland woods. As long as a plane was on the ground, I alone had the decision as to whether it could take off. Once a captain was in his plane and had the motor started, he was in charge. I had an argument with just one captain, but after that the word got around: I was in charge.

The Pan Am captain brought the map to me shortly thereafter. I laid it on the table and explained to the group why we were going to have to send them to Foynes instead of Lisbon. Mr. Churchill started to argue that they could get around the storm.

Sir Winston Churchill

I listened him out and then said, "Mr. Prime Minister, that Boeing will be carrying tonight the single most-valuable cargo to our war effort that has ever crossed the Atlantic. I may be just a Navy lieutenant from Tennessee, but I have now 'talked' enough Boeings across that I know how treacherous these Atlantic Ocean skies can be. I do not question that General Marshall has the authority to remove me from my post in a moment. But as long as I am in charge here tonight, your destination will be Foynes, Ireland—not Lisbon."

In the silence that followed, Prime Minister Churchill looked me straight in the eye, and that great bulldog face was motionless. Suddenly he laughed, then turned to General Marshall and said, "George, we're not going to Lisbon tonight; we're going to Foynes, Ireland."

That was the end of it.

After dinner, Churchill said he would like to say a few words. So about 15 or 16 of us went into the staff lounge. It was a cold night, and there was a fire in the great fireplace. Mr. Churchill stood with his back to it and began to tell us about the war, where things stood at the moment and where he hoped they would be over the next year.

Then suddenly he switched his tone and said, "Let me tell you boys about how important small outposts such as yours are during wartime. If you are doing your job here, and doing it well, you are just as important as the men on the front line. You're a vital part of a long chain of command, without which there would be no front line." It was a presentation of stark drama such as only Churchill could create, and most of us were in tears.

Then he said to General Marshall, "Get up here, George, and talk to these boys." Later, looking at General Alsobrooke, Churchill said, "All right, Brookie, it's your turn." By the time they had all finished, we felt we had the single most important job in the war.

After that, it was time for them to go. I ran back and brought out another double Scotch, which Churchill drank while walking to the plane. When we reached the aircraft, he said, "John, send a boy back to get us some ice. I forgot we have champagne on board."

Once the ice was on board, the plane moved away from the dock. Churchill emerged once again and stood on the short wing in the semi-darkness to give us a final victory sign as the B14 taxied away. It was one memorable evening.

* * *

The following morning, a Pan American B14 seaplane was shot down by German aircraft just outside of Lisbon. Leslie Howard, the English actor most famous for playing Ashley Wilkes in *Gone With the Wind*, was in the plane. A month or so afterward, a report was printed in the *Times* that the Germans thought it was Churchill they had shot down that morning.

We never know what seemingly minor twists of fate can swing the outcome of a war and possibly even rewrite the script of history. When I read that German report I had some deep and unsettling thoughts.

What if that storm had not been on the path to Lisbon that night? What if the Prime Minister had simply overruled me or general Marshall removed me and ordered the plane on to Lisbon anyway? What if my better judgment had been overcome by the intimidating presence of Mr. Churchill, General Marshall and two great generals?

What suddenly gave a young naval lieutenant, who knew very little about what he was doing, the guts to stand up to the Prime Minister of Great Britain and three of the most powerful generals in the world?

Only the enigmatic hand of fate will ever know.

JAMES FORRESTAL

If I were ever put in charge of running a war, I would try to bring Jim Forrestal, secretary of the Navy, back to life.

Jim had the shape, size and appearance of a stubby middleweight boxer—clean but tough. He started out as a runner for an old New York investment house and ended up as chairman. After a couple of drinks one night in some strange place, he told me, "They really didn't want me, John, because I was from the wrong side of the tracks. So I worked nights studying the investment business. When I began to produce substantial profits for the firm, they finally had to recognize me."

I spent weeks with this man and never once saw him deviate from the war effort. He spent 20 minutes a day on exercises, but aside from that he was always studying facts and figures, trying to make the U.S. Navy more effective in the war. In the beginning, I found him difficult to work with, but the key to our friendship was performance. I learned much from Jim Forrestal about knowing every detail and performing on time. No alibi—except maybe death—was acceptable to him.

In war, no one could move fast enough for this remarkable man. In 1944, we dropped into Oran in North Africa en route to Naples for the "secret" second landing in southern France. As we walked down the DC-4 steps, I saw eight to 10 cars lined up with drivers, all dressed in white, standing at attention. There were only the two of us and the crew on board the aircraft. We were greeted effusively by a delightful old Navy admiral who rode in the first car with the secretary. I sat in front with the driver.

We had just started to the admiral's headquarters in the hills above Oran, when I heard him begin to tell the secretary about its interesting history. He managed to go on about it for maybe two minutes before Forrestal said:

"Admiral, I'm not a damn bit interested in history at this time. We have a thousand ships about to make a landing. All I want to know from you is the condition of your ship-repair facilities. How many ships have you handled in the last 30 days? The last three months? What do you need to double your capacity? How many men? How many more floating docks? We may have immediate need to even quadruple your capacity here, and this can be a critical port. Please let me have all the facts on this port immediately. And if you have any aerial photographs of the base, I would like to have them too."

I was laughing to myself in the front seat. When we reached the magnificent chateau that was the admiral's headquarters and left the car, the secretary said, "John, bring me that material as soon as they have it—no matter what the hour!"

I finally went to bed about 2:30 a.m., with no sign of the figures Forrestal had requested. The next morning, they were still not available. The admiral assured the secretary that he would send the information to us in Naples on his plane.

After a quick breakfast, we went straight to the airport. As the secretary started up the steps, he turned to me and said, "John, I want to remove that admiral immediately. I will wait in the plane while you send the dispatch."

"Mr. Secretary, let me do that from Naples," I suggested. "He's an old man with many years of regular Navy service. Let me work it out to let him down lightly."

Forrestal turned on me like a tiger. "Did you hear what I said? Do it right now!"

"Yes, sir," I said. I went over and sent a dispatch to the chief of Naval Operations that read: "On receipt of this dispatch, you are to remove command of this post, Admiral W. C. Wilson. Within one hour you are to have the Navy's best replacement available, experienced in ship repair, to take over this command. Time is of the essence. Advise me at NAS, Naples, Italy, when complete."

When I gave the secretary a copy of this dispatch, he smiled and said, "I'm glad to see, John, that you have finally learned how to carry out orders."

The secretary insisted on going in on the landing in southern France.

Because our intelligence had not been the best, I was worried. I grew even more so when I went into Naples to buy Frances a pair of those wonderful Italian gloves, and the young lady who waited on me said casually, "Are you going in on the landing tomorrow?" I almost forgot what I was buying!

Forrestal and I rode in the landing craft of the third wave, and everything went almost perfectly. The Germans had moved out many of their forces, and while there was some resistance, it was not even remotely comparable to the fierce fighting and deaths we had sustained in the first landing in Normandy.

However, the landing vessel just ahead of us hit a mine, and several of its passengers were killed. It could just as easily have been Secretary Forrestal.

GENERAL DWIGHT EISENHOWER

Back in London two days later, Forrestal and I were taken across the channel in a tiny plane to the headquarters of General Dwight Eisenhower, supreme commander of the Allied invasion of Europe.

We met him in an apple orchard in Normandy, and there seemed to be only a few guards around. A black fellow served us Jack Daniels and water. I think that was his principal job.

After dinner, Eisenhower took us into a war tent with many maps all around. He started out by taking us over to the largest map, telling us the objectives and pointing out where our forces were at the moment. There were two lines, a blue one and a green one, extending about equal distances into Germany. There was also a red line that ran probably 100 miles ahead of the others.

"The blue line is Bradley. The green is Montgomery," said the general, referring to the respective forces of Generals Omar Bradley and Bernard Montgomery. "They are stopped at the moment because neither one will move unless he has at least a week's supply of gasoline.

"The red line is George Patton. I know many people have criticized me for sticking by him after he slapped that soldier in the hospital. The truth is that if we win in Europe, and we will, it will be to a large extent because of George Patton. He is out there tonight, and probably half his tanks are out of gas, with no backup supplies and knowing it will probably take a day or two before we can get more fuel to him.

"If the Germans knew that, they would cut him off in a moment and probably crush him. But they don't know that, and with his reputation, they are afraid to take the chance. George Patton knows more about war strategy—about how to win—and he has more real guts than all of the balance of our generals put together."

General Eisenhower switched subjects. "I had an interesting visit, Jim, just before the second landing," he said. "Mr. Churchill flew over and said he was now convinced that we were making a major mistake by going into Toulon. That we should go in on the other side of Italy at

Piave, and move straight toward Russia. That we would save thousands of miles of territory and millions of people from Russian domination.

"I told Mr. Churchill he could well be right, but that we were too far along; the landing was set. If President Roosevelt wanted to change the plan that was another thing. Otherwise, we would land in southern France. He made some very strong arguments, and he may have called the president, but I heard nothing further."

When you look at a 1944 map, you can see that Churchill was almost 50 years ahead of his time in his strategy.

ROSA MORLEY

Every night we were overseas, I tried to get Secretary Forrestal to break his work routine and go out for dinner. Every night it was the same story. He would tell me he'd try, but five minutes before we were to meet, he would call with apologies that urgent phone calls had to be made or that new papers had arrived.

London proved to be no exception. His "Unable with regrets" was delivered to me in the Grosvenor House bar. We had come to London after the landing at Toulon and checked into the Grosvenor House. I had invited the secretary to dinner and made reservations at Les Ambassadeurs, which was one of several clubs owned by John Mills.

As I came downstairs to wait in the lobby, I saw what I knew must be the most beautiful girl in the world. Tall, stately, her every movement pure style, with a mink coat to the floor and gorgeous brilliant red hair flowing everywhere. I was so struck with her beauty, I could only stare.

She finally saw me and gave me a slight smile. I walked directly to her and said, "Pardon me, but would you like to have dinner at Les Ambassadeurs tonight with the secretary of the United States Navy?"

She laughed and asked, "Are you the secretary?"

"No, but I'm waiting for him to come down."

"Thank you. I'm waiting for Lord Stone."

My heart was beating fast. "Well," I said, "why don't we both sit in the bar together and have a drink? You can wait for Lord Stone, and I'll wait for the secretary."

"Let's go," she said, taking my arm.

That was my introduction to Rosa Morley, London's leading actress of the day, whose life-style was as colorful as she was beautiful. It was said that she was courted by more famous men than any other woman in Europe. She was one of the two women in all my life with whom walking into a room was always an experience.

Every eye, male and female alike, would always turn to see Rosa Morley make her entrance, just as they would when I began watching Pat

Kerr make her entrances. Whether it was by way of the dress they were wearing, the style and excitement with which they entered, their smile or the amusing way they laughed and tossed their heads, both always gave their audiences their money's worth. I always had great fun and pride in sharing their spotlight. With Pat, I still do.

That first night I saw Rosa Morley, we made a late date at the Milroy, London's best wartime nightspot. For the balance of the four days the secretary and I were in London, whenever we were not busy, Rosa and I spent our time together.

On the way from London to Preswick, I told Secretary Forrestal I would like to take up duty in London if he had no objection. So for the last seven months of the war, I operated the European and Middle Eastern Division of the Naval Air Transport Service for Jock Whitney and the chief of Naval Operations.

The Germans had just started shooting their V-1 missiles at London, which caused much physical damage, in addition to being one of the greatest psychological tools of World War II. As we lifted off from Bovington Field in London, Secretary Forrestal said to me:

"For the first time in my life, John, I have been really frightened. When I heard the last of those putt-putts of that little gasoline motor in the V-1s, I knew it was coming down close to me—how close was the problem. I can't tell you how relieved I am to be leaving London."

I found Rosa had a luxurious new apartment in what was formerly the Garden Club. She suggested I move in, but I thought the U.S. Navy would prefer that I have a residence of my own. She and I went around on a Sunday and gave a 10-pound note to each of the hall porters in six of the most desirable buildings on Park Lane, requesting that they call Rosa's apartment secretly if they heard of anyone who was going to move.

Sure enough, it worked. Within 10 days, I had moved into 60 Park Lane, the best building in London. My place was a beautiful flat owned by a princess who had been frightened out of town by the V-1 missiles. The princess had left behind a wonderful housekeeper named Mrs. Story, who made my life very easy.

My next move was to get a place in Paris, and the mayor of Orly found me one close to the airport. A gorgeous estate taken from a Nazi sympathizer when the Allies retook Paris, it had room for my staff and pilots, both trans-Atlantic and local. We were then sending flights every two hours between London and Paris, seven flights each way a day.

My last move was to acquire part of a two-bedroom suite at Shepherd's Hotel in Cairo, which I shared with Claude Bernheim. Claude operated the French Transport Aerien. I had a two-motor plane at my disposal, and for all intents and purposes, I was "King of the Walk," as the English expressed it.

After Rosa and I lived in separate apartments for two weeks, I came home from Cairo one night, and Mrs. Story met me at the door. "Oh, Mr. Tigrett," she said. "The place is in a mess, and I haven't had time to get it straight. Miss Morley moved in with us today."

So she had. And though she never gave up her own apartment, we lived together at 60 Park Lane until the end of the war. Rosa was a delight, and we had endless fun together and a very deep love for each other.

A WILD FLIGHT ACROSS THE INDIAN OCEAN

The chief of Naval Operations gave me an assignment to make a preliminary report on the possibility of the Navy starting a PB4Y seaplane operation from a river in Calcutta, India, to a lake at Kumming, China. The Navy brass was seeking an operation that would compete with the Army Air Force's much publicized Burma Hump Operation out of the Chabour Valley in northern India.

It was understandable that the Navy would want to match the Air Force on that route, but it was impractical from an operational standpoint. I wrote most of my report before ever reaching Calcutta, because I knew the area and the aircraft that would be involved. Our slow-moving seaplanes would have been sitting ducks for the Japanese.

While in Calcutta, I received a message from the chief of Naval Operations that I was to join General Kuter, the head of war plans, on a flight from Ceylon to Australia to carry a secret dispatch to General Douglas MacArthur at his headquarters in Brisbane.

With dispatch in hand, I flew to Columbo, Ceylon, where I met General Kuter and his aide, Captain Miller. The night before our departure, we rounded up about 20 guests for a memorable dinner. The curry, whiskey and wine flowed as freely as on any occasion I have witnessed, before or since. I think they were serving about the 27th course when General Kuter and I were able to unsteadily make it to our feet and make our departure.

We were to take off the next day at 5 p.m. on what was to be the first DC-4 flight between Ceylon and Australia. Our plane was a new DC-4 stripped bare inside except for three lightweight, uncomfortable wire seats, six life preservers and a rope ladder for climbing down to the ground upon landing. Some of the very first trial long-range fuel tanks were attached beneath the wings.

The airfield had short runways, and we were carrying an exceptionally heavy load of extra gasoline. In order to give us every inch of runway for takeoff, the pilot backed up the plane as far as possible to one end, until the tail was touching a palm tree just off the runway. Even so, the pilot predicted we would not be able to clear the palm trees at the other end of the runway. Sure enough, we clipped the tops off several upon takeoff.

Still, we were airborne and proceeding toward our destination when first one engine went out, and then another a few minutes later. There was no choice but to dump our extra fuel and head back for Ceylon. Over the next three days, we attempted four more takeoffs, and every time the same problems turned us back.

Finally, a young mechanic resolved the difficulties. Observing that the wet heat in Ceylon was causing vapor lock in the fuel lines to shut down our engines, he came up with a plan to ice the gas tanks. That did the trick, and we took off successfully at last.

We were admiring an unbelievably beautiful sky over the Indian Ocean that night when the plane's navigator (who looked about 16 to me) burst through the cockpit door and announced in a frightened voice:

"General Kuter, we are approaching the Kneeling Islands, and our radar shows a plane has just left the ground and is rapidly coming up toward us. It appears to be a Jap Zero. We're going up to get in the clouds and do our best to hide there. If they spot us though, your life rafts are under your seats. I would get them out and be prepared to use them. That's all."

With that, he returned to the cockpit and closed the door behind him as the plane veered sharply to the left and upward. General Kuter, Captain Miller and I were speechless, knowing our lives were at stake. The general and I attempted to retrieve our life preservers as instructed, only to find they were glued to the seat bottoms.

As we struggled to free the life preservers, Captain Miller decided to take more heroic action. He found his .38 pistol in his travel bag, removed the plastic plug in the window beside his seat, and poked the barrel of his pistol out through the opening. Vigilantly he kept the pistol pointed at the skies, prepared to gun down the Jap Zero if it appeared.

After an hour and a half of our pilot making sharp, evasive turns back and forth, the skies were dark enough for us to move out of the clouds and resume our course toward Perth, Australia. However, we had used up so much fuel while evading the Zero that the pilot doubted he had enough left to reach Perth. That left us facing quite a dilemma, as we were 14 hours from Ceylon and had no chance of turning back. The pilot told us he was going to try to make Exmouth Gulf, Australia, where his maps showed a small American submarine refueling station with a short airstrip.

For an hour and a half, we sweated out whether we would make it or not. And when the wheels of our DC-4 touched down on the grass airstrip at Exmouth Gulf, every tank on the plane was empty. The strip was so short, the pilot was barely able to stop the big DC-4 some 20 feet from the water's edge.

We climbed down the rope ladder, and just as I put my feet on the ground, I heard someone say, "Well, I'll be damned! Johnny Tigrett. What in the world are you doing here? I haven't seen you since the Memphis University Club dances three or four years ago."

I turned to see it was Jack Myer, an old friend of mine.

"What can I do for you fellows?" he asked.

"How about some ham and eggs, with some hot biscuits on the side?" I said.

"Come with me! I'll give you the finest breakfast of your life."

He did just that, while our plane was refueled. After breakfast, we flew on to Brisbane and my meeting with General MacArthur.

GENERAL DOUGLAS MACARTHUR

I had heard a great many stories about General Douglas MacArthur, the commander of Allied Forces in the Pacific. Whatever he did, he did it with great determination and vigor. He was said to be a disciplinarian beyond belief, and his tough, unbending manner bore that out.

I had heard that officers in the Army and Navy were always nervous or frightened when in his presence. Those were the thoughts in my mind as I went up the steps of his headquarters in Brisbane.

Three security MPs checked my credentials. Two of them then began asking intimidating questions, but I held my ground. I told them I represented the chief of Naval Operations, and I was there with a secret dispatch for General MacArthur, to be given to him and to receive his reply.

They finally gave up and took me to a small anteroom next to the general's office. I waited for about an hour. When the door to his office suddenly opened, it was the general himself.

"Come in, Lieutenant," he said. His office and desk were most impressive and warm with mementos and pictures. My first thought was that he couldn't be quite as cold a character as I had heard and read. He motioned for me to sit down.

I sat in the chair opposite his, opened my small case, took out the CNO dispatch and handed it to him.

The dispatch was almost three pages in length, and the general read it carefully. Then he looked up and said, "Are you familiar with the contents of this dispatch?"

"Yes, General, I am," I replied. The Navy was very annoyed, to say the least, at the fact that it loaded its aircraft on a priority basis in every theater in the war except General MacArthur's. When a Navy transport entered his theater, his officers would often unload Navy material and personnel and load on their own.

The chief of Naval Operations' dispatch suggested a compromise: A prioritized board with equal Army and Navy representation to load the aircraft in his theater of operations.

"Lieutenant," General MacArthur said, "we will have a dispatch ready for the chief of Naval Operations tomorrow morning. But let me also tell you in person; as long as I am responsible for any aircraft or personnel entering my theater of operations, it will be under my command. There has never been any exception to my policy, and there never will be. That will be the language of the dispatch for your return."

"Thank you, General," I said. "I will carry your message to Washington."

I got up to take my leave. Just when I reached the door, I turned and asked, "Pardon me, General, but have you had any word on General and Mrs. Pat Seales?"

He looked quite surprised and asked, "Do you know them?"

"He is my uncle by marriage, General. We have been trying everywhere to get some information," I replied.

"Come sit down, Lieutenant," he said. "I'll tell you about them."

I have never seen a personality change as I saw at that moment. From the tough, hard, disciplined General MacArthur, he suddenly grew tender, kind, considerate and worried over his friend of many years.

"General Seales was more than my executive officer," MacArthur began. "He was my closest friend. We were together at West Point and shared many assignments. His wife, who, as you know, was in a wheelchair, was equally dear to me.

"When the Japanese closed in on us at Bataan, we escaped in one plane, and General and Mrs. Seales and their staff were in the second seaplane. They took off just behind us. I have wished a thousand times since that we had all been in the same plane.

"En route, their plane developed motor trouble, and they were forced to land and try to repair it. They landed in a lake on a small Philippine island; we were not sure if the Japanese had any troops there. To compound the misfortune, as they taxied to shore, they struck a hidden rock that ripped out part of the pontoon.

"The last time they were seen, General Seales had Mrs. Seales in his arms, and he was headed toward the hills to try to hide out for as long as they could. Two days later, the Japs found them. My intelligence people tell me they have been moved three times to different prison camps. They have both been tortured Japanese style—never enough to take their life.

"We know where they are, and I have worked on many plans to try to get them out, but I cannot justify the many American lives it would take in the gamble. I can only pray, as I do each night, that those Jap bastards holding them—who have no humanity and no souls—will let them live until we can win this war."

He paused for a moment, then asked, "How did you get here?"

"I came with General Kuter on the first DC-4 flight from Ceylon to Australia. We landed at Exmouth Gulf," I replied.

He smiled and said, "I was first going to send you back to your quarters, Lieutenant, but stay for lunch and tell me about your flight."

The great general of the Pacific could not have been more kind or attentive or warmer. He even came close to apologizing for his position on loading Navy aircraft.

"I'm sure Washington looks on me as a tyrant," he said. "I would like to be able to go along with what the chief of Naval Operations proposed, but out here thousands of miles away, I am the sole person held responsible for my theater. If I make a mistake, I want it to be my mistake—not someone else's for whom I will surely be blamed."

Before I departed, General MacArthur had me give him my home address and promised that if anything happened to General and Mrs. Seales, he would see that I was advised.

True to the general's word, when the Pacific war was over, we received word from Washington that the Seales had finally been released and were proceeding home. By that time, they had been fed so poorly that Mrs. Seales weighed less than 80 pounds. General Seales, a large man when captured, was down to 125 pounds.

Mrs. Seales breathed her last breath of life just as their plane landed in San Francisco. The general took her body in his arms and carried it from the plane to the waiting ambulance.

GLENN MILLER, FAREWELL

When Pearl Harbor brought us into World War II, I had not seen Glenn for five or six years. He too joined the cause and served as a captain in the Air Force. He put together a band of enlisted men that entertained Allied troops in the war zones. So both of us spent the war zigzagging around the world. But somehow our paths never crossed.

Our nearest encounter occurred while I was running the Atlantic Naval Air Transport Service from London. We had a commuter operation with planes leaving every two hours between London and Paris.

Early one morning, I came into Bovington Field, our London Hub located about 16 miles north of the city, on my way to Paris. As usual, I stopped to speak with Mary, the pretty girl who served doughnuts and hot coffee for the Red Cross.

"I'm so excited," she said. "I just saw Captain Glenn Miller. He came by and had coffee and doughnuts."

"You don't say?" I replied. "Where did he go?"

Mary said she thought he went to the operations room, so I went there and asked, "Where's Captain Miller?"

"He was booked on one of your planes, Lieutenant, but he took a Norseman instead," an officer there said. "A fellow came in and said he was going to Paris, and Captain Miller said, 'I'll ride with you.' As a matter of fact, you can see them right there at the end of the runway, they're just getting ready to take off."

"Well, I'll catch up to him in Paris," I said.

I called my people in Paris and told them to watch out for a Norseman coming in from London, explaining that Captain Glenn Miller would be aboard. "I want you to meet him and give him the super deluxe treatment." I said, "Don't tell him I've arranged this—just tell him you have a big surprise for him, and hold him there until I get over."

When I arrived in Paris, I went straight to the NATS office and asked, "Where's Captain Miller?"

They said that he hadn't shown.

Glenn Miller

"Why, he was on that Norseman that flew over here ahead of me."

"No, sir. We've been tracing that plane, and something happened to it. They didn't reach Orly. Not only that, but we haven't been able to find it anywhere."

"You mean it went off the radar?"

"Yes, sir, it went right off the screen."

I spent hours checking with every alternate field, but it soon became evident that the Norseman with Glenn and the pilot had gone down.

A number of resources were at my command at that time, and I was determined to do everything possible to find him. I had three planes available and sent them up immediately, along with others that the Air Force sent. A total of six planes combed every quadrant of the English Channel, but that is a very rough place to search for anything. Basically, the Channel is simply the Atlantic Ocean tied up into a narrow passage with a sharp wind that doubles and triples the waves. At the time of year Glenn was lost, it almost always has fog over it, and the seas are unrelenting.

We looked for five days without ever finding a trace. The fate of Glenn Miller, my dear friend and one of the greatest jazz musicians the world has ever known, remains a mystery to this day.

Laughter and Tears With Rosa

Every night I was in London, Rosa and I would go out to dinner after the theater. Two or three nights a week, we would go dancing, usually at the "Dorch"—the Dorchester Hotel—or the Milroy.

Rosa had a driver, a big, tough Northern Englishman named "Abe," who picked her up each night from work and helped fend off the "stage-door Johnnies" who hung around outside the theater and sometimes found their way to either her apartment or ours. Rosa was always getting roses or letters or other gifts from admirers.

I came in from Paris one night to find our apartment filled with flowers and the refrigerator packed with caviar, smoked salmon and other delicacies not available in wartime London. I said to Mrs. Story, "Where did all this come from?"

"From that enormous Polish-Jewish man," she said. "He came to the apartment twice while you were away. Miss Morley saw him both times, but would not let him in. The last time they had words. He threatened her if she didn't go out with him, and she told him off. He's scary, Mr. Tigrett."

I figured out pretty quickly that the large Polish-Jewish man was probably John Mills, the owner of Les Ambassadeurs and the Milroy, who was said to control the black market in London. Rosa came in from work that night, and we decided to have a bottle of champagne and dance at the Milroy.

I never mentioned John Mills or anything about the flowers and food to Rosa that evening. We started home about 1 a.m., and just as we approached the stairs (the Milroy was on the second floor), Rosa said, "Wait a minute. I want to go to the ladies room."

As fate would have it, just ahead at the top of the stairs stood John Mills. As we passed him, he said to Rosa, "You stuck-up bitch. You're nothing but a goddamn whore."

With that, I took one grand swing at him and caught him off balance, sending him tumbling down the stairs. The next thing I knew, Rosa had me by the arm, rushing me down the stairs—past Mills, who was out cold—and into the street. Right behind us came four of Mills' goons, and they quickly surrounded us as we tried to reach a taxi.

Rosa took charge. "If any one of you bastards so much as touches this officer of the United States Navy, your operations will be closed down tomorrow morning and you will never open again." With that, she turned and pushed her way through them with me in tow, got us in the taxi, and away home we went. The four goons stood there speechless.

* * *

Victory in Europe came when Germany surrendered on May 7, 1945. That night in London was unbelievable. Lights that had been kept dark through most of the war were lit everywhere. Music, shouts and screams filled the air. Hordes of people headed for Buckingham Palace. Everyone was drinking, happy and crying. Rosa and I stood in front of the palace in the mob as the king came out and gave his dramatic victory speech.

Rosa and I were crying, too, for we both realized it was the end of our wonderful and exciting life together. I had always told her of the obligations I felt in Tennessee to all my folks, my three wonderful young sons and my loving wife. I had thought about that every time Rosa and I were together. It was not what I wanted to do, but the obligations of life cannot be carelessly cast aside, and I finally decided I could not hurt so many people. It was too much to walk away from—even for love.

Before I came into Rosa Morley's life, she had been courted ardently by a wealthy and very famous Frenchman named Jean LaBoussier. He was a hero of the Free French Air Force, having shot down the most German planes. After Rosa moved in with me, he came to see her only once, and she had him to our apartment. He had been shot up and was on crutches at the time. I was away, but when I returned, Rosa told me of his visit and how he had asked her to marry him. When she told him she loved him but loved me more, he cried.

Two days after V. E. Day, I caught a plane for Paris after calling Jean

LaBoussier and asking him if I could come by his apartment for a few minutes. He was shocked that I called him, and as a Frenchman could not understand my visit.

I told him quite simply that I loved Rosa but that I could not walk out on the obligations I had back home. This might seem strange to a European, I told him, but to a Southerner it was part of his honor. I promised him that I would never see Rosa on a serious basis again, and that I hoped he would call her that very day and go see her, for I knew she would be very lonely. I said I hoped they would marry and that he would always be kind to her and look after her. On that note, with tears shed by both of us, I left him and went straight to my plane bound for the U.S.

As we reached the end of the runway, a car came tearing toward the plane. A Navy chief leaped out, shouting, "Commander, what'll we do with your Mercedes?"

I had a marvelous Mercedes convertible that we had taken in occupied Germany. I had the keys in my pocket. I tossed them to the Navy chief through the open door of the plane.

"It's yours," I said. "Goodbye."

For me, the war was over. Once again, I headed back to Jackson.

* * *

Three months later, I received an invitation to the Paris marriage of Rosa Morley and Jean LaBoussier.

PART TWO:

The International Citizen

Part Two

In Part Two, we see John return home, though he is not the same person he was when he left. By the time the dust of World War II has settled, he is truly an international citizen, a role he will expand upon for the rest of his life.

But first he takes his family to Chicago and sets about building the American Trailways bus system. "For a young man from Jackson, Tennessee, there was no better training than the United States Navy and the bus business," John says. "The Navy trained me in the world. Every foreign city, every town, every place of any consequence—I was either in it or close to it or knew about it. When I moved into the bus business, I learned about America—the towns, large and small, in 48 states and what makes them tick."

This period in John's life brings him into dealings with a continuing cast of characters, from Howard Hughes and Adlai Stevenson to gangster Joe "Bananas" Bonanno and Teamster head Jimmy Hoffa to a continuing string of audacious hustlers. Con men "have cost me millions of dollars," John writes, "but somehow I feel nothing except good will toward them."

Why? Because, whatever their shortcomings, the con artists in John's life have always been entertaining. "And if like me, you are born with genes that require you to be happy and have fun," John says, "then that is the direction to take. I recommend it without qualification."

After American becomes prosperous, John transforms a sideline interest—novelty toys—into a multi-million-dollar business. The story of the remarkable Drinking Duck, one of the •most successful toys of all time, provides a classic example of striking gold with entrepreneurial instinct and drive.

John's spectacular success with this attention-grabbing enterprise soon makes him a centerpiece in the dominant national media of the day, the general-interest magazines in America. Once his story goes out across the land, he finds himself scrambling to escape a bombardment of 50,000 letters, telephone calls, cables and visits—most uninvited and undesired.

John learns to survive this too, however, and soon establishes such a comfortable, secure life that, at 50, he begins to figure he has done enough for one life. Then, Inez Robb, one of the best-known newspaper columnists, invites him to a lunch that forever changes John's view about how to live life to the fullest.

— ROBERT KERR

4

Postwar Adventures

WHEELS, "WHEELS," WHEELS

Three days after my release from the U.S. Navy, I had a call in Jackson from a Mr. Wheelock Whitney in Chicago who said he wanted to come to see me.

He arrived two days later, along with a Mr. Glore and a Mr. Watson. These three gentleman had come to ask me to join their group in building a transcontinental bus line to compete with Greyhound. How they chose me I never knew for sure, but I assumed it must have been Secretary Forrestal's suggestion.

"Wheels" Whitney was the heir of his father's interests in Northern States Power. His family and I became great friends from the start, and he remained my warmest and dearest associate until his death from cancer. I loved "Wheels" as did so many others. He was the kindest man I ever met in business.

Charlie Glore was the most prestigious banker in Chicago and head of Glore, Forgan and Company. Jack Watson owned a famous old shipping company known as the Munson Lines.

They made me an offer I could not refuse. I decided to leave my small investment company, pack up my family and try my hand at the bus business. Ten days later, I was in Chicago with an apartment at 1550 North State, an office on the top floor of the IBM Building on Michigan Avenue and an airplane at my disposal. I had made a four-year agreement to try to acquire enough local bus companies to put together a national carrier.

Apart from Greyhound, there was only a large group of local bus carriers at that time, mostly owned by former taxi drivers or small transfer companies. Most started out carrying baggage and trunks to hotels from their local railway station. As roads were built, they added buses to take passengers to nearby towns. They either operated independently or as part of a loosely affiliated association known as Trailways. The three men who came to see me had played important parts in financing the building of the Greyhound Corporation, and they had decided it might be done again. They were interested in additional profits, but also in keeping the government from bringing antitrust action against Greyhound.

One of the first things I did when I reached Chicago was to go to see my old friend Eric Wickman at Greyhound. I had met Eric back when I wrote a history of the Greyhound Company for *The Saturday Evening Post* and *Reader's Digest* titled "Everything Happens on a Bus." Eric and I hit it off from the first time we shook hands.

This intriguing little Swedish immigrant originally came to America to work in the iron mines outside Hibbing, Minnesota. He put in five hard years, saving every penny to go back to Sweden. Then one day, a slick salesman came to town and sold Eric not only a Hupmobile, but also the Hupmobile franchise for the county and the Goodyear Tire franchise for the three adjoining counties. By pure coincidence, I'm sure the price of the transaction was almost every cent Eric had saved.

Two weeks later, it dawned on Eric that the only automobile in the entire county was his Hupmobile. Further, there was not a single car in the three counties where he owned the Goodyear Tire franchise. Realizing his prospects for tire customers were limited, he looked for another way to generate a return on his impulsive investment.

Sheer necessity made him decide to gamble on driving passengers in the Hupmobile over the barely negotiable road between Hibbing and Alice, a distance of 11 miles, in competition with a horse-and-buggy company. Eric's first route ran from the post office in Hibbing to the First National Bank Saloon in Alice. The service proved so popular that he had to take on a partner, Andy Anderson, who fortunately was a mechanic.

Their system was simplicity itself. At the end of each day, they would take the pennies, nickels, dimes and quarters they had earned to their room at Mrs. Brown's Boarding House and put them in a trunk underneath the bed where they slept. At the end of the week, they would pay off the gas, oil and repair bills, then split the balance 50-50.

By the time I moved to Chicago, Eric's one-Hupmobile operation had grown into the Greyhound Corporation, a large company that, with its associate companies, completely dominated the industry.

Greyhound's executive staff occupied the top floor of the great Greyhound Tower in Chicago. According to Eric, his executives had all learned the business from the wheels up.

The president was simply the best bus mechanic around. "He can repair a bus motor with no parts," Eric said. The executive vice president was the best "bag-grabber" who ever lived.

This was a reference to the days when the competing lines had "bag-grabbers"—men who would compete with each other to carry passengers' luggage for a fee as far as three or four blocks from the bus station. The fellow who got the bag would also lead the way to his employer's station for the bus-ticket purchase. The competing carriers were usually located just across the street from each other, and the competition was fierce.

Those days were not so far in the past at the time I agreed to help build a new national bus line. It was still a rather "wild and woolly" business.

HOWARD HUGHES—NO DEAL!

About the same time I accepted the proposal to move to Chicago, I had a call from Carl Lueder. In the early days of my war service, when I had been thrust into the assignment of assistant director of the Naval Air Transport Service under Captain "Showboat" Smith, I could never have survived without Carl's exceptional help and advice. He was a very skillful airline operator, an ever modest man, and my great friend.

Before the war, Carl had been executive vice president of TWA under Jack Frye. He knew every phase of running an airline, from the design and structure of the planes to controlling a pilot's ego. Whenever I had to write operations directives, Carl told me exactly what to say. His instructions always worked beautifully. After the war ended, we left the Navy at about the same time.

"John," he said, when I picked up the phone, "I need some help. Howard Hughes has sent me word that he wants me to come in as president of TWA. As you know, he is a tough cookie. And worse still, for some reason, he frightens me to death. I was wondering if you would consider negotiating an employment contract for me? I'll be glad to pay your fee."

"There will be no fee, Carl. I could never repay you for the help you gave to me in NATS. When do you meet Hughes?"

"He's a very strange man. He sent word for me to meet him day after tomorrow at 10 p.m. in the bar of the Meuhlbach Hotel in Kansas City."

"I'll meet you at the Meuhlbach at 7 p.m. that day," I said.

Carl told me at dinner what he wanted: a five-year contract with a salary of $150,000 (which I raised to $250,000), a car with a driver, plus certain family health and retirement benefits.

Then Carl said, "I want one other thing—probably the most important of all. I want to run the airline without his constant interference."

I said, "From what I've heard about Hughes, that will be very difficult. If your mind is made up though, let's try it, but in a different way. Write briefly on a piece of paper exactly what you want in that regard.

Let me trade on everything else, and then at the very end, you give him the note. We may have him so far down the road that he will agree."

Promptly at 10 p.m., we arrived in the Muehlbach bar. At 11 p.m. we were still waiting in the bar—and we were still there at midnight.

At about 12:30 a.m., Howard Hughes, dressed in a pair of wrinkled blue trousers with a hole in one knee, very old tennis shoes and a work shirt, finally rolled in, without any apology whatsoever. His manner was as arrogant as I had been told.

Carl introduced me as his old Navy friend who handled contract matters for him. Hughes obviously did not like my injection into the matter, but he accepted it.

I laid out the basic details of our proposal in less than 20 minutes. Hughes' only comment was, "I think the salary is high, but I'm willing to try it. Everything else is okay."

So I said, "There is just one other thing, Mr. Hughes, that Carl feels is reasonable and that I would assume you certainly would want anyway. Carl, give him your note."

Hughes took it and read it. Then he reread it.

After less than a minute, he viciously crumpled the sheet of paper, threw it on the floor and said emphatically, "No deal."

With that, he got up and walked out of the bar. Neither Carl nor I ever heard another word from him again.

* * *

I felt badly about the Hughes outcome, because flying was Carl's life. When the Coca-Cola Company of Chicago approached me about taking over one of their West Coast operations, I recommended Carl. He was given a most attractive proposal to run Coca-Cola in Oakland, California, which he accepted.

However, Carl had been on the job just two days when he had a massive heart attack and died. He was a very dear friend.

HOW YOU BUILD ONE

When "Wheels" and the others came to me, they had already purchased control of a company known as the American Bus Lines. The company ran from New York to Los Angeles but had only interstate rights. This meant it could only handle passengers traveling across state lines. The plan was to purchase all the small or large lines that had intrastate rights, so our company could sell tickets for travel between any two points.

My job was to trade for the companies along our routes and to fight for intrastate rights from the state highway commissions. The first company purchased was a big one, Burlington Trailways, and in the next two years we bought some 40 or 50 more companies. Some of them had only 15 to 50 miles of route, but had the essential intrastate or "grandfather rights" we needed.

A typical bus line purchase was the Mohawk Trailways of Springfield, Missouri. It was owned by Floyd Jones, who was one of those pioneers in the business who started by carrying baggage and trunks from the railway station to the hotel. Floyd was later a partner in the Tucson Rapid Transit Company with me.

In an effort to buy his bus line, I flew to Springfield to negotiate with him. Floyd took me to his cabin in the Missouri hills about five miles off the main road. I spent three days with him—drinking bourbon from about 3 p.m. on and hunting coons at night. Floyd hadn't received a statement from his company accountant in more than a year.

As he explained to me with a shrug, "My one-legged bookkeeper is an alcoholic, John, so you can't really believe his statements anyway."

On the second night, I asked Floyd what he wanted for his bus line. I saw his lips tremble.

"John, I want a half-million dollars cash," he ventured.

"Is it worth it?" I asked.

"John, I expect you'll find a lot more than that when you check it all out. For the last year or so, I've just been drawing a thousand dollars a month out of it to look after me and my sister."

"Okay, Floyd," I said, "I'll buy it. I have complete confidence in you."

I meant it. The next morning, I sat down at the cabin to write out an agreement. Floyd came in and said, "John, I forgot something last night, and I can't go through with that deal on the basis we agreed."

My heart fell as I asked, "What? What did you forget?"

"My desk and chair. It belonged to my father, and I can't sell it."

I laughed with relief. "Well, Floyd, you are just too strong a negotiator for me. I will specify in this agreement that in addition to the Mohawk garages in Springfield and in Memphis, your personal desk and chair and the contents therein are not included in this purchase."

I finally sobered up the one-legged bookkeeper and found out where he had carefully stashed everything. There was more than $400,000 cash and other hard salable assets worth another $200,000 to $400,000, all this in addition to three buses and the "grandfather rights" to intrastate passengers across Missouri.

JIM OATES AND ADLAI STEVENSON

The other crucial element in building a national bus system was preparing the cases and trying the applications that we made to the various state commissions requesting intrastate rights. These applications were vigorously fought by Greyhound and many other carriers, particularly all the local ones along our routes that we had been unable to purchase.

Because of the legal time involved and my time, this proved to be an unbelievably large undertaking in terms of expense. The attorneys decided to use me as the principal witness, so over a period of two years, I was on the witness stand more than 250 days.

There is no finer training school in the world than being on a witness stand day after day, cross-examined by an endless series of lawyers, all with different mind patterns. In the process, I also became well-acquainted with most of the small towns and cities in the United States. It fascinated me to build this network of intrastate rights that linked them all together and in my mind to see America come alive!.

Fortunately, I had enormously competent attorneys working with me. Sharing this trial by fire, we became warm friends. The best one was widely known in the Midwest as the busiest lawyer around. His name was James F. Oates.

For three years, Jim and I traveled the roads and worked out our cases. In every bus-company purchase, he was the one who finally wrote the documents by which we lived. He finally devoted 100 percent of his time to this job.

We became a remarkable team, hardened by a number of defeats. In the long run though, we won a great many more of the cases than we lost. When Jim told me he had an offer to become chairman of the People's Light Gas and Coke Company, the largest company in Chicago, I cried.

It was something he could not turn down, but I certainly missed him. After two years with People's Gas, Jim went on to become chairman of the Equitable Life Insurance Company in New York. He built that business to where it was one of the two leaders in the insurance business in the United States.

When Jim left, I used local attorneys in the various states. Meanwhile, his firm—Sidley, Austin, Burgess and Harper of Chicago—was constantly sending me young attorneys to try as Jim's replacement. I finally reached the point where I didn't even take them with me to trial. After lunch with them, I would usually decide that they were not tough enough to handle a particular job. Jim had been so good that, in most instances, I doubt I really gave the replacements a fair chance.

Then one day, Jim called me and said, "A friend of mine has just come back from the United Nations, and I think he might be able to do the work you want, the way you want it done."

"Well, Jim, I'm so tired of talking to these fellows," I replied. "Don't waste time telling me about him, but if you think well of him, have him meet me Sunday afternoon at Midway Airport for the 3 p.m. Braniff flight to Dallas. If I don't feel he's right for the job, I'll tell him so there. Otherwise, I'll take him on to Dallas and talk to him on the plane."

That Sunday was a rainy day. Back then, you went to the gates at Midway Airport and walked out a distance to the steps to the plane. At the entrance for the Dallas flight, there was a man in a beat-up raincoat with a funny hat and worn-looking shoes. He was asking everybody who came through the little gate, "Are you Mr. Tigrett? Are you Mr. Tigrett?"

I looked him over and almost didn't admit who I was, thinking I could slip on by. But at the last minute, I guess I felt sorry for him and said, "Yes, I'm Mr. Tigrett."

"Jim Oates sent me to go with you," he said. "I have my ticket."

"Well, let's board, and we'll talk on the airplane. By the way, what is your name?"

"My name, sir, is Adlai Stevenson."

At that time, Braniff had one of the first Boeing airplanes with a lounge in the back. I took him there and started telling him about the particular application we were seeking on this trip, for intrastate rights from Dallas to El Paso. I had been over the route and knew it fairly well. I told him about each little town and about the schedules Greyhound was running at that time, as well as about other competition in this area.

When we reached Dallas, "Ad" and I went to the Baker Hotel, where we were given two of the smallest rooms I have ever seen. I took out a fifth of Jack Daniels, and we sat in my room and talked and talked and talked. About 1 a.m., I finally said, "Look, we must get some sleep."

The next morning as I was shaving, it hit me. I thought to myself, "My Lord, what have I done? We sat there drinking and talking for hours, and I have no idea what this fellow is going to say!"

I reminded myself that I had a former governor of Texas who was familiar with this case as associate counsel, and I decided that I could not gamble with this Stevenson fellow, whom I had not even known 24 hours. However, we had breakfast together, and the more I saw of him, the better I liked him. Finally, I decided to give him a try on the opening statement and see how he performed.

When our turn came, the hearing room was crowded. It was a joint hearing before the Interstate Commerce Commission and the State of Texas Highway Commission. "Ad" stood up and apologized, explaining that he had just come in on the case the previous night. Then he proceeded to give the finest opening statement I have ever heard on the bus business and why we should have an intrastate franchise.

He talked for almost an hour. He remembered every fact, every figure and the name of every town. He spoke quietly and with great dignity. When he finished, I was so excited with his performance that I jumped up, threw my arms around him and kissed him.

"You are one of the very best at this that I have ever encountered," I exclaimed. "From now on, you are my man."

And he remained my man—until he ran for governor of Illinois and was elected. Then in both 1952 and 1956, "Ad" was nominated by the Democratic Party for president of the United States.

Even when he was running for president, and I was with him several times, he always looked as if he had just slept in his clothes and hadn't had time to get them pressed. But once he started talking, he had you. You forgot the rumpled suit, the scuffed shoes, the battered raincoat and the hair out of place. He spoke with enchanting wit and persuasive intelligence. He and Jimmy Goldsmith are the two most erudite men of my life, each possessing a unique mastery of the English language. "Ad" and I had a lot of fun together. He was a man of great stature and would have made a remarkable president.

For me, those 10 years in the Navy and the bus business gave me an unbelievable education. They also gave me as many useful experiences as you can crowd into one lifetime. For everything that could happen, did happen—and I loved every minute of it.

EVERY MAN IS A THIEF

My stout little secretary, Rosemary Olsen, was very protective of me. She did her best to screen all my Chicago visitors.

One day she came in and said, "Mr. Tigrett, there's a gentleman out here who wants to see you. He had no appointment. He will not tell me his name, and he will not tell me what he wants to see you about."

"Then, just let him wait," I said.

About 30 minutes later, I looked out the door and saw the fellow. He was a reasonably nice-looking man, well-dressed, and I decided for no reason at all to see him.

Rosemary showed him in, and he said, "My name is George Johnson. That's not my real name, but that's the name I will use in this meeting. I want to talk to you about thievery in your bus system."

"Well, I'm not interested," I said. "We don't have any thievery, to speak of."

"Yes, you do, Mr. Tigrett," he said. "I expect on a system as big as yours, it amounts to between 10 and 20 million dollars annually."

"That's absolutely ridiculous," I argued. "It couldn't be so."

"Mr. Tigrett, you discover some strange things in life, but I'll tell you one thing I know for sure," he continued. "You will find that every man is a thief."

"I don't believe it," I said.

"It's true; every man's a thief of something. He may pick up a pencil," he said, "and slip it in his pocket, or food in a grocery, or he may pick up loose change. But, every man—and every woman—is basically a thief."

"Well," I said, "You'll have to prove it to me."

"That's why I'm here, sir," he said.

"Where do you want to do it?" I asked.

"I'll do it anywhere you say on your system," he replied. "I'll show you that your bus drivers are all stealing money from the company."

"That's just not possible," I insisted.

The week before, I had been in Omaha where we had Burlington Trailways, a big division. I had given away some five-, 10- and 15-year pins to the drivers and other employees—as fine-looking a group of American workers as I ever saw. After the presentation, there was a lovely dinner for these straight-up, honest folks. I was positive there couldn't be any thievery in that group.

So I turned to Mr. Johnson and said, "All right, you try out the division that I just left last week in Omaha. Check those bus drivers."

"How many do you have?" he asked.

I checked on it, then told him we had 55 drivers based there.

"I'll tell you what I'll do with you, Mr. Tigrett. I'll make you a proposition. If I prove to you that 90 percent of those drivers are stealing money from you every day, you owe me $50,000. If I don't, you owe me nothing."

"Mr. Johnson," I replied, "I'll give you $25,000 if you give me incontrovertible proof."

"Oh, the proof will be incontrovertible," he said.

"On that basis," I retorted, "you have a deal."

"Okay, Mr. Tigrett. I'll make the first deal with you for $25,000," he agreed. "I'll call you when I'm ready."

After his visit, there was not another word from him for more than a month. Finally I received a call, though he was still so guarded, he wouldn't even give his name on the telephone to Rosemary.

"Just tell Mr. Tigrett I want to talk to him about Omaha," he said. "He'll talk to me."

She put him on, and he said to me, "I'm ready, Mr. Tigrett. When can you come to Omaha?"

"I can be out there day after tomorrow," I answered.

"All right, sir, we'll be at the Plaza Hotel. I'll meet you in the lobby at noon, and I would like you to also invite the union's district agent," he said.

We met at the Plaza, and Johnson took me upstairs to a suite of rooms with a desk and chairs at one end of the living room and drawn curtains at both ends. He also had some sort of control box on the desk.

"I made appointments through the union agent, and the drivers will start coming in here at 1 p.m.," he said. "The union agent will sit here by me. You will sit on this side, and the driver will sit right here in front of me. His chair is on a swivel so he can look at the screen. Behind the curtain at the back of the room is a projection operator," he said.

At 1 p.m., the first driver came in, a fine-looking man wearing a 10-year pin. I greeted him and told him how happy I was to see him and how proud I was of him. When he sat down, I said, "I know nothing about what this man wants to do. Whatever it is, the union and I will find out at the same time."

Mr. Johnson started out by saying to the driver, "On the 21st of this month, you drove the run from Omaha to North Platte and then on to Cheyenne."

"Yes, I think I did," he said.

"You think you did, or are you sure?"

"Let me look in my book," the driver replied, and after checking, he said, "Yes, I drove that run."

"Do you recall just outside of Ashland picking up three Indians who had a lot of luggage?"

The driver thought a moment and then said, "No, sir, I don't believe so. I don't remember exactly, but if I do remember, I don't believe I did, sir."

"You don't recall picking these people up at all, and you don't recall letting them off somewhere close to Broadwater?"

"No, sir, I don't remember that at all."

"Well, let me refresh your memory a little bit."

With that, Johnson pushed a button, and the curtains separated to reveal a large projection screen. The lights went out, and he told the operator to start the projector.

The first thing we saw on the screen was the daily newspaper for the 21st of that month. Then we saw three Indians waving down a bus. The bus stopped. The Indians had a lot of boxes and things that they couldn't carry on the bus, so the driver got off. A close-up left no doubt that it was the man sitting in the room with us.

Then we saw him picking up a suitcase and some beat-up boxes, and with the Indians' help, loaded them in the cargo area under the bus. Everyone got on the bus, and it proceeded. The next thing we saw were the same three Indians getting off the bus on the roadside. The driver came off first and opened the underneath storage, took the suitcase and boxes out and handed them to the Indians, who then departed.

The driver's report for the 21st of that month then came on the screen. It showed his name, number of tickets taken on that date and the fact that he made no roadside pickups or discharges. Johnson then asked the driver, "Do you know the fare that you charged them?"

"I guess I just slipped up and forgot to put it on the report—I'm sure I turned it in," the driver replied.

"No, you didn't turn it in," said Johnson. "You turned in only the tickets shown on your report. It does not include the fare the Indians paid you, which was $22.10."

"Well, I guess I just overlooked it, sir," said the driver.

Signaling the projectionist to start again, Johnson said, "Can I show you what you did on the 23rd?"

With that, the driver started crying. "I didn't mean to take anything from the company," he wailed. "I just didn't have any way to get it recorded."

Johnson had caught him, just as cold as you could possibly catch a thief. He went on to prove conclusively that of the 55 drivers there, 53 were stealing money from the company. I was so disheartened and discouraged, I could not sleep for nights.

"You have certainly earned your fee and given me a great education," I said to him.

I arranged to send him a check for that amount, and he gave me his real name and address in Louisiana. I decided to use him on a few other divisions far from the one in Omaha. I knew that the word would get out very quickly. I paid him a total of $150,000, and our revenues in those areas picked up on an annual basis by about $3 million. The drivers had been stealing small amounts, but altogether it added up to a lot of money.

I then called Johnson and offered him a different deal. "My friend, you have now established your reputation with our drivers," I said. "We have 15 garages scattered throughout the territory in which you work. From now on, every time you walk through one of our garages and speak to the people there — just spend 30 to 45 minutes chatting with them— I will pay you $500."

He laughed and said, "That's the best deal I have ever made."

He didn't abuse it, but every time he did a walk-through anywhere, our revenues would pick up there 1 to 3 percent. We didn't prosecute any of our people, but we did have to fire a number of them.

We also had to rebuild, motivate and train new drivers, and it was a chore to get good ones. However, for the most part we solved the stealing matter by simply letting Johnson walk through the garages.

JIMMY HOFFA

As the years went by, our bus business thrived. I also did well with the Tucson bus company in which I held interest. And then the Mafia began to get wind of how well we were doing, and decided to move in.

Joe "Bananas" Bonanno ran the Tucson Mafia, as well as being involved in the Las Vegas and Los Angeles organized crime. Through the use of "blind pigs" (the local name for hidden ownership), he was reportedly the majority owner of a leading laundry and the principal soft drink company in Tucson, in addition to some other major businesses in town.

A call came to me one day from an attorney reputed to be one of Bonanno's men, saying he wanted to come to see me. I met him the next day, and he told me he had a client who wanted to buy the Tucson Rapid Transit Company. I replied that my partners and I had no interest in selling since we wanted to keep an interest in Tucson. However, when he left, he said, "I think you would be wise to give this matter further thought, if you want to avoid any trouble."

About 30 days later, our labor contract expired and the Teamster drivers walked off the job. I had been in this situation before and had settled it with no problems in less than two weeks. This time, though, it was different.

Someone cut up our bus seats and tried to burn the garage. It all culminated 10 days later when two of the replacement drivers were killed. All hell broke loose in the newspapers and television, convincing me to call Jimmy Hoffa, head of the Teamsters. He agreed to meet me at the Adolphus Hotel in Dallas three days later.

I took the audited statements of the company with me, and we met in his room. He was alone. I told him to look at the statements of the company first and then to tell me what settlement he thought would allow the property to continue to operate. He sat with the statements for some time and made a number of calculations on a yellow pad.

Finally, he looked up and said, "I don't see anything unreasonable in your overhead and maintenance figures. You've got a very low operating cost. You can probably give us another 12 cents an hour and still oper-ate, but it will be tight." That was two cents more than my final offer.

"Okay," I said. "I'll try it." We shook hands. That was the negotiation.

We had completed in one hour what I had failed to do in days of meetings with representatives for the drivers. Hoffa then said to me, "I'm sorry about that violence and those two drivers. It should never have happened. It was all the fault of that son-of-a-bitch who's the Western manager of my organization. I just found out he has been working with the Mafia, and through them, with 'Bananas' in your town. I'm on my way to L.A. this afternoon, and that bastard will be lucky if I don't shoot him myself. I'm going to kick his ass out of the job and clean up that whole West Coast mess."

He then added, "If you have any trouble getting the new contract through, don't call the regional attorney. Come directly to me."

That is my memory of Jimmy Hoffa—a tough guy but, in my book, also a fair one and a good businessman. He represented his people well.

Two months after the settlement, a well-dressed, gentlemanly Swede from Minneapolis came to see me. He was recommended by a prominent banker there and said he had a group that wanted to buy the company. By this time, I was tired of dealing with labor disputes. A week later, we worked out a sales agreement that was satisfactory to me and my part-ners, Kim Whitney and Floyd Jones.

Several months later, I was told that the purchaser was a very close friend of Joe "Bananas" Bonanno.

Reverend Samuel King Tigrett (holding the child) and members of the First Baptist Church, Tigrett, Tennessee, on July 4, 1895

John Burton on one of his many trips to Moscow, trading for Occidental Petroleum Corporation, Armand Hammer and others

(Left) The marriage of Pat Kerr to John Tigrett by Dr. Norman Vincent Peale in the great Marble Collegiate Church (29th Street and Fifth Avenue, New York City), November 24, 1973

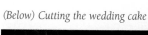

(Below) Cutting the wedding cake

(Left) On the way down the aisle, the bride to the groom, "I hate being married."

(Above and right) The beautiful bride,
Pat Kerr Tigrett

Pat (right) and her sister, Jana, would later become Pat Kerr, Inc.

The Tigretts' beautiful London home, One Cumberland Place, Regents Park, NW1

Lord Roy Thomson; the Sheik of Umm al Quayne, Trucial States; and Dr. Armand Hammer at the signing of an oil concession, 1970

Isaac Tigrett and Johnny Carson at one of the famous July 4th parties at One Cumberland Place in London

A unique group of old friends on a white-wing dove shoot in Mexico

Harrison Kerr Tigrett, age 7 days, with his proud and loving mother,
Pat Kerr Tigrett, 1977

Yawning Kerr Tigrett with his mother and two godfathers, Sir James Goldsmith and
Dr. Armand Hammer

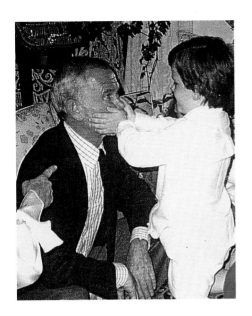

(Left) Kerr Tigrett thanks Johnny Carson for showing him a new card trick.

(Below) Kerr au naturel, 1978, with his mother

(Above) Kerr with his songbird friend, Andy Williams, 1982

(Right) Pat, Kerr and Kerr's godfather, Jimmy Goldsmith, 1984

(Left) John Tigrett; Sir John Foster, famous Queen's Counsel and senior warden of Oxford University; and Lord Roy Thomson, Cairo, Egypt. The trio was trading for a half interest in El Ahrum, the leading Egyptian newspaper.

(Right) Jim Goldsmith, John Burton and Jim's son, Maness Goldsmith, in Mexico, 1995

Pat Kerr Tigrett with the three men in her life, 1994

5

Fun and Games

ADVENTURES IN TOYLAND: THE DRINKING DUCK

Over the years, the Chicago Mafia also put a great deal of pressure on me. Eventually I grew tired of the hassles and returned to Jackson to devote more time to a sideline of mine—toys and related products. It would prove hugely successful in the 1950s and make me a little more famous than I ever desired.

Weekend ventures have always been my passion. During the week, I keep my mind focused on my current mainstream project. But on Friday night, I turn those off like a water spigot. Then for two days, I completely change my pace and mind-set, with new excitement and fun.

One Saturday morning in Washington, D.C., in the early 1940s, I was dictating a story for the *Saturday Evening Post* and *Reader's Digest* to Miss Emily Binko, the public stenographer in the Park Hotel.

As I dictated, I noticed my concentration swerved every few minutes toward a nearby "ping" that sounded as though someone was tapping a glass lightly.

"Miss Binko," I finally said, "what is that pinging noise?"

"Oh, Mr. Tigrett," she said, "that's my 'bird.' "

With that, she went over to a file cabinet behind me. I turned around just in time to see the "bird" work once as she reached to stop its motion.

"Wait a minute," I said quickly. "Let the 'bird' work again."

I moved over to the file cabinet and saw a glass tube about 6 inches long with a bulb on one end covered by a small piece of toweling. It was attached to a glass of water with a little wire cradle made from a paper clip. The liquid would run up the tube, causing the towel head to dip in the water; with that, the seal was broken, and the liquid would run down again, starting the process all over.

I reached for the telephone, called my friend Dos Hatfield, a patent attorney, and asked him to come over right away. We both spent some time watching it work, but could not figure it out.

"Dos," I said, "somewhere in the world, a fellow has a patent on this bird. Find him and buy it."

A month later, Dos called. "I found your 'bird' inventor," he said, "His name is Charles Harold, a well-known concert violinist. He also told me how it works. He made up a few of the gadgets, one of which he gave to Miss Binko's boyfriend. Harold owned only half of the patent, so I bought it from him for $800. The other half he gave to a college chum of his who runs the Moonbeam Broadcasting System located on 42nd Street in New York. I haven't been to New York lately, so I haven't had a chance to get the other half."

"Good job, Dos," I said. "Send me a patent-ownership transfer form, and I'll tackle Mr. Moonbeam when I'm in New York next week."

I couldn't find the Moonbeam Broadcasting System listed in either the telephone book or the Yellow Pages, but I had an address and decided to make a visit.

When I reached 42nd Street, I thought there had been a mistake because the address turned out to be a porno theater featuring "Live Girls in the Nude Every Hour!"

I noticed a dark and rather rickety-looking stairway next to the theater, so I decided to explore further. At the top of the stairs, I found several offices that seemed to belong to old-time theatrical agents. In the

The Drinking Duck

middle of them, in the largest, heaviest gold letters you could get on a glass door, was a sign announcing the office of the Moonbeam Broadcasting System.

I knocked and was greeted by a very friendly little man about 5 feet tall, wearing large, round horn-rimmed glasses. He identified himself as the president of the Moonbeam Broadcasting System.

"What can I do for you?" he asked as he stepped into the hall.

"Do you know a man named Charles Harold?" I asked.

"I do know Charles Harold. We were in college together. But there is no need for us to stand in the hall. Please come in my office."

The door to his windowless office opened directly into the hall. I could see the office was about 4 feet by 7 feet, with a large length of pipe running through one end. There was just room enough for his desk, squeezed between the doorway and the pipe. To allow a visitor to enter the office, the president of the Moonbeam Broadcasting System had to push his office chair under the desk. I could then slide through the narrow space to reach a small straight chair between the pipe and the wall.

We talked a bit about show business and Charles Harold, then I said, "I think I might be able to do something with the Harold glass-bird invention of which you own half. What would you want for your half?"

He seemed shocked but replied, "Well, as you know that invention has great potential—great potential. However, I am not in the position to do anything with it. Would you pay me $250 for my half?"

"Will you sell it for $250?"

When he said he would, I reached in my pocket and countered, "Well, I won't buy it for that. But here are eight $100 bills. You are entitled to the same price we paid Charles Harold."

Except for the fact that the pipe was between us, I think the president of the Moonbeam Broadcasting System would have kissed me . . . or fainted.

Within six months, I found a specialty glass manufacturer in Detroit, and we developed a stamped cradle that looked like legs. We also added a bottom bulb to make it work better.

To the flocked top bulb, we had added a duck bill, a funny hat and two crossed eyes. With a bit of paint and the addition of feathers to the bottom bulb, we were ready to introduce The Drinking Duck to the world.

At that time, the busiest traffic corner in the U.S. was said to be at State and Randolph streets in Chicago. Walgreen, with its large windows on both streets, was located there. Mr. Moss, the manager, rented me all his windows on State and Randolph for three days beginning on Monday.

Late Sunday night, we pulled down all the window shades. Inside, we installed specially designed troughs with a reserve water supply in each end so the troughs would stay filled for 48 hours. Then we arranged more than a thousand Drinking Ducks, all rocking and "drinking" out of these troughs in perpetual motion.

We finished about 5 a.m., with the shades scheduled to be raised three hours later. I went back to the hotel exhausted. Just before 9 a.m., the phone rang and rang. When I finally picked it up, I heard the desperate voice of Mr. Moss, the Walgreen store manager.

"Mr. Tigrett, please, please come over here immediately," he begged me. "There is a mob scene outside our windows," he begged. "The police are about to arrest me for creating a public nuisance."

By the time I reached the store, Randolph Street had been blocked off, and about 10 policemen were trying to keep the State Street crowd from being run over. They had arrested Mr. Moss, but had not yet taken him away. The store was in absolute havoc.

I quickly asked that the shades be pulled and the window doors locked from the store side. Slowly the crowd began to disperse, and order was restored to the Walgreen Drug Store. All the window-display units had been sold, as well as all the backup stock. Several hundred more people paid their $5 and received a receipt entitling them to a Drinking Duck as soon as Walgreen could get more in stock.

That was the beginning of one of the most successful toys of all time. We went on to sell more than 20 million units of the remarkable Drinking Duck.

* * *

Of all the amusing and interesting stories that were told about this toy, I think I most enjoyed the one about Albert Einstein. His son wrote a book about his famous father, and one of the anecdotes included was about his father's Drinking Duck.

Einstein's son said the great scientist spent several days trying to figure out how the Drinking Duck worked. Finally, he gave up.

YOGI BIRD

With the success of the Drinking Duck, I began to look around for other unique toys for Tigrett Industries. I had established the company to develop unusual toys and related products. I received a telephone call from a man named Fritz Weigel, who said he was head of research of a division of the B.F. Goodrich Company in Cleveland, Ohio. He thought he had a potential toy, and he wanted me to look at it.

What arrived was a little balsa-wood box. Inside was a small sprocket with five suction cups on it. The instructions said to put it on a mirror or glass surface, and it would "walk" down the surface. When I tried it, it worked perfectly, except that I decided I wanted it also to walk up.

A couple of weeks later I met Fritz Weigel in Chicago, and he said he could add a spring and a winding string if we wanted it to walk up. I was impressed with Fritz, and finally that evening asked him if he would have any interest in moving south to work with me.

"I would move out of Cleveland even for less money," he said. "It has the most abominable weather and dark surroundings of any city."

Thirty days later, he was research director of Tigrett Industries in an old church building in Jackson. He had come up with the idea for the toy we dubbed the Yogi Bird while working for B.F. Goodrich. The company was the largest maker of suction cups in the world. Fritz had figured out that if you put a tiny hole in the cup, it would release after a fraction of a second. This was the heart of what made the Yogi Bird "walk."

At one time, more than 500 workers were assembling Yogi in Jackson. We sold more than 10 million, and started selling them in Europe.

When I reached Paris, I licensed the product to a leading toymaker, and took on the job of showing him how to sell it. First, I asked for the name of his best toy demonstrator in town.

"Unquestionably, it is Pierre LeQuoix," he replied. "But I must warn you, he is a very strange fellow."

The next day, I met Pierre. He was an enormous man of about 6 feet 8 inches and well-dressed, except he had a little watermelon hat sitting on top of his head. With him were four midgets, and I mean *midgets*.

The Yogi Bird was the perfect product for the Champs Élysées, with its two-story glass windows. About dusk, when the Champs was filled with people, Pierre and his group set out. They picked the Renault Showroom, with endless expanses of glass. In less than five minutes, they had attracted a crowd that blocked the broad walk.

Besides being boss, all Pierre ever seemed to do was stand in the crowd and watch the midgets put the birds on the window, then look intently as the toys climbed upward. When the spring was exhausted, and the bird jumped off the window, Pierre would throw his head back so that the watermelon hat would fall off, and cry out, "Amazing! Amazing!" Then they would start finding the hat.

They sold 3,000 Yogi Birds that night, and another 3,000 the next afternoon. I gave Pierre $3,000 in francs, which was his share. However, when I started to look for him that night, I could not find him.

I called my friend and said, "Where's Pierre? I gave him $3,000 for one night and one afternoon's work, and he has disappeared."

"Oh, you gave him his limit."

"What do you mean 'limit'? "

He laughed. "Remember how I told you he was the envy of every Frenchman but a very strange fellow? Well, he has his own philosophy of life. Once he has made $3,000, he gives the midgets $1,000 and stops work. Then he goes some place on the Left Bank, gets drunk with three or four women and stays there until his money runs out. When he sobers up, he will come back to work again."

I was intrigued—I had to stick around and wait for my new friend Pierre to return. Sure enough, three days later, just before dark, he showed up at my hotel looking immaculately dressed with his midgets, ready to go to work again. Pierre took up his stand at the Renault Showroom on the Champs Élysées. The last view I had of him as I headed for the airport, was Pierre in the midst of a large crowd, his head jerking back just enough to make his watermelon hat fall off as he shouted, "Amazing! Amazing!"

THE ENDORSEMENT GAME

One year, at the Wimbledon Tennis Championship, I was at a luncheon in super-agent Mark McCormack's tent. Upon hearing my name, he exclaimed, "From Jackson, Tennessee?"

When I said that was correct, he announced, to my complete surprise, "My friends, this is John Tigrett. He is the man who put me in business. He was my first customer and gave me confidence to give up the law and take on a new career."

Back in the 1950s, I had decided that the best way to sell our sporting goods line was to get star endorsements and use them in television spots. The first athlete we used was Willie Mays. I made a deal directly with him for $2,500 to endorse a device called the Pitchback. Willie had no manager at the time. The Pitchback had a nylon net that was attached around the edges to springs on a frame. When a ball was thrown against it, the Pitchback would return the ball.

We filmed the spot in Florida, where Willie was in spring training. As he was practicing on the Pitchback, a fellow player came by and asked, "Willie, what is that thing?"

"I don't know," Willie answered, "but it sho' do pay good!"

When the Pitchback proved successful, we developed a large frame featuring a nylon net without springs, into which you could drive golf balls. The net absorbed the energy of the balls, and they dropped down to the ground.

Arnold Palmer was the brightest new golf star of the day, and I decided to use him in a television spot if he was available. When I reached him he said, "You will have to deal with my agent. He's a lawyer in Cleveland named Mark McCormack."

I called McCormack, explained the product and told him what we wanted Arnold to do in the television spot.

"I understand," he said, "I'll get Arnold to do that for $5,000."

"I'll give you $2,500," I retorted.

"I'll take it," he replied, and that was the beginning of the sports marketing empire McCormack has since built.

Once the papers were signed, we found out that Palmer was playing in a tournament in Mobile, Alabama, that week. So Albert Stone and his assistant took our television people down to shoot the spot.

I was in New Orleans at the time and, at the last minute, decided to go by Mobile on the way home. The television shot had just been set up when I reached the Mobile Country Club. As I stood in the back of the crowd, Palmer was teeing up the ball. He took a couple of practice swings and then finally hit a mighty drive. The ball went straight through the net and down the fairway a couple of hundred yards, where it bonked a man on the head. I turned quietly, slipped out of the laughing crowd and caught a taxi to the airport.

Later on, it cost me $5,000 to settle with the man Arnold hit.

THE SPRING MAN

My secretary in Jackson came in my office one day and said, "There's a nice, tired-looking little man outside who wants to see you. He's from Austin, Texas, and has ridden the bus all night to come see you."

I was busy at the time, and I told her, "Let him wait." I forgot about him until I came out for lunch. Here was this unimpressive gentleman, patiently waiting. I introduced myself and apologized. He said his name was Edwin Foster and that he was the inventor of something he wanted to show me.

I didn't know why, but there was something enormously appealing to me about this man. I said, "Come have lunch with me and tell me about it. You can show it to me later."

At lunch, Edwin told me he had been exploring spring steel for some time. It was his contention that by pulling it through a dye that curled it slightly, he could get an almost constant amount of energy from it. This was unlike spring clocks, for example, which are most powerful at the start but gradually run down to nothing. At lunch, he showed me a small roll of spring steel he had cut off, which when unrolled was stiff as a stick. By the time lunch was over, I had no doubt that Edwin Foster had hit on a simple and remarkable process. If there were not too many conflicts in spring patents, he could make a small fortune.

The next weekend, I went to Austin to understand fully what he was doing and to look at his laboratory. What I found was a very small house in a modest neighborhood with a makeshift laboratory in the basement next to the furnace. Edwin's muscular son, Wilbur, was his assistant, and the die he was using was two pieces of wood held in a vise. When I asked Edwin why he didn't make any of the steel pieces longer than 6 feet, he said, "That's all Wilbur has the strength to pull through the die."

I never had a written agreement with Edwin. We trusted each other implicitly. He was one of those people you meet infrequently who are not impressive in appearance or conversation, but who immediately draw on your sympathy with their modesty, earnestness, and soft, hesitant voice. You know almost intuitively that their life has been a struggle, but they have never complained.

I gave Ed an advance to make some better models and told him I would pay his travel expenses. I also told him I would want to be paid 6 percent. We soon licensed his spring steel as the "Spirator" to the Lufkin Rule Company for all rules over 10 feet. My Zurich associate, Louis Habegger, also licensed it for similar purposes in France, Germany, England and Japan.

Ed installed a "Spirator" in an Eastman Kodak movie camera, enabling it to feed an entire 25-foot film without rewinding. At that time, the spring used on the Eastman unit could only feed about 7 feet of film before it had to be rewound.

We staged a demonstration for Kodak in Rochester, New York, in front of about 15 department heads and engineers. Ed took one of their cameras and replaced the Kodak spring with his "Spirator"; then he put the unit so everyone could see it work. I explained that he had found a way to get more work from a piece of spring steel and said, "Run it through, Ed." Ed wound the camera, turned it on, and the whole 25 feet of film fed out onto the conference table.

"That's not possible," said the head of their research department.

I laughed and said, "Run it through again, Ed," which he did, with the same results.

Hundreds of uses were found for the "Spirator." I later built a small plant in Jackson to make Ed's Lineator, a 3-foot or 6-foot rule that coiled itself, yet could remain stiff when rolled out. Sometime later, I sold that business to Lufkin Rule, which today is part of Cooper Industries.

I was once told that the American flag placed on the moon had a Lineator at top and bottom so it would stand out straight for the photos.

The last time I saw Edwin Foster, he owned what possibly was the largest house in Austin, built on top of a tall hill with a spectacular swimming pool and a marvelous view overlooking the town. He also had a real research laboratory, which was automated—so Wilbur didn't have to pull the steel through the die by hand anymore.

CHARLES AND RAE EAMES

Charles Eames and his wife, Rae, were one of the most distinguished teams of architects in the world. I had never heard of them until they wrote me saying they had a toy they would like me to see.

About a month later, I was in Los Angeles and called Charles. He came by and took me to his lovely home. His small plant was located nearby at Pacific Palisades, where he showed me models of three beautiful toys:

• The House of Cards—playing cards with striking photographs that had slots in each card so you could build with them in any direction;

• The Giant House of Cards—a much larger version of the original cards;

• The Toy—a building set of dowels and large sheets of tough paper, the dowels giving support on the edges were tied together with pipe cleaners.

I liked all three models, so we came to an agreement and he began to perfect them for manufacture. Charles Eames was acclaimed throughout the world at that time for his molded plywood chair. That afternoon, he showed me his experiments with a molded fiberglass chair.

He tried and tried that day, and for some days later, to get me to join him in producing the chair. However, I knew so little about that market and had my hands so full at the time that I diplomatically turned him down.

Later, Charles found a partner in Herman Miller Furniture Company in Michigan, and began one of the most successful manufacturing ventures ever. No telling how many chairs they sold. They are in every airport, every school, and hundreds and hundreds of other places. In the history of chair making, there has never been a chair so popular. Every time I see one now, I regret letting that opportunity go by.

As for Charles Eames' toys, they were successful, but primarily as "art objects." They never made it to Woolworth's, but they are still being produced in Germany today.

T H E   P L A Y - A - R O U N D

A product that revolutionized an industry was the Play-A-Round. The idea came about when our son Johnny fell and cut his head on a wooden spoke on his playpen.

At that time, all infant beds and playpens were made of wood. I was convinced that a nylon net could replace the wood. After many trials and the help of the Sears research laboratories, we finally came up with a round playpen that had three steel legs supporting two aluminum rims and a masonite bottom. The top rim was covered with vinyl, and a heavy pad on the bottom made it childproof.

We shot more than 10,000 feet of movie film, from an unobserved position, with infants in the Play-A-Round in order to see their reactions. It was fascinating. Those films wrote the book for infants from six months to two years of age, and gave us product after product. But first I had to sell the Play-A-Round.

Harry Sundheim was able to get a large order for the Sears catalog. However, the catalog was months away; in the meantime, no retail operation would touch our playpen. So I took a Play-A-Round to New York, wrestling it in and out of taxi cabs, and went to every buying office. Without exception, they turned me down.

I then took on the major department stores: Macy's, Gimbel's and Saks. They had exactly the same reaction: No!

It was odd. Every rejection only made me more confident. Watching those tiny humans in those films had convinced me that the Play-A-Round, for safety alone, was a needed product.

I decided to try Chicago, where I had a few friends, and took my well-worn demonstration model along to show a few more times. The president of Marshall Field was an old social friend, so I called him.

"My friend," he said, "our infant buyer is a tyrannical German woman of about 60 who has been here 20 years. She is so tough that no one has ever had the nerve to fire her. But if you want to try your pitch on her, come on over."

I went by his office and kidded him into coming along with me. His description of Mrs. Fisher proved to be an understatement. She paid no more attention to the president than she would an office boy. To me, she said, "I have only 10 minutes to give you for your demonstration. Get with it."

As I went through the demonstration, she kept making remarks to her milquetoast male assistant loud enough for the president and me to hear. "I've never seen a more ridiculous product," she barked. "No infant would stay in that thing for five minutes. I really shouldn't even spend 10 minutes watching this foolish demonstration."

By the time I had finished, I was as red as a beet with pure anger.

At that point, Mrs. Fisher said, "Mr. Whatever-your-name-is, you apparently know nothing about infant products. I would not even have this monstrosity on my floor."

I bowed low and said, "Mrs. Fisher, you are so kind, and I do value your opinion. But as far as I am concerned, you've got the damn unit on your floor, and it's going to stay there. Let's go, Tom." I took my friend by the arm, and we walked away quickly.

The next afternoon, I was in my office when I overheard my secretary say, "Yes, ma'am, you want another Play-A-Round?"

She turned to me and explained, "There's a Mrs. Fisher from Marshall Field on the phone. She said some crazy woman had come in and bought the Play-A-Round, and she wants us to send her another one."

I laughed and said, "Tell Mrs. Fisher she will have another one within 30 minutes."

Marshall Field sold 10 Play-A-Rounds the first week, and from then on, we never looked back. Within less than three years, the net playpens and beds had revolutionized the industry, seizing more than 95 percent of the market for such products. It remains so today.

6

A Few Good Con Men

For some reason, I seem to be a magnet for con men. Somehow, I pull them out of a crowd of thousands and make them my friends.

They have cost me several million dollars, but somehow I feel nothing except goodwill toward them. For along with almost believing in their own fraud, they are, in general, the most charming, imaginative, convincing people on this earth.

Not one I ever met thought small. They all dealt in stupendous processes that, if for real, could produce vast and immediate fortunes. Plus they usually exuded that boundless kind of enthusiasm that sometimes creates miracles in and of itself.

If like me, you are born with genes that require you to be happy and have fun, then that is the direction to take. I recommend it without qualification.

Still, my friends are always questioning me: How did a grandson of a Baptist preacher, raised under the strictest conditions in a small Tennessee town, end up making a business of representing world-famous rascals, double agents, gamblers, takeover kings and entrepreneurs?

The answer is very simple.

It dates from that day in Alamo, Tennessee, when the deal on the Hatchie Bottom Drainage District No. 1 bond issue showed me I could deal for myself. I determined I would never be salary bound and would only consult with or represent interesting and daring minds.

My associates have almost all been people who were not impressed with regulations or bothered very much about the law. They figured that—with enough time, money and lawyers—there was always a way out of anything.

I have enjoyed laughing at life with these rascals, the most intriguing, devious and exciting minds on this earth. To me, "rascal" is a term of endearment, for I loved them all. And for reasons unknown, despite their ever suspicious minds, they trusted me implicitly.

It is only a short step down from being a world-famous rascal to being a plain confidence man. However, even with the con men, I have not one single regret. I learned something from each one, and it was worth the price.

Let me tell you about a few.

A Smooth Old Game

Albert Noe, owner of the New Southern Hotel in Jackson, called one day and asked me to come have lunch with him and meet an oil friend, Cliff "Tex" Henson, from Kentucky.

Albert's friend stood about 6-feet 3-inches tall. Tex was appropriately dressed for an oilman of the time: boots, Levis, Western shirt and string tie. He also wore what appeared to be two big diamond rings on one hand and a third ring on the other.

Tex explained that he had been very successful in Kentucky and that he had discovered the "trend line" that came down into West Tennessee. In fact, he said, Madison County, in which Jackson is located, lay at the very heart of this "trend."

So Tex wanted to check out the area and take some leases. With that, he produced a large-scale map of Madison County marked with a great number of red Xs in four areas. He pointed out how he had discovered by "coincidence" that one of the marked areas was part of the 2,500-acre Albert Noe farm.

Tex told us he had brought with him the very latest computerized device for finding oil. He said that industry leaders no longer used the old-fashioned seismic shots to find "highs" for drilling, and he had one of the vastly superior new machines that did exactly the same thing with "Zeon gas rays."

Tex continued to explain at length the intricacies of the new machine until Albert finally said, "Why don't we try it out on my farm?"

"Well," Tex said, "why not? We won't find anything on such a casual outing, but at least you can see how this unbelievable machine works."

We went out into the parking lot to Tex's stretch Cadillac. I sat up in the front seat with his driver, while Tex and Albert rode in the back. Between them sat a machine about 2 ½ feet square. It was constructed of very shiny metal and had lots of impressive-looking gadgets, dials and lights on one side. When it was turned on, the bottom emitted what looked almost like lasers—two red and two green.

We headed for an area at the back of Albert's farm. It was a rough area, but our friend's map had many Xs there, so he thought it might be the heart of the "trend." Tex explained that the floor in the car affected the beams, but that they were so strong they could at least begin to locate the crucial "highs" in an oil field. If the lasers turned red, it meant there was a "high" at that point.

As we rode along, Tex constantly turned a little handle on his machine, which was shooting out tiny beams of light intermittently. Suddenly, Tex yelled, "Stop!"

He began turning the handle even faster and said, "Now, go a little bit farther." Finally, he said, "Now, wait a minute . . . stop right there and let me take the machine out of the car."

Tex had a rig in the back with wheels. He put the machine on it and began excitedly walking back into an area we couldn't reach in the car. He was turning the crank all the time. I never saw a man get more excited than Tex did when all the lights on the front of his machine lit up.

"My God!" he yelled, "I've never seen that before with this machine. There must be a limitless amount of oil here. Let's move around."

By this time, Albert was just as excited. I knew a little bit about the oil business and had never heard of this machine. So while I appeared excited, what I was really trying to do was to see what was inside.

"I've never witnessed this before in my life," Tex continued. "There must be more oil here than this machine has ever found before, and it is absolutely foolproof."

We returned to town and Albert began calling his friends. Among them, they soon had $250,000 to get Tex to bring in his rig and explore the area. I tried my best then and many times later to get Albert to slow down and check out Tex further, but it was all to no avail. No matter what his station in life, once a man is sold on something he believes might make a quick fortune, no one can stop him.

Tex brought his rig down, and I think the final amount that Albert and his friends put into the operation was $2 million dollars. They never found any oil except what dripped out of Tex's leaky rig.

Ions

Joseph Hilton was executive vice president of the Continental Illinois Bank in Chicago. I knew him when I was there in the bus business. He called me in Jackson one day and said he wanted to send down a friend he thought had a remarkable invention. Joseph and friends had agreed to back the man up to a million dollars, but he wanted to first see what I thought.

Several days later, his friend—a man in a loud purple Hawaiian sports shirt, blue jeans and open-toe shoes—came to my office. The first thing he did was give me a lecture on the mind and body's reaction to positive and negative ions in the air. He intrigued me, for I had never heard of ions. He lectured for some time, until I finally asked if he could demonstrate what he had been explaining.

A few minutes later, I was sitting in the back seat of a new Buick sedan under a device attached to the roof that was roughly 18-by-18-by-3-inches. Wooden leaves on the bottom had been turned to face downward. It was a cloudy day, about to rain, as we started driving down the highway.

"On days like this," he explained, "the negative ions are present everywhere. They depress everyone. I can look at you and see that you feel like you are carrying a heavy weight. Your breathing is not free and easy. Am I right?"

"Well," I said, "I don't feel too bad, but I have felt better."

"There," he said. "What did I tell you? That's those negative ions working on you. Now let me turn on the positive-ion machine."

With that, he turned on the switch of the box over my head and a soft breeze came from it.

"Now, leave the windows open. It will take about 10 minutes to drive the negative ions out of the car," he continued. "After that, you'll begin to feel better."

Ten minutes later, he said, "Now, put up the windows and you'll begin to feel the positive ions. If you stay under this machine for an hour, you'll be a new man—thinking positively and wanting to get busy doing many things."

After several minutes of positive ions, I suggested we turn around and head back to the office. On the way, I asked, "Does this device have any commercial applications?"

"Oh, yes," he said. "My brother has it installed in a plant in Europe, and it has had amazing results."

"Tell me about them," I said.

"Well, the first week it was in use, the employees felt so good that production increased about 10 percent," he said. "The second week, the workers voluntarily reduced their lunch period from 45 minutes to 30 minutes so they could get back to work sooner. The production then went up 20 percent. By the time the positive-ion machine was in place for a month, the workers were taking only 15 minutes for lunch, and production had gone up 40 percent.

"I have not personally checked on these installations lately, but I have heard that now the workers no longer want any lunch period. The production at the plant is almost twice what it was before they installed the positive-ion machine."

"Where is this amazing plant located in Europe?" I asked.

"Oh, I'm sorry, my friend. That is the deepest of secrets. Until our patents are granted, we cannot reveal that location to anyone," he replied.

I wrote my pal in Chicago and reported word for word my experience with his friend and the ion business. I never heard from him again.

THE RE-IGNITABLE MATCH

Batton, Barton, Durstine and Osborne was one of the largest advertising agencies in the U.S., and the company's president was an old friend of mine. He took me to lunch one day at "21" in New York and told me of a remarkable device he had just seen in Sweden.

The device was a small stick about 2 ½ inches long that you could strike like a match and use repeatedly. My friend had the Reynolds or Liggett account at that time and wanted to put one of these sticks in with each pack of their cigarettes. He had already paid $100,000 for first refusal of a 60-day U.S. option on the process and was so excited about the prospects that he wanted me to organize a private company to manufacture the matches in Jackson. He said he could raise all the capital required, and he gave me copies of the filed patent applications and several trial units.

Three weeks later, I found myself registering at the Grand Hotel in Goteborg, Sweden. The next morning a man named Paul Swenson, who said he was the attorney and brother of the inventor, called on me at the Grand. I had just introduced myself to him in the lobby when he put his finger up to his lips and said, "Come with me."

He took my arm, and we walked for several blocks in silence. We finally reached a small park and selected a bench isolated from the others. He looked around everywhere and finally he said, "We were being followed from the hotel, but now it's all clear."

I breathed a sigh of relief and said, "What's all this cloak-and-dagger business?"

Looking around first, he then whispered in my ear, "The Swedish Match Company—they are everywhere. They will stop at nothing to get my brother's secret formula. I fear his life is in great danger. You may be sure that everything in your hotel room will have been searched by the time we return. I certainly hope you did not leave any confidential papers there."

"No," I said. "I have with me the option agreement and my passport."

"I'd like to see your passport," he said. "I'm sorry. We can never be too cautious."

I handed him the passport and he reviewed it with great care, looking at every page. He finally asked me to sign my name on a piece of paper just as it was on my passport. This I did.

He examined both carefully and finally handed back all the papers and said, "My brother will not be able to see you today. I will contact you tomorrow." With that, he walked away quickly.

As I sat on the park bench, I thought, "This is something I really don't need—an undercover spy operation, with double agents and shadow mystery men. I'm going back to Jackson."

By the time I had walked back to the hotel and found my things untouched, I decided to spend another day checking out the scene.

Paul picked me up the next day about 10 a.m. He felt again that we were being followed, but I saw no signs. He drove us on a strange and curious route, always looking around very suspiciously and at last pulling into the dock area where he stopped before a large tin building.

Two well-armed guards there spoke to Paul. We went into a small room where I was searched. From there they took us through three doors with big padlocks. My thoughts were of Sherlock Holmes, Earl Stanley Gardner, James Bond and all the mystery characters I had read about over the years. Here I was in my own spy novel.

After we cleared the third massive metal door, we walked into a large brightly lit room. It had a row of beautiful, shiny Swedish machines that mixed and formed the re-ignitable matches and carried them by belt from the cut-rolling machine to the packing machine, which wrapped them individually and dropped them into boxes of 50.

Ivan Swenson, the inventor, was a large Swede with golden hair and a very kind face. He was an impressive-looking fellow. He took me carefully through every step of the process and would pick up a re-ignitable match from the belt every now and then, strike it and blow it out. It was a great show. The machinery was spotless and worked with remarkable Swedish efficiency. Anyone would have been impressed. I watched the process for more than an hour and finally said to Ivan, "Okay, I've seen enough. Cut it off, and let's go where we can talk."

Shortly thereafter, we were at his home for a late lunch. His wife and daughter, typically Swedish in appearance and manner, were there. After lunch, we began negotiating a deal. He asked for $5 million down and 20 percent royalties. We finally reached agreement on a payment of $1 million down, 15 percent royalties and a salary for him as advisor of $100,000 a year for three years. I wrote the understanding on a notepad, and we both signed it. We agreed we would have the final closing in Jackson, Tennessee, where he could also help develop the layout of the plant and begin to talk to the base personnel about any problems. The machine was to be moved as soon as the operating space became available.

Three weeks later, Ivan Swenson was in Jackson. The president of BBDO had raised the funds as promised and deposited them in the First National Bank in Jackson. I agreed to take my $250,000 fee in company stock. We were ready to formally close the next morning.

Somehow, I began to feel insecure about the whole deal. Things had gone too easy. I had been amazed he agreed so quickly to my terms of $1 million instead of the $5 million he originally requested. I decided the secrecy in Goteborg was all fiction. Ivan had worked for the Swedish Match Trust for 20 years. Why didn't he sell to them? I thought of all this and more while worrying about closing.

Ivan was staying in my home in Jackson, and that night we had a dinner party for him. I had Fritz Weigel, our research man, and his wife Peggy in the group. As they left, I walked them to the car and told Fritz of my last-minute concerns.

"Have we tested everything? If you think of anything more we can do, Fritz, call me tonight no matter what the hour," I said.

At 2 a.m., the phone rang. It was Fritz. "John," he said, "after we left you, I went down to the lab and put a few of the matches in the oven at temperatures that would approximate leaving them in a closed drawer for several months or in a car on a hot day. I took one out and struck it, and it went off exactly like a bomb. In fact, it burned my hand so badly that I'm talking to you from the emergency room at the Jackson Madison County Hospital. Fortunately, I had on protective glasses, or it would have caused serious eye damage as well."

"Fritz, I'm distressed that you were burned, but you have found the answer."

The next morning, Ivan Swenson and I were having breakfast on the side porch. After the usual pleasantries, I turned on him like a tiger.

"Ivan, what is it about your match that you haven't told me?" I asked.

"What do you mean?" he said. "I have told you everything."

"Not quite," I said. "You haven't told me of one deadly defect—that if you leave these things around for six months or even less, they turn into a bomb. My associate, Fritz Weigel, almost had his hand blown off last night after he left here. Could you live with yourself if you had us put these things out to the public, and hundreds of people were maimed or killed—or even just one? Do you want that?"

Tears came into the old man's eyes, and after a long silence he said, "I have worked night and day for five years trying to find an answer, but I could not. I'm so tired, I let my need for money overcome my good judgment."

Ivan left for Goteborg that afternoon, and I never heard anything from him or anything about the wonderful re-ignitable match again.

WATER TO GASOLINE

This story occurred many years after I had left Jackson for London, but it is a classic account of a master con man at work.

William Rahman, a man always on the "fringe" of the oil business in London, called me one day. Excitedly, he said he had just seen the most remarkable oil development of his life and asked when I could come look at it.

I felt sorry for Rahman, for while he kept trying, he could somehow never deliver. I told him if I was in London the next Sunday, I would look at it. I forgot the matter until he called me again and said he had the demonstration set up about an hour's drive outside London.

He asked what kind of car I would come in, and I told him we would probably be in a Rolls Corniche. "That would be very difficult," he said. "Since this is a fuel demonstration. It would be much easier if you could come in a two-tank Jaguar. We need to have one tank completely empty."

I told him I would try. I found such a car at Avis, and rented it. It had two completely separate gas tanks in the rear, and you could switch from one to the other. My instructions were also to bring a can with me containing exactly one gallon of regular gasoline.

I arrived at the English country inn with Eric Levine, a lawyer, and a friend of Eric's, who was an oil engineer. We were introduced by Rahman to George Barnhill, who described himself as a nuclear engineer. This fellow looked like a country bumpkin until he started talking. He then explained that water was made up of hydrogen and oxygen, as we all knew, and the problem had always been to separate the two.

Barnhill had worked on a separation formula for 10 years before nuclear ions had been found, and he had applied these to water in a nuclear laboratory near Kent. He had found, after three years' work, that he could split the water atoms with unbelievably high temperatures and mix the results with gasoline. He said he could mix up to 85 or 90 percent of this new material with regular gasoline, and it would power a car or other units just as well as current fuels.

The next thing Barnhill did was take one of four glass jugs from a corrugated box and pour the liquid into three paper cups. "Try it," he said. "It will not hurt you." The other two men sipped sparingly, but I took a full swallow and declared it tasted the same as water.

Barnhill then took our can of gasoline and started pouring it slowly into one of the jugs, explaining that his liquid was only to be 75 percent of the new material. The balance was to be the gasoline we had brought in. He was very careful to put only one-quarter of the gasoline into the jug.

After more lecturing on the chemical process, he said, "Do you have a car outside?"

When I said I did, he replied, "Then, let's go try it."

He handed me a jug, and we went to the Jaguar. Barnhill's assistant got under the car and turned the tap on one of the tanks, letting the gasoline run out. He put the tap on again, and Eric poured in the new liquid. Eric drove and I sat beside him on the front seat. Barnhill's assistant was in the back.

"I don't want you to think there's anything contrived in this experiment," Barnhill said as we drove off.

Eric drove to the highway and accelerated the car up to 60 or 70 miles per hour and said, "The Jaguar runs better on this stuff than on gasoline."

We returned to the inn, and I told Mr. Barnhill I would like to option the process. The engineer, Eric and I were all convinced and enthusiastic about the process. We agreed to return the next Sunday with the papers, and I would bring down a different group for one additional demonstration.

The next Sunday, I brought down two chairmen of prominent oil companies and the same engineer. The remarkable demonstration was the same except Barnhill expanded on his discussion of the nuclear aspects and said he had gained access to the British government's nuclear laboratory, which was in the same area. He asked for £100,000 good-faith deposit on the option and an initial payment of

$5 million. We were to finance a £10 million plant in Florida, and he was to retain a 25 percent royalty of the overall result.

On the way back to London, the two oilmen, both my old friends, had quite an argument as to whose deal it was. They both wanted to put up the whole amount. I finally settled them down by telling them that I would put up the £100,000, and we would make a consortium with each partner owning 20 percent of the operation. Together with the Occidental Oil Company and investor Lord Roy Thomson, we would put up all the money required for the downpayment and the Florida Plant.

We were one excited group, especially the oil boys. They laughed and laughed about how they would have their way with the "Seven Sisters" (as the world's seven largest oil companies were called). They wanted one more demonstration for two of their directors, and I arranged it for the following Saturday. Meanwhile, I would pay the £100,000 so they would feel secure about the option.

The last demonstration went off very well, but to our surprise, a group from Florida was also there, and they were prepared to pay more for the rights. This group was headed by a doctor from Clearwater who said he was prepared to pay £250,000 for the option. I took him aside, and we finally worked out a deal to cut him in for 20 percent. He was to come to London the next weekend to sign the papers.

That Saturday night I did not sleep well, for reasons unknown. I began to wonder for the first time about the four gallon jugs Barnhill had in the cardboard box. Had we actually used the same one in the gas tank that he used to pour us the water to drink? Or did he have methylene in a separate jug that he somehow switched on us? Was it a simple case of jug switching, the oldest trick in the book? I rolled and tossed, and on Monday morning called John Smith at his home.

John Smith was a man Jimmy Goldsmith and I had used to check out the top management of every deal we made. In a few days, he could give us a highly personal dossier on any president or chairman—what sort of person they were, what hobbies they had, who were their girlfriends, and what were their drinking habits. This remarkable fellow helped us immensely, and the information he developed was always correct. Today he has possibly the largest corporate detective business in Europe.

All I gave John Smith that Sunday morning was the name George Barnhill and the address he had given me. I did not tell John anything about the deal, for I still felt confident Barnhill was on the level.

On Tuesday about noon, John Smith reached me. "I'll have you a complete rundown on Barnhill by Wednesday," he said. "Have you paid him any money?"

"Yes, £100,000," I answered, as a sinking feeling came over me.

"Don't pay him another penny, and do not talk to him if he calls on the phone. I'll figure out a way to get your money back."

Shocked, I said, "Tell me more."

"I'll see you Wednesday. Meanwhile, just follow my instructions."

On Wednesday morning, John came to my office and gave me as complete a dossier as I have seen on anyone, including newspaper clippings, a prison record and bankruptcy papers for a period of 20 years. George Barnhill, the "innocent country bumpkin," was one of the greatest confidence men Europe and the U.S. had ever seen.

"Now, about your £100,000," John said. "Get your lawyer on the phone, and I'll tell him how to get it back."

Eric Levine was away, so I called an old friend of his, a tough woman lawyer named Gillian Benning.

John asked me, "What lawyer did Barnhill use when you paid the money?"

I gave him the lawyer's card, and John said, "Ms. Benning, this is a case of extortion by a famous confidence man named George Barnhill. He has been in personal bankruptcy, and as you know under our law must report to the court every expenditure he makes over 50 pounds."

John explained the situation in great detail and finally said, "Just call Barnhill's lawyer and tell him if he doesn't have the £100,000 back by noon tomorrow, you are going to bankruptcy court and take over everything he has, including his shoes!"

The next day at noon, the lawyer brought the £100,000 along with an agreement that I would not reveal to the newspapers, or others, any of the details of the transaction. I signed. Ms. Benning sent a runner to the bank with the check, and we collected the £100,000.

However, great confidence men never give up. About a year later, I had to appear before a grand jury in West Palm Beach, Florida. To my surprise, the Florida doctor who had nearly come in on our deal with Barnhill had paid him more than £1 million before recognizing the fraud. Barnhill would never hand over the formula. In my opinion now, there never was any formula.

I went before the grand jury in West Palm Beach, and the district attorney tried very hard to get me to say I knew the formula didn't work.

"I can't say that," I replied, "because I don't know. I never saw the formula. All I know are two things: One, whatever he had in that gallon jug worked as well as gasoline. And two, that if Barnhill were to come in here today—to this grand jury—and put on his act, every single one of you would invest."

My testimony brought down the house. The grand jury failed to return an indictment.

Six months later, I was summoned to appear before the grand jury in Dallas, Texas. It seemed Barnhill had persuaded a member of the wealthy Hunt family to put a reported $5 million into his scheme. Barnhill used the same old routine, drawing in his victims, then always refusing to deliver the formula.

However, this time Barnhill had grown a little overconfident and careless. Enough evidence was produced against him for a conviction that sent him to federal prison for 10 years.

7

Fame, Fun and Changes

WHEN IT RAINS, IT POURS

Tigrett Industries was grossing $2 to $3 million a year, and my association with unusual, original products began to be of interest to the
national magazines.

Soon my old associates at *The Saturday Evening Post* called and sent
Art Baum to do a color story. Around the same time, Charles Eames
called about *Life* wanting to do a cover article. *Look* also asked to write a
feature on our childproof-testing operations, and my friends at *Reader's
Digest* also sent down a writer.

Here were the four leading general-interest magazines in America, all
wanting stories at the same time. I was afraid to let any of them know
that the other was doing a story, so I staggered their visits to Jackson over
a couple of months. All had different lead times, and I thought they
would probably space themselves out.

During this two-month period, while I was in New York, *The New
Yorker* and *Time* also interviewed me. In addition, my dear friend Inez
Robb, who had a column in 220 newspapers, did an interview with me
after a Sunday lunch at her penthouse on 13th Street.

There was no publicity agent involved in any of this, nor did I make any effort to attract even one of these stories. They just happened.

Weeks went by and nothing appeared, so I was beginning to think our little operation must not have made a very good story after all. Then suddenly, within a two-week period in 1953, every one of the articles appeared in print.

There were seven color pages in *Life,* six color pages in The *Saturday Evening Post,* five black and whites in *Look* (where they dubbed me "Toy Tycoon Tigrett"), a feature story in *Reader's Digest,* plus articles in the *New York Times, The New Yorker* and Inez' widely distributed column.

To say this media blitz turned my family's life upside down would be a considerable understatement. I began receiving calls all day and all night from everyone you can imagine.

I had to change my telephone to an unlisted number, and for a month had to hide out from all the people who came uninvited to my office and my home to see me. I was inundated with more than 50,000 letters, telephone calls, cables and visits.

Once the last of the articles appeared, I decided I had reached the pinnacle in publicity, and from that day on I would never grant another interview to anyone. I stuck to that pledge for nearly 40 years.

* * *

No matter how high you think you're flying, however, someone can always bring you down to earth.

About a week before its color article on Tigrett Industries actually appeared, *The Saturday Evening Post* began doing local promotions in Jackson for it and other upcoming articles. One morning, to my surprise, I discovered my picture on a poster tacked onto telephone poles wherever magazines were sold in Jackson.

The posters announced: *Read about John Burton Tigrett and his Crazy Way To Make a Living.*

I always bought my weekly magazines at the neighborhood drugstore, Lehnings. It was run by a Mr. Ray, a large fat man who had bad

The Saturday Evening

POST

42

March 28, 1953 – *15¢*

It's a Crazy Way to Make a Living

By ARTHUR W. BAUM

Every year John Tigrett sells $2,000,000 worth of curiosities like hoppity birds that climb walls, ducks that teeter on the edge of a glass, Zoomerang coils that flick in and out like a cobra's tongue. Here's the inside story of one of America's daffiest businesses.

THE youngish chairman of the board, thirty-nine years old, two hundred pounds, curly hair and freckles, walked over to the office wall. "Got a new one," he drawled in a creamy Southern voice, and pulled from his pocket a bright plastic shell, less than hand size, in the form of a big-beaked, leering bird.

"Watch this," the chairman said and, after winding it up, he pushed its underside lightly against the wall. The creature stuck there for a moment and then, with rather slow, lurching hops, began to climb, like a downy woodpecker scanning a tree trunk for larvae. Up it went, slapping down one suction foot with nice timing just as it pulled the previous foot free. It was apparent that it had several feet arranged on a wheel in its insides, and as the wheel revolved it picked up one foot as it smacked another one onto the wall. Step by step it humped along, almost to the ceiling. When finally it fell off, its rubber-band motor exhausted, the grinning young man caught it in his hand.

Once again he wound it, placed it on the wall and stood away. This time the bird walked down, still with groggy hops, but a little faster. Again it was wound. This time it lurched sideways across the wall.

The young chairman beamed with pride. "Isn't it astonishing?" he demanded.

It was astonishing indeed, but not so much so from this particular source as it would have been from elsewhere. For the wall-climber was the latest curious product of Tigrett Industries, Inc., a Ten-

nessee toy-manufacturing firm which specializes in eccentric motions. The chairman, also the founder, was John Burton Tigrett, of Jackson, Tennessee, in which city, for reasons of home-town devotion, Tigrett has located the chairman and company factory. Founded only three years ago in Chicago, where the main office remains, the company is launched on a career of toys and motions that only recently resulted in the hoppity bird on the wall.

The new gadget, however, is descended from a line of authentic eccentricity. Tigrett also produces the Zoomerang, a plastic-paper coil on a stick that is only two inches long in repose, but which flicks out to an alarming five feet or so at the flip of a wrist, and instantly returns. He is also the owner of that almost departed drinking duck of a few years back, the creature that perched on the edge of a glass of water and bobbed up and down unassisted as long as it could get its beak wet.

Jacksonians were only mildly surprised to find Tigrett returning home a couple of years ago as a thriving manufacturer of toys. Fellow townsmen, having known him ever since he arrived from Memphis as a months-old baby, had observed him in so many roles that the number of characters remaining in which he might appear was growing limited. He had begun as a book salesman and investment counselor and had ultimately gone to the big city as an official of a nationwide bus company. He had enjoyed incarnations as hotel owner, author and

PHOTOGRAPHY BY BILL SHROUT

Florida real-estate operator. He was involved in a transit company in Tucson and had drilled for oil. For three years he h.d been a Navy lieutenant, but even here he bounced around, for the Navy lent him to the State Department and to Intelligence. For one service or another he has been around the world several times, though he has never yet set foot on a Navy vessel.

This restless record has left no mark on Tigrett, who is quiet and placid, but it may have been good background for the toy business, since toys are a peculiar and unpredictable industry. The toy market, influenced heavily by customers who buy on momentary impulse, is mercurial—it has not been too long since the leading seller by a margin of millions of units was a plastic hen laying plastic eggs. Thus there is no safe way of calculating the fate of the recently introduced wall-walking bird except to note that some prior Tigrett motions have succeeded quite well.

According to Tigrett, the Zoomerang line, for example, is currently the country's largest-selling toy, a surprising record to be popping out of the quiet town of Jackson, Tennessee. The Zoomerang coil has several applications. Already, 15,000,000 have been sold and 3,000,000 are being produced annually. The coil is a toy in itself, manipulated by hand. Or it is a sort of nonexpendable projectile in a gun, shooting out and coming back as a captive missile. It is also made as a captive arrow in a miniature bow and arrow, and Tigrett has one or two more forms which will appear later. (Continued on Page 172)

Johnny and Frances Tigrett and their sons, John, Jr., Isaac and Hewitt, playing with—naturally—Tigrett toys, in their Jackson, Tenn., home.

Tigrett treats the children of the Alexander School in Jackson to a toy free-for-all, designed to test the popularity and durability of his products.

feet and wore the toes of his shoes cut out. He never smiled, and only rarely spoke.

On the day of the *Post's* arrival, I proudly went down to Lehnings to purchase several copies. I was pleased to see five or six of these posters with my picture and name had been tacked up just outside the front and back entrances of the drugstore.

I was feeling elated and famous. After all, wasn't I "Toy Tycoon Tigrett"? I picked up three copies and saw Mr. Ray by the cash register.

Hewitt Tigrett with Hopalong Cassidy
and the toy guns made by Tigrett Industries

"Hmm," he said. "Are you sure you want three copies of the same magazine, Mr. Tigrett?"

"Yes, thank you, Mr. Ray," I said, anticipating some compliment from him.

"Must be something mighty interesting in there, Mr. Tigrett, for you to buy three copies—that's expensive. I never read it myself."

He made my change and returned to his business. I started to open a copy of the magazine and show him my story, but changed my mind.

There should be a Mr. Ray in everyone's life. They help us put things back into perspective when we begin to imagine we are important.

Dr. Norman Vincent Peale, Lord Roy Thomson, and John share stories in London.

APPLE PIE AND MILK

The late Dr. Norman Vincent "Doc" Peale and his wonderful wife, Ruth, were close friends of mine for 30 years. I doubt that any of us know where or how we met, but we all came from the same heritage of positive thinking. We have had more fun times in more places together than I can count.

Doc was the leading force in the world for making people believe in themselves. With their books and Guideposts, the Peale empire continues to offer a strong dose of courage every day to millions who need it.

Some years ago, I noticed that Doc was scheduled to speak in Nashville and I decided to go up and surprise him. The talk was scheduled for 8 p.m. in the War Memorial Building, and I arrived after he had started. All 4,000 seats were filled, so I stood in the back.

Whenever Doc finished talking, his admirers would always gather around him to get some private word or sign, or just to touch him. On this night, about 20 minutes after he had finished, he remained surrounded by a large group waiting to see him. As I moved through the crowd behind him, I said in a loud voice, "I'm sorry, Doctor, but if you don't come now you'll miss your plane."

Doc turned around and gave no sign of recognition, but said to the crowd, "I'm sorry, my friends. They tell me I have to go. God bless you all." With that, I took him by the arm, the crowd parted and we went out the back door. He put his arm around me and asked, "What would you charge to come up and save me once a night?"

"You couldn't afford me, Doc. But if you were a pretty girl, I'd work for free," I said.

"Where are you taking me?" he asked.

"I thought we would go down to the Andrew Jackson Hotel and have some apple pie and milk."

"One of your best ideas, Johnny Boy. Let's go!"

We walked the block to the Andrew Jackson and found it closed. "There must be some place open at 10 p.m.," I said, "but I don't know this town at all. Anyway, let's walk toward those lights by the side of the Capitol."

We walked along laughing and talking until finally we found a small place with a cafe sign out front. I opened the door and saw two or three small tables and a large woman standing behind the counter.

"Pardon me, ma'am," I asked. "Could we get some apple pie and milk here?"

She looked bewildered and mumbled, "Apple pie and milk . . . Wait a minute and I'll see."

Returning a few moments later, she said, "Yes, we have some."

We went in and sat at one of the tables. A few minutes later, the large woman served us each a small glass of milk and a flat piece of apple pie that looked as though it had been in the refrigerator for at least a fortnight.

Before we started, Doc said, "Let's have a word of prayer." We bowed our heads, but out of the corner of one eye, I noticed two girls had joined the large woman. Before Doc finished praying, one more appeared. They stood silently in back of the counter watching us eat the pie and milk.

John and Isaac Tigrett with Dr. Norman Vincent Peale (seated)

When we finished, Doc, being his usual cordial self, went over and introduced himself, then shook hands with each of the women. He asked what church they went to on Sunday. After a few moments' silence, one of them chirped, "I'm a Baptist."

The others did not offer any indication of religious affiliation, so Doc said, "Well, may God bless you all. Let's have a little prayer before we go".

After the prayer, I paid the $4 check, left a dollar tip on the table, and we walked out.

"That was a rather interesting cafe, Johnny Boy," Doc observed, "even though the pie was not too fresh."

"Yes, Doc," I said, smiling. "You're right about the pie. But it was not too bad for a whorehouse. I'm happy you had the prayer and blessed all the girls."

THE WORLD'S GREATEST SALESMAN

On many occasions, Dr. Peale and I discussed philosophical matters. Once, I said to him, "Doc, you and Billy Graham are possibly the best salesmen of Christianity around today, but your converts often hold for only relatively short periods. Why can't you sell like St. Paul? He made it stick.

"Here was a Turkish Jew, with a bad stomach, selling Gentiles a new religion. His only talents seemed to be his mind and voice. He was in a world that didn't want him, competing with established religions and goldsmiths and silversmiths making perfectly good idols. Yet, wherever Paul went, he was so convincing that he made Christianity dominate the inhabitants' minds, and almost everyone he touched became another missionary.

"Let's assume he had the power of the Lord behind him, but I would certainly hope that you and Billy have it as well. One day, I think I'll follow the path of one of his journeys just to see what he was up against. I want to see where he carried out his mission after asking that classic question of Jesus, 'What do you want me to do?'

"I want to discover, if I can, how he sold an idea—not to a group or a community or even a city, but to the whole Western world. In so doing, he became the greatest salesman the world has ever known."

Some months later, my quest to learn about the greatest salesman began. I started out from Jerusalem in two Range Rovers with the distinguished professor of ancient history of Ankara University and the professor of religion from the American University in Athens. Each one had an assistant, lots of books, tents, food, arms, et cetera.

We went to most of the places that St. Paul mentioned—and some he did not. Many of those locations in Turkey no longer exist. The sands of time, or the sea, have buried them forever, at least physically.

The mission of those two outstanding historians each evening was to reconstruct verbally the life of a town or village in the period of St. Paul's journey: How did these citizens make a living? What was the political situation? How were they taxed? What amusements did they have? What was their sex life? What religions were in town? Who were the leaders? What was their social life? What did the merchants sell? What were the food staples and the holiday foods? How many people were using idols?

They were to tell us everything they could to place the scene in perspective at the time St. Paul was there.

One night we were all sitting around the campfire on a plain south of Ephesus. Close by was a pile of rocks—all that was left of the former town. As I listened to the brilliant Turkish historian Dr. Kayaal describe the life there as St. Paul found it, I was impressed with how, overall, the living structure was remarkably similar to that of my hometown.

I interrupted him: "Doctor, with all due respect, you're telling us about this dead town in Asia Minor as St. Paul found it, but you sound to me like you're talking about Jackson, Tennessee. I could take you to the Jackson Country Club tonight, and you would hear the same arguments going on that you tell me were going on in the meeting place here.

"You would hear the same envy, the same greed, the same gossip. Their food here was perhaps a bit better because it was purer. But the politics were the same. The complaints about taxes and politicians were the same. Those about education were the same. The similarities are very close."

By the light of the fire, I could see my wise friend's eyes brighten. He smiled and said, "John, each generation lives only in a passing facade. It is like a movie set. Every succeeding generation calls it progress, but actually they have only placed the furniture a bit differently, perhaps added some new amusement, and sometimes painted their room of life a different color.

"The basic human mind, however—the mind of envy, desire, greed, sex, forgiveness, belief, generosity, drive, religion and all other human qualities—has never changed. And never will change."

"Does anything every really change?" I asked.

"Only the calendar, my friend. Only the calendar," he answered.

FINISHED AT 50!

For a good many years, Inez Robb was the highest paid newspaper columnist in the United States. Two hundred and twenty of the largest newspapers in the U.S. published her column.

From the first argument we had, while she was interviewing me in the old United Press Building in New York, we developed a mutual admiration society. Her husband, Addison Robb, for reasons unknown, was always after me for advice.

In the late fifties, I had scaled back my involvement in Tigrett Industries, and my family and I moved to a new home in Tucson, next to the Tucson Country Club. When Inez and Addison decided to move west as well, they came to Tucson because of our friendship. I helped negotiate a house for them down the street from the country club.

One weekend while I was in New York, Inez called and asked me to come to a party Saturday night at the penthouse they kept there.

"Thanks, Iny, but no thanks. I am 50 years old, and I'm tired out. I don't want any more social life or business life. I'm finished. I just can't take it anymore."

"Well, will you come to Sunday lunch tomorrow?"

"I might. I will be down in your neighborhood anyway. I'm going to hear Doc Peale preach Sunday morning."

That Sunday morning, I went to the Marble Collegiate Church on 29th Street, sat with Ruth Peale and listened to Doc give a "fire burner." Afterward, I visited with him for a few minutes and then took a taxi down to Inez' penthouse on 13th Street.

When I arrived, Inez was at the elevator as I stepped off. She greeted me and led the way toward the drawing room, where I noticed the French doors were closed. She put her hand on the door handle and then turned back to me.

"Johnny," she said, "you told me yesterday that you were 50 and finished. Well, I want you to meet two of my dear friends who are a bit older and who want to talk to you about being 'finished.' "

She opened the door and said, "This is Roy Howard, Chairman of Scripps Howard. He's 85 and still works every day. And this is Bernard Baruch, the well-known consultant to presidents. He's 87 and is still going like a house afire."

At that time these gentlemen were two of the most distinguished Americans alive. Spending time with them that afternoon convinced me that never again would I say—or even think—that I was "finished."

LET ME OUT OF THIS PLANE

Tucson, Arizona, in the late 1950s was still a Western cowtown with middle-class folks and a high degree of basic Americanism. One day I was enjoying life at our new house, just relaxing by the swimming pool, when our cook brought out the phone. The call was from Kemmons Wilson, chairman of Holiday Inn.

"John," he said, "I'm going to give you just one last chance to help us get Holiday Inns into Europe," he said.

"What would you like me to do?" I asked.

"Meet me at the Pan American ticket counter in New York tomorrow at 7 p.m. and go to Europe with me."

Life to me has always been like a Ouija board. Sometimes I have said "yes" and other times "no" without even thinking. For reasons still unknown to me, I said okay to Kemmons that afternoon and hung up.

The next evening, I was at the Pan American counter at New York's Kennedy Airport. Kemmons bought two coach tickets for us, and away we flew to London. We never discussed business of any kind on the plane. In fact, both of us went to sleep almost immediately.

The next morning, after we landed at Heathrow Airport, Kemmons told me, "We're going on to Paris. I have to meet Dr. Armand Hammer, the chairman of Occidental Oil there. Do you know him?"

"No," I replied. "Albert Gore has been trying for years to get us together, but our paths have never crossed."

When we landed at Orly Airport in Paris, Dr. Hammer had a man meet us to take us to his private plane, an old converted B-25. That was the first time I met Dr. Armand Hammer and his wife, Frances. It would prove to be the beginning of a long, sometimes rewarding, sometimes maddening, but always interesting relationship with Doc Hammer.

We climbed aboard the B-25, and I overheard that our destination was Rabat, Morocco. Kemmons had not spoken a word to me about going there.

Toward the front of Doc's crowded old B-25 was a small table on one side of a narrow aisle. He and Kemmons sat on one side of it, with me on the other. I started the conversation by asking, "Tell me about the deal you want to make in Morocco."

Kemmons answered, "Well, John, we are going to build four 300-room Holiday Inns in Morocco. The king has agreed to get us the land at a reasonable price in all four cities, and we, in turn, are going to put up $20 million apiece. We're going to build one in each of the cities of Casablanca, Tangier, Fez and Marrakech."

I interrupted: "Let me be sure I understand you, Kem. You and Dr. Hammer are each going to take $20 million of your stockholders' money and put it in four hotels in a relatively poor third-world country."

"Yes, that's it," said Dr. Hammer. "We'll build a great tourist business there with these modern hotels."

I had just met the plane's navigator, Frank Meyers, who was sitting on a small jumpseat in the aisle just in back of the pilots. I called to him, "Frank, where are we now?"

"We are just coming up on Nice, Mr. Tigrett," he answered.

"Ask the pilot if he can land there and let me off," I said, as the two faces across the table went completely blank.

Doc Hammer finally asked, "What did you say?"

"Doctor," I said, "I don't want to be any part of taking $40 million of American stockholders' money and putting it in four hotels in a rundown third-world Arab country like Morocco. I'm not mad. I'll pay my way back home, and I won't charge you a cent. I just don't want my name connected with that kind of a deal."

"What would you do?" he asked.

"I would make them put up every penny and pay you for providing the plans, supervising the construction and managing the hotels. After all, this is their opportunity, not yours. In addition to these other things, you're tying them in to the largest hotel reservation operation in the world and an international oil company to help make it successful."

"What about our previous discussions with King Hassan?" asked Dr. Hammer.

"Those were just preliminary discussions. Now we're up to bat. Give me three days to handle the negotiations and a promise not to run around dealing behind my back. If I can't deliver the deal within three days, you can go back to what you were going to do, and I'll go home."

I negotiated the Holiday Inn matter with Morocco's minister of finance, a man named Mamoun Tahari. He had a bright mind and was most ingenious in his understanding and financing. King Hassan appeared to have absolute confidence in him. Mamoun's help made our negotiations move easily, and we settled quickly.

On the morning of the third day, Kemmons, Dr. Hammer and I had breakfast at Mamoun's home. I went back to his bedroom and wrote out a two-page letter of intent on an old Smith-Corona typewriter stating that two Moroccan insurance companies were to put up all the money and agree to pay Holiday-Occidental $1.5 million for their participation. The deal would be split 50-50 with the Moroccan government.

As we walked out of the house after the signing, Dr. Hammer put his arm around me and said, "John, how about moving to Los Angeles as executive vice president of finance at Occidental?"

"Thanks, Doc, but no thanks. Just be sure I get my $500,000 fee for handling this deal paid promptly."

PART THREE:

Starting Over – From Despair to Determination

Part Three

Part Three of this collection of stories begins with unimaginable tragedy. After a long string of fabulous successes, John realizes that into even the most charmed life crushing blows of misfortune can sometimes fall.

He recovers from this dark chapter in his life by making dramatic changes. At age 52, he sets off from Tennessee with little more than the clothes on his back and $10,000 of the fortune he has built. He leaves behind everything he has known and owned.

In New York, he writes simple notes offering his services to three chairmen of large corporations, and sets off for London. From that beginning, he launches a phenomenal career as an international financier and negotiator.

John's wheeling and dealing with Occidental Oil chairman Armand "Doc" Hammer alone could fill a book. Their relationship takes John into Russia, across the Middle East and Africa, and to virtually every other corner of the globe. It leads him into international Cold War intrigue and to a witness stand before the Watergate Grand Jury and the SEC.

Yet an even bigger challenge presents itself in Hammer's ego. The oil magnate "took credit for everything, no matter who had conceived or executed it," John recalls. "Armand Hammer was not just mean, he was evil . . . absolutely ruthless in both business and life . . . a man of no loyalty except to himself, who worked inside and outside the law."

It is an experience that sharpens John's ability to work closely with one of the most powerful con men in the world without ever letting down one's guard. But there are fringe benefits of inestimable value, such as a bear hug from Leonid Brezhnev after giving the Soviet president a red Mercedes convertible.

John is part of the story when, for the first time in history, a personal Swiss bank account is opened on order of the Swiss Supreme Court for U.S. investigations into the dealings of John, Libya and American billionaire Bunker Hunt. Even so, the pertinent details of John's dealings elude investigators.

John is called upon on more than one occasion to convince Libyan dictator Muammar-al Qaddafi to see reason and pay debts he owes Western business interests.

It is also in this period that John forges a lasting relationship with Sir James Goldsmith, the man John calls "the very finest financial mind I think I have ever seen." This leads to a series of ventures between the two involving the highest stakes, transforming business after business in the cataclysmic era of the corporate takeover.

Such remarkable individuals are but a few with whom John does business in these chapters of his life.

— ROBERT KERR

8

No Exceptions

Life is made up of triumphs and tragedies, in about equal amounts. No matter what you try or how you try, it will always come out about the same. No one escapes. But, for a time, I foolishly thought I might be the exception.

It was 1964. Here I was with a beautiful, devoted wife, three remarkable children, knock-out homes in Tucson and Jackson, profitable and growing businesses in both cities—and warm friends everywhere.

We had just moved to Tucson for the winter, and I was in California on business when I received a telephone call. I have never been the same since.

My son, Hewitt, age 13, had been playing in a sand bank of a small stream that ran through the country club grounds in back of our house. He was throwing things up to the children on the top, when the bank caved in on him and he was smothered to death. Nothing they were able to do could save him.

Hewitt was the light of my life. He had more on the ball at 13 than any person three times his age. He was a charmer. He talked to everyone

John and Frances' three sons: (from left) Isaac, John Jr., and Hewitt

and somehow made them feel better. He was a straight-A student and was always trying to help before anyone asked him. He was always spreading love everywhere.

At 13, he had it all—everything I would want for him as a child or as a person. He was both, and he gave himself to everyone he met. He had no jealousies, no hate, no envy. Only love.

Doc and Ruth Peale came to Jackson and dedicated the chapel Frances and I built as a memorial to Hewitt.

Tragically and incomprehensibly, within six months of Hewitt's death, we received word that John Jr., our oldest, had died in an accident at Huatabampo, Mexico, while making a documentary film.

At the time of his death, Johnny had just won the Venice Documentary Award, and his movie was featured at the Museum of

Modern Art in New York City. He was great friends with George Lucas, the producer-director of *Star Wars* fame; they had worked together at the UCLA Film School.

Johnny was a completely different child from Hewitt: highly sensitive, a constant reader and as well educated and knowledgeable as one could be at his age—absolutely brilliant in every respect.

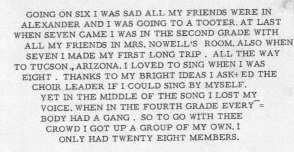

THE NAMES IN THIS LIFE HAVE BEEN CHANGED

TO PRO TECT THE GUILTY ★ INFANT FURNITURE
★ PLAY EQUIPMENT
★ SPORTING GOODS
★ TOYS

JACKSON. TENNESSEE

PLEASE ADDRESS REPLY TO
P. O. BOX 1251
JACKSON, TENNESSEE

THE LIFE OF HEWITT TIGRETT

byHEWITT TIGRETT
I WAS BORN IN THE YEAR OF 1951 WHEN T V WAS
WATCHED BY ALL. THE TOWN WAS YANKEE. WE KNOW
IT TODAY AS CHICAGO ILL. whenI WAS TWO INTO
JACKSON, TENNESSEE I CAME EAR, NOSE AND TOES,
WHEN I WAS THREE I FELL OUT OF MY PLAYPEN
CRACKING MY FRONT TOOTH, WHEN FIVE I STOPPED
SUCKING MY THUMB(I NEARLY BURN'T THEM OFF).

GOING ON SIX I WAS SAD ALL MY FRIENDS WERE IN
ALEXANDER AND I WAS GOING TO A TOOTER. AT LAST
WHEN SEVEN CAME I WAS IN THE SECOND GRADE WITH
ALL MY FRIENDS IN MRS. NOWELL'S ROOM. ALSO WHEN
SEVEN I MADE MY FIRST LONG TRIP . ALL THE WAY
TO TUCSON ., ARIZONA. I LOVED TO SING WHEN I WAS
EIGHT . THANKS TO MY BRIGHT IDEAS I ASK+ ED THE
CHOIR LEADER IF I COULD SING BY MYSELF.
YET IN THE MIDDLE OF THE SONG I LOST MY
VOICE. WHEN IN THE FOURTH GRADE EVERY =
BODY HAD A GANG . SO TO GO WITH THEE
CROWD I GOT UP A GROUP OF MY OWN. I
ONLY HAD TWENTY EIGHT MEMBERS.

MY GIRL IN THE WORLD THEN WAS MACALL.
THEN CAME HIGHLAND PARK AND SHE MOVED
AWAY. INGRADE FIVE MRS. FAIR'S ROOM WAS THE
LEADER IN ALL OF THE FIFTH GRADE SPORTS. THE GI
L THEN WAS MAC PUD(JUST AS P. A.) AND STILLIS
(SORTA) TODAY. MY GREATEST VACATION WAS
IN DISNEYLAND. AND THIS IS THE GREATEST LIFE
A TEN YEAR OLD COULD WANT.

SHORT FACTS
PARENTS
JOB
FATHER
MR. JOHN B. TIGRETT   TOY MANUFACTUER
MOTHER MRS. FRANCES TIGRETT   HOUSEWIFE
ALSO TWO BROTHERS

Hewitt Tigrett

He was also a schizophrenic, a mystic, a boy so delicate I wanted to clutch him to my breast, and I did so every time we were together. We took him to every specialist we heard of and to every hospital we could find looking for a cure. I was forever trying to protect him from the world.

I will always feel I failed him, though. I tried desperately, but no one could ever find the key to save him. Somewhere, somehow, we lost the way. There must have been a right road, but we could never quite find it.

There is one thing though that I know for certain, I alone failed him. He had a soul that should and could have been saved. It will haunt my conscience forever that I did not do more.

At the funeral tent in Jackson, I read his last letter on the fortunes of life and how to meet them. Johnny had written it to me from a Mexican jail. His letter said it all as a final goodbye, written in his wise and brilliant style.

Eagle Scout John Tigrett, Jr.

"*If you will just open your mind, the spirit will lead you and your knowledge and heart will be blessed. Once the learning process begins, the deeper areas of the mind are opened, and intelligence, understanding and love are set free to reach even higher planes than you ever thought possible.*"

— John Burton Tigrett Jr.
From his last letter to me

THREE NOTES

After losing two sons within six months, Frances and I drowned ourselves in sorrow both mentally and physically. I have never stopped crying for those two great guys. The years have made no difference in the depth of my sorrow, and even today I cannot think of them without tears.

How the human mind can move from despair to determination, I do not know. I only know that one morning in Jackson, Tennessee, I awakened with a determination to change my life and start over again.

That afternoon I told Frances I was leaving. I had made a bit of money, but I agreed she and my other son, Isaac, should have it all. I wanted only $10,000 cash, my bag, some clothing—and a divorce.

I left the next morning for New York, never to return again. I was 52 years old.

On the plane, those cold shivers of loneliness came over me. At that moment, I had only a vague idea of where I was going, no job and just enough of a "stake" to probably get me to my destination. When I sat down in room 232 at the St. Regis Hotel that night, I began to think about what I would do next.

I decided to write three brief notes—one to Kemmons Wilson, then chairman of Holiday Inn; one to Martin Condon, then chairman of a prominent snuff company, Conwood Inc.; and one to Dr. Armand Hammer, chairman of Occidental Petroleum Corp. All contained essentially the same message:

> I am moving to London to try to rebuild my life. If there is anything I can do for you or your company in Europe, you can reach me in care of Paul Curry, 235 Bayswater Road, London W1 Telephone: 625 0943.
>
> Always, my best,
> John Tigrett

Paul Curry was an old friend who represented a magazine or two. He had offered a bed in his attic until I could get situated.

I then decided to call two or three friends to help me get through my loneliness. My last phone call from the St. Regis that night was to a young lady I barely knew. Why I made that call was a mystery to me then and is now, for it changed my life.

For years I had contributed substantially to the Jackson Junior Chamber of Commerce's "Miss Tennessee" beauty contests. In all that time, I think I went once. Just the year before, however, I had been asked to back the chamber's Tennessee winner for additional training before the Miss America Contest at Atlantic City.

She was a young lady from Humboldt named Rita Wilson. I agreed, and she was sent to meet me. She did not win, but we kept in touch. I had dinner with her a time or two in California where she was making television commercials.

When she came on the line that night, I outlined the facts. I had left Jackson. I had $10,000. I was headed for London. I had no prospects and no guarantees. After I had given that bleak outline, I laughed and said, "Would you like to go with me?"

Without hesitating, she gave me the shock of a lifetime, replying, "Send me a ticket, and I'll join you tomorrow." The next morning I booked passage for two on the Holland American Line to Southampton.

When we reached Paul Curry's house, I found a letter from Kemmons Wilson and a cablegram from Martin Condon, and Armand Hammer's secretary had been calling twice a day for me. All three wanted me to do something.

Kemmons wanted me to make Holiday Inn deals for him in Europe. Martin wanted me to buy a snuff business for him in England. Armand wanted me to look after Oxy's operations in Libya and arrange oil concessions for him.

The next day, I called all three and gave them all the facts. I was broke and needed an advance on whatever I would end up doing for them. I asked Kemmons for $25,000, Martin for $50,000 and Armand for $100,000. All of them came through without a question. Now I had "walking-around money," and Rita and I started looking for a house.

On the way to London, I had told Rita she could stay with me as long as she wanted. I said that while I didn't want to marry again, if she ever felt insecure, I would marry her. Then and now, I felt a substantial obligation to this unsophisticated young girl from Humboldt. Not many would have taken the gamble she did.

We lived happily together for several years, and somewhere along the line she did decide she would like to get married. I doubt it was insecurity, but more likely her upbringing in the Humboldt First Methodist Church.

We were officially married in the registrar's office in London according to the English custom. Then, at a small picturesque Episcopal church off Bayswater Road, we had a social wedding. I assembled all of my friends at the time and had as groomsmen Armand Hammer, Jimmy Goldsmith, Baron Alexis DeGunsberg, Bunker Hunt and Sir John Foster. It was a very unusual crew, and they carried off the wedding reception at Claridge's in grand style.

Two or three years later, Rita met a young man on a ski trip and fell in love with him. Certainly we loved each other, but we were not *in* love. We parted with much regret on both sides, and she went to live with the young man. We were later divorced in Humboldt, Tennessee.

I continued to look after her family, providing them a house and finally giving it to them when I had paid off the mortgage. But since the day the divorce was granted, I have never seen Rita again.

Dr. Armand Hammer and his wife, Frances

ARMAND HAMMER AND
THE RUSSIAN CONNECTION

When I wrote those three notes on that lonely night at the St. Regis, I had no idea the note to Armand "Doc" Hammer would develop into such a close association with him. We became almost as two brothers for more than 18 years.

How could I possibly have imagined, for example, that my acquaintance with Doc would lead to endless trades, more than 20 trips to Russia and an unusually close association with Chairman Leonid Brezhnev. Doc and I also worked together in every country in North Africa, from Morocco to Egypt, making oil concessions or trading phosphate, and in every one of the nine Trucial states, as well as Iraq, Iran, Kuwait and Saudi Arabia. I lived in these strange lands for 10 years, and we finally established a solid working relationship with the leader or oil minister in every country.

However, I'm not so sure I would have written that third note to Doc Hammer if I had known that it would lead me to five or six appearances before the Security and Exchange Commission (defending Occidental, Hammer and myself) or to the witness stand for two days before the Watergate Grand Jury—where I was saved from a long jail term only by the brilliance of the late Edward Bennett Williams.

Armand Hammer was a Russian Jew whose father had been head of the Communist Party in the United States. Jimmy Goldsmith always thought Armand was a double agent, which indeed he was, and which I knew almost from the beginning but never revealed to Jimmy or anyone else. With his family background and early associations, he simply had to be.

I accepted it, and it made a difference to me only once—an occasion when he tricked me. In truth, I never saw that it helped or hurt in anything I closed for Oxy in Russia or anywhere else.

When the Russian KGB records were recently opened to my friend Ed Epstein for his book *Dossier: The Secret History of Armand Hammer,* he found a good many payment slips for worthwhile amounts payable to Armand Hammer.

In the world of great egos—and I have had a close personal friendship with 10 or 15 of the world's most famous—Doc Hammer's ego, by far, surpassed them all. He took credit for everything, no matter who had conceived it or executed it. He spent hours developing stories to make himself appear the genius that he really was not.

In the 18 years that we were together until his death, Doc always had writers working on a book about him. I made the arrangements for a couple of these would-be masterpieces. Doc dictated nearly every word that went in them, but even then he was never satisfied because they could not possibly make him appear as great as he considered himself to be.

I have never read even one of these "tomes of greatness" out of fear that I would never be able to stop laughing or be able to recognize his version of the deals I made.

Armand Hammer was not just mean, he was evil. They are not the same thing. I found him to be absolutely ruthless in both business and life. He was a man of no loyalty except to himself, who worked inside and outside the law. He called me over from London on several occasions to settle the contract of his latest promised successor as chairman of Occidental. The president or vice chairman's job was truly a revolving door, and he always had the same request: "John, come over here and get rid of this son-of-a-bitch. Settle his contract. I'm not speaking to him anymore."

Doc was also as malicious as anyone can get with his family and girl-friends. He sued his brother's widow while she was in a nursing home for what little money she had inherited. Doc said the amount was owed to him by his brother. He also sued the niece of his late wife, Frances, to whom Frances had left her own inheritance and a house Los Angeles. His grounds, as best I could determine, were that Frances should have left her inheritance to him—even though it was Frances' money from a for-mer husband. Doc completely disregarded the fact that he had used Frances' money to finance his purchase of Occidental and almost every-thing else he did in business.

If this was the man's character, why would I maintain an association with him for 18 years? Just one reason: He fascinated me, as he did so many others. His mind was the most devious I have ever encountered.

Further, working with Doc was always a challenge. Over the years, we developed a real affection for each other, but it was never so strong that I let down my guard or ever really believed anything he said.

I was one of two people in the world—his wife, Frances, being the other—who did not take him seriously. We both laughed at him. Frances was a remarkable, wonderful, fine woman who was much smarter than Doc. She was also as straight as a die. I am sure she stayed with him for the same reason I did.

Once, when Doc was being given some great honor (which he had actually had me buy for him) by the head of a European country, Frances and I were sitting together in the audience. She leaned over to me and said, "Johnny, if they knew as much about Armand as you and I do, they wouldn't be giving him a medal—they'd be hanging him!"

I could write a book about Doc Hammer as thick as those he has written about himself. We were involved in many amusing incidents and deals, and it is an undertaking to try to select even a few of the best stories about him.

When I worked with him in the semiformative stages of Occidental, Doc was traveling around trying to impress people with his old beat-up converted B-25 bomber that leaked oil.

When he finally became such a burden that I quit working with him, he was moving around in a long-range, luxurious Boeing 727 with a beautiful bedroom, a pretty hostess, and a private chef.

This was Doc Hammer, double agent, and as mean and evil as they come. He was a human being with no conscience, who never had a real friend—except perhaps for me.

9

Dealing With Doctor Hammer

CALLING CARD— THE HAMMER COLLECTION

For "Doc" Hammer, the Hammer Collection was an original calling card for himself and for Occidental. The company financed the major acquisitions in the collection, and it was used as a business tool.

We were always trying to get oil or coal concessions in different countries, and the art collection gave him a strong introduction. The collection was effective in advancing negotiations on many issues, and it certainly gave him absolute access to many world leaders.

One day when he had a falling-out with his curator girlfriend, he called me in London to ask if I would be his temporary curator. I agreed to act for two weeks or until he could find someone qualified. It took him more than a year to find a replacement.

Meanwhile, on top of everything else I was trying to do, I had to open the collection in Stockholm and at the National Gallery in Edinburgh, the national Gallery in Caracas and other exhibitions. I organized a routine, and it was always the same: cocktails, preview of the collection, black-tie dinner, major politicos, brief speech by the museum head, Doc's speech, cash gift to the museum and back to London.

My limited knowledge of the Hammer Collection began at the Smithsonian, after the opening of its initial showing. When Doc called me the next day, he was livid. The art critic of the *Washington Post* had critiqued the major paintings and declared the show "second class."

I went over to Doc's suite at the Watergate Building, where he was putting together his response in the form of an advertisement for the *Post*. I tried to dissuade him, but his ego had been badly hurt,and he was hell-bent to answer. The ad ran—a full page—the next day in the *Post,* and I left the same day for London. Fighting with American newspapers was never my cup of tea. There is no way to win.

I knew then, and now, nothing of substance about art except that there are great pictures I like and enjoy. I had, however, seen enough of Doc's operations to give me, rightly or wrongly, serious doubts about his own art judgment. The article in the *Washington Post*, I learned, was not only written by a well-qualified critic, but it also read like he knew his subject. He had carefully and most objectively reviewed the collection.

Two or three weeks later, Doc was in London and had quieted down. I said to him at Claridge's, "Doc, who are considered among the best art authorities in the U.S. and Europe?" He named the director of the National Gallery in Washington and four or five others.

"Why don't you pick out three of the best, and I'll make a deal to have them review the Hammer Collection?" I asked.

"I'll think about it" was all he said.

However, about six weeks later, I was in Paris and ran across one of the art people he had named. "John," he said, "Dr. Hammer employed three of us to review his collection for quality and tell him what he might do, if anything, to improve it. Quite frankly, between us, it is a very poor collection. He is going to have to trade up in every area."

I then asked, "Did you ever read the review of the Hammer Collection in the *Washington Post* when it opened at the Smithsonian?"

"Yes, I did," he replied. "That critic was dead right. In fact, Dr. Hammer didn't need to employ us—all he needed to do was follow what that fellow recommended. He gave him all the answers."

THE MILLION DOLLAR SUITCASE TRICK

Doc Hammer had a number of very strange acquaintances.

From time to time, they would surface and contact me. Nearly always, it would be in connection to some unusual mission I had agreed to carry out for him. At least half of Doc's requests I turned down, usually on the basis of not having the time. He was always very gracious about it and said, "I understand, John." The simple fact was that we both understood I didn't like the look of what he proposed.

Every time I did undertake a "special" task for him, one or two strange characters seemed to come right out of the "woodwork" as part of it. They embodied many of the phases of his odd underground career and included, among others, two federal judges, two highly placed political lawyers and Las Vegas operators, and at least three members of what I'm sure were Mafia. In Europe, it was endless Russians posing as art dealers or bankers. He had quite a group of unusual associates.

Still, Doc Hammer was hardly the only world magnate who had such unconventional associates and methods. During that same period of time, I worked closely with J. Paul Getty, Lord Roy Thomson, Bunker Hunt and several others. All thought they were above the law and often acted accordingly. And on their way up, they had made some strange acquaintances.

Maybe it was the orphans home or the tramp steamer or something else, but I learned early in life to be very cautious without appearing to be. I also had a lot of luck, for in all my time with Hammer, Getty, Thomson, Hunt and others like them, I was only tricked three times.

One morning I was in the Zurich office of Louis Habegger (he ran our patent-licensing company, among other things) when I received a call from Doc. "What are your plans, John?" he asked.

"I'll be in Zurich until about 7 p.m. tomorrow and then on to London," I said. "I plan to go from there to New York on the Concorde the next afternoon to finish up some work for Jimmy Goldsmith."

"That's perfect," he said. "I have a friend in Zurich who has a very valuable piece of sculpture for me. I will have him deliver it to you at the Baur au Lac at 5 p.m. tomorrow. Just keep it with you, handle it carefully, and do not check it under any circumstances. I'll call you in London tomorrow and tell you where to deliver it in New York."

"Okay, Doc. I'll be glad to," I said.

The man who delivered the suitcase to me that evening could easily have passed for Sam Giancana's hit man. I watched him for a few minutes through the Baur's glass doors before going into the lobby. He was sitting next to the wall and constantly looking from side to side, checking everyone who came in the room. I went up to him and said, "My name is John Tigrett, and I assume that you have the sculpture Dr. Hammer wants me to take to New York."

"Do you have identification?" he asked.

"Yes. Here are a couple of cards, and any of the hotel employees will vouch for me," I said.

He gave me the bag. "Here's the key. Do not open the bag under any circumstances, for it has an unusual alarm. Do not check the bag at any point. Always keep it in your sole possession," he warned me in what I recognized as a Russian accent.

"I will," I said, as he turned and quickly left.

When I picked up the large bag, I found it so unusually heavy that I had to have a bellboy help me with it to the limousine.

The next morning I had another call from Doc. "John, I will meet you at the side door on 57th Street of the Manufacturer's Trust Company at 57th and Fifth. If your plane is on time, you should get there by about 4 p.m."

"Okay, Doc. I'll be there," I responded.

He called back a few minutes later and said, "I'll have someone meet you at the plane to help you through customs."

When I reached New York, they were calling my name before anyone left the Concorde. At the door was a small man in large dark glasses who helped me with the bag and said, "Your friend, Judge McDonald of the New York Supreme Court, has given you 'freedom of the port,' Mr.

Tigrett. He sends his warm regards." I noticed another Russian or Middle Eastern accent.

"Well, that's very nice of the judge." I said, "Give him my best in return."

I had never heard of any Judge McDonald and knew nothing about being granted "freedom of the port." All I know is that the little man who met me went directly to a special desk where my passport was stamped. Customs was completely bypassed. He had a boy pick up my personal luggage, and a few minutes later I was in a limousine en route to 57th and Fifth with the bag on the seat beside me.

When we reached there, I saw Doc watching from inside the rear door of one of the bank's offices. "Hello, John. Have the driver bring that bag on to the safety-deposit-box area downstairs," he said.

A rather large safety-deposit box was opened by the bank officer standing by, who then quickly left. Doc first turned off the alarm on the bag, which I saw was next to a small wheel on the bottom. I gave him the key, and as he opened the bag out popped at least a million U.S. dollars in hundred dollar bills.

The country boy from Jackson, Tennessee—loyal American and grandson of a Baptist preacher—had just brought in a million dollars, which was destined to support the Communist Party in its work in the United States against our government.

I was livid! I looked at him very directly. "Doc, if you ever trick me again, I'll kill you."

"John," he said, looking straight into my eyes, "I think you would."

L E N I N – B R E Z H N E V   L E T T E R S

I believe Doc Hammer was the first American the Russians allowed to land in Moscow in his own private plane, but it was not easy making the arrangements. It took six months of negotiations that included Doc working with the Russian ambassador in Washington and with me doing the same with the Russian ambassador in London.

The Russians first made an offer to allow us to go in through Copenhagen using their pilots with the windows blacked out. They even suggested they would send a plane for us from Moscow. It was not that Doc was not known to the KGB, but they were always suspicious even of their own.

We held out, and finally they gave in. In the end, we flew in from London via Copenhagen, with Doc's own great pilot and the windows uncovered.

We had two adjoining suites in the National Hotel in Moscow, where every room was bugged by the Russians to pick up the slightest whisper. Our major objective was to trade super phosphoric acid for ammonia. The phosphoric acid (which we couldn't sell in America) was being made from a new process in a plant in Lakeland, Florida. The ammonia was in good supply in Russia.

In principle, the Russians were agreeable, but their bureaucracy made ours in the States seem like Simple Ned. Every time we thought we were getting close to an agreement, some other bureau got involved and raised objections.

Our method of handling the KGB's "bug" operation was basic. We never talked about anything but the most innocuous things when we were in the hotel. When we were in the room and wanted to talk business or do some planning, we would go to Doc's bathroom. I would turn on the bath and wash basin full force so they would make as much noise as possible. Doc sat on the toilet and repeatedly flushed it while we whispered in each other's ear.

It was in one such "high-level conference" that I said to him one day,

"Doc, we're getting nowhere. Every time we get approval from one group, another pops up, and we are back in the soup again."

"What if we persuaded Brezhnev," he said, flushing away, "to write me a 'Lenin letter.' " Back in the Twenties, Vladimir Lenin had written a letter designating Hammer as their official contact in dealing with Western capitalists.

"Doc," I said, "maybe you have the answer. Let's try it."

We then sent a request for an audience with Soviet President Brezhnev, and two hours later we were in his office explaining our problem to him. He called for his secretary and dictated a short note that read:

> *Dr. Armand Hammer is our great friend. He is trying to help us in the development of our new agricultural objectives. If you cannot do what he requests of you, please come to see me.*

Brezhnev signed the note, and from that moment on, we made endless trades in Russia for everything under the sun with scarcely a single snag. A letter like that worked as well in the Seventies as it had in the Twenties.

A RED MERCEDES FOR THE CHAIRMAN

Early on, I learned never to ride to an airport with Doc Hammer unless I was going on the same plane. All the so-called "vital matters" he had to talk to me about would be lost in a snooze within five minutes after the limousine started. As a consequence, he would have to hold up the plane while he scribbled notes on the front and back of Claridge's envelopes that he would send back to me by the driver.

Along with his request, he would include three or four sheets of Occidental Petroleum stationery, which were blank except for his signature at the bottom as chairman. One was always used to appoint me as agent with unlimited powers to handle the transactions.

I received a lot of these notes and saved one or two. I wish I had saved them all. One read, "John, what would you think about us giving Brezhnev a Mercedes? See if you can get one!"

The next morning, I stopped by the Mercedes showroom on Park

In this note Doc Hammer asked me to negotiate, contract and conclude a $16 million interest in a project of Getty's in Algeria. It also requested that I initiate negotiations with Paul Getty to merge Occidental and Getty Oil Companies. If I had been successful, it would have made the third largest oil company in the world.

Lane and looked at the range. The one I liked the best was a 350SL convertible. I ended up ordering it in fire-engine red with bright-red leather upholstery. Several weeks later, we had it picked up in Germany by a man I sent from London. He had with him all the necessary papers to drive it to Moscow.

A few days later, I flew into Moscow with a note handwritten by Doc to Brezhnev. Brezhnev's assistant met me at the National, and we drove out in the Mercedes to his dacha. It was a small, lovely house just outside Moscow, deep in the woods. When we arrived, Brezhnev was sitting on the porch. I gave him Doc's note, and after reading it, he said something in Russian.

"Come try it," I said, and then took him to the car and showed him the operating features. He was a great bear of a man, and I moved the driver's seat as far back as it would go so he could get in comfortably.

He then asked me to go along, but I said, "No, try it out alone and see if you really want to keep it." He drove off and burned rubber as he turned out of the grounds. Twenty minutes later, he returned at high speed and brought the Mercedes to a sharp stop.

I opened the door, and Brezhnev had a big grin on his face. As he got out of the car, he suddenly put his arms around me, gave me a great bear hug, kissed me on the cheek and said, "John, tell Armand I love it, I love it, I love it!"

GIFT OF A "MILLION-DOLLAR" GOYA

Doc developed a bad habit of calling me four or five times a week, usually in the middle of the night. No matter where I was, he would track me down.

As I sleepily answered, he always asked the same question: "Were you asleep, John?"

"Yes, Doc," I would answer. "It's 3 a.m. here." He never apologized, but simply proceeded with the conversation.

On one such call, he said, "When we were with Dr. Piotrovsky, the curator of the Hermitage, the other night, he said the one great painter that they did not have was Goya. What would you think if we gave them a Goya and made a big act out of it—American to Russian friendship?"

"Good thinking, Doc. I'll see if I can find one," I replied, then said goodbye and went back to sleep.

I put the word out in Europe to several sources that I was looking for a Goya—not the best on the market, but still a good one. Two weeks later, I had a call from an art dealer who worked for the Prince of Liechtenstein in Vaduz. They had one they were willing to sell. I flew to Zurich and drove down to Vaduz to see the Prince's collection at his castle.

They met me, and after some negotiations I bought what I thought would fit the bill for $160,000. It was a painting of Goya's mistress, a rather pretty and distinguished-looking woman. I had it packed and sent by air to Doc in California, where as usual he hung it in his dining room.

Several weeks later, he called and said, "I had a great Goya expert look at that painting, and he said it was worth at least $300,000."

"Okay, Doc. Then we made a good buy," I said.

About two weeks before we were to present the painting to the Russians, Doc said, "I had a fellow who really knows Goyas look at that painting today, and he said in his opinion it was worth a half-million dollars."

"Great, Doc" I said. "Would he pay that much for it?"

No answer.

The Russians had set a date of October 25 for the presentation. We flew into Leningrad the afternoon of October 24. They had a big suite for the Doctor and a smaller one for me, both at the National. After dinner, Curator Piotrovsky and Director Suslov gave us a surprise by opening up the Hermitage that night just for the three of us.

On four massive tables, they had laid out their Greek jewelry collection, which had never been shown before. They said it was the first time the boxes had been opened in more than 50 years. It was unbelievably beautiful with the most original designs I have ever seen.

We were then given the run of the Hermitage. Frances and Doc went to see the 26 Rembrandts, and I went to look at room after room of Impressionists. Director Suslov also took me up to see the room for the next day's presentation. It was a large room lined with great columns that had been refinished with gold leaf. They had worked night and day on the room for more than six weeks. It was quite impressive, and the whole evening was a most memorable one.

Later that night, I was in a deep sleep when the phone rang and rang before finally awakening me. Frances Hammer was on the line. "John, I'm sorry to call you at this hour, but Armand is quite ill," she said. "Can you possibly find a doctor?"

It was 3 a.m. in Leningrad, and the only word I knew in Russian was *nyet*. I rushed down to the lobby and with much difficulty was able to have my problem finally understood. An hour later a physician arrived.

After the examination, the Russian doctor said Doc had some kind of Russian virus—at least that was what we thought he said. The physician gave Doc a shot, left some pills and his phone number, and was gone. I went back to bed.

As the day progressed, Frances and I checked on Doc every hour. He was not getting any better, and his fever stayed up close to 102 degrees. We were scheduled for the Hermitage Museum at 2 p.m. An hour before that, I went to his room, and Frances said he still had fever.

I woke him and asked, "Can you make it, Doc?"

"Can't we delay it?" he said.

"No, Doc. Everybody who's anybody in the Kremlin crowd is here. It's not a question of delaying it. You've got to make it. Between us, we have blown a few deals. But this is one we can't blow. Let's start getting you dressed."

Frances and I pulled his legs out from under the covers. I got him into his underwear and socks, and with difficulty, we proceeded to complete the process of dressing him. For some reason I could not tie his tie, and Frances finally came to my rescue. Frances and I each took one of his arms and managed to get him to the elevator and the limousine waiting outside.

By the time we reached the Hermitage, I could see he was beginning to gain strength. When we finally reached the curator's office, it seemed like the entire Russian government was lined up against the walls to greet us. Everyone had on their decorations, and Doc said, "Let me handle this alone. Don't help me."

I stood aside and put Frances behind him. He went around the room shaking hands with every single one and saying a few words in Russian to charm them. Meanwhile, I was worried about how we would get him up the long red-carpeted stairs to the presentation room. When he had finished and reached the steps, he said quietly, "I don't think I can make that, John."

"Hold tightly to Frances," I said. "I'm going to put my hand on your butt and push you up the stairs."

It worked. We entered the gorgeous golden room and were greeted by enormous cheers, two television stands and photographers galore. There were more than 1,000 people, and you could hardly squeeze by them. From that moment on, Doc Hammer became a changed man. It was as though he had just had six shots of adrenaline and a pint of Russian vodka.

We moved up to the 20 microphones in front of the veiled painting as the cheering and clapping continued on and on. Finally, the mayor of Leningrad stepped up to the microphone and, in Russian, gave a most flowery introduction. Then Doc was on stage.

For 20 or 30 minutes, this very remarkable old rascal talked in fluent Russian. He told many stories about the hard times in the 1920s, including a particularly poignant story about a child that Doc found on the street freezing, who had been without food for days. He took him back to his apartment, warmed and fed him, then took him home and gave the family enough to help them through. He had everyone in the house in tears. My translator could not even finish the last few lines.

Then he switched and talked about the new Russia. He eloquently spoke of its great future and how he was going to try to help, as he did in the 1920s, and how important it was that the U.S. and Russia support each other.

Finally, he said, "I give you today one of the great masterpieces of Goya for the most famous museum in the world—a museum that stands apart from all others. In the eyes of this beautiful woman, I hope you will always see the human kindness that represents both our countries, a kindness that I believe will always join us together as one."

He then unveiled the painting, and the place went up for grabs—clapping, shouting, cheering. No moment in my life was more dramatic than that one.

I took Doc's arm and said, "Let's get out of here before you collapse."

"You're right," he said.

We started through the crowd for the stairs when I saw a little Russian woman whom I had noticed standing just behind the painting while Doc was speaking. She kept trying to get to us, and finally I said, "Hold up, Doc. There's a woman behind us who is desperate to see you."

We stopped, and she worked her way to us. When the woman reached Doc, she held out a little yellow pencil and said, "Dr. Hammer, I have saved this and waited for more than 40 years to give it to you today."

Printed on it were the words: *The Armand Hammer Pencil Factory.* It was a product of a Russian factory made after Lenin gave Hammer Russia's pencil concession in return for Doc's help in the Twenties.

The next day, the Russian physician said Doc would have to stay in bed for a few days. My job was finished, and Doc offered me the Gulfstream back to London, but I told him I had space on a commercial flight. When I reached London, I went by Annabel's for a drink, where Louis, the maître d', always saved me a copy of the next morning's *London Times*.

On page three was a half-page picture of the Goya headlined: *Armand Hammer Gives Million-Dollar Painting to the Russians*.

Watergate Indictments
and Heart Problems

The political winds of guilt by presumption blew hard during the Watergate years. Once the Democrats had Watergate as a front-burner scandal, they went after anyone who had even been friendly with President Nixon, much less contributed to his campaign. They passed a law that decreed any corporation or individual making a political contribution of more than $1,000 after April 7, 1972, was liable to severe penalties.

Doc had met with the secretary of commerce in Washington in the latter part of March of that year. He agreed to give the Nixon campaign $50,000 in cash. But the secretary asked for more and suggested that if Doc's contributions reached a total of $100,000, he could be in the president's "club" and sit with Nixon the night of the election. It was too much for Doc's ego to resist, so he agreed and asked the secretary to send a "collector" by to see him in California to collect the second $50,000.

According to Doc, a former governor of Montana came to collect on April 3. So Doc went down to his bank lock box on the ground floor of the Kirkeby Tower, took out $50,000 and gave it to the collector. This story, I'm sure, is true, for it is exactly the way Doc would have operated.

The collector's version, however, was different. He claimed that Doc gave him $5,000 in September, $10,000 in October, $10,000 in November, $15,000 in December and $10,000 on January 21.

To me, this was obviously so different from Hammer's way of doing things that it made no sense—until we learned that this collector was in a jam and had to stick to his story in order to avoid his own indictment.

On my instructions, thousands and thousands of dollars were spent checking every air passenger list available in Los Angeles and surrounding airports on the April 2, 3 and 4 in question, as well as all private aircraft landings on those dates. Detectives were hired to cover every potentially incriminating Montana angle. They found the former governor had been short of cash during that period in April from building a motel and buying a radio station. However, he was an old political hand and had skillfully thought through every possibility and covered his tracks. We could not even get a trace of evidence.

Doc told me the story over and over. The collector had called him at home the night before making the April 3 pickup, and Doc had agreed to meet him the next morning on the ground floor of the Kirkeby Building. At the appointed meeting time, Doc had drawn out $50,000 in cash from his lock box in the bank while the collector waited upstairs. Doc then returned and made the payment, but did not ask for a receipt because they were old friends. No one else witnessed the transaction. The collector had obviously planned it with great care so that it became a case of his word against Doc's.

Doc was indicted in Washington D.C. with the collector's testimony, and was due to go before a federal judge who had a record of stiff penalties for this kind of political case. It became urgent that we get the case transferred to California where Doc might receive more leniency.

Arthur Groman and Louis Nizer, Doc's lawyers, delayed the Washington trial through various legal maneuvers, and finally were successful in having it transferred to California for sentencing.

One morning during that time, I was in Doc's house in Los Angeles when he had just finished swimming his daily 25 laps in the indoor pool. We were trying to figure out what position to take at the sentencing, so that the judge would not send him to prison.

I asked him, "How's your health, Doc, after all the strain you've been under? You know, frankly, you don't look well." Being the remarkable rascal he was, he picked up on the idea and ran away with it.

"Yes, John," he said smiling, "I have been having some chest pains lately."

"Well," I said, "Let's get a prominent Los Angeles physician to look into the matter."

Within seconds, he was on the phone asking for recommendations on the best-known heart specialist in L.A. Within an hour, he arranged for him to come by to see him that evening.

Whether Doc ever had a heart problem, I do not know. If he had, he never mentioned it to his wife, to me or to anyone close to him, as far as I know. I know further that he would not take the heart pills that were prescribed for him. I tried to get him to take them on several occasions, but he always responded by saying, "I don't need those things."

Shortly after the specialist's visit, we put Doc in a small Catholic hospital near the courthouse where he would be sentenced. The room was very Spartan, with a bed, a chair, a little radio and a telephone. When no visitors were around, he continued to run Oxy operations all over the world by telephone. Whenever anyone else was in the room, however, Doc would suddenly appear gravely ill, and we would only let them stay a very few minutes.

When the sentencing day arrived, we arranged for a large station wagon, a wheelchair, heart monitors, two nurses, and a doctor. As we reached the courthouse, the nurses wired Doc up to the monitors and put him in the wheel chair in his pajamas and robe. We then rolled him into the courtroom with a doctor standing attentively by his side, checking on him every couple of minutes.

When Doc's case came up, the judge asked, "How do you plead, Dr. Hammer?"

In a voice that sounded as though he had one foot in the grave, Doc croaked almost inaudibly, "Guilty."

"I can't hear you, Dr. Hammer. Can you speak up?" asked the judge.

"Guilty, Your Honor," Doc repeated in a hollow voice.

"I won't dwell on the various aspects of this case," said the judge. "The media have already covered it fully. I am sentencing you, Dr. Hammer, to three years' probation. You are to report once a week for the first two years to an officer of this court. Next case."

"Thank you, Your Honor," Doc replied feebly.

We carefully wheeled him out of the courtroom, put him in the station wagon and headed back to his hospital room. When he had been unhooked from all the medical apparatus, and the nurses and doctor had gone, Doc stepped out of the wheelchair, turned some jazz music up loud on the radio, and cried out gleefully, "Let's dance, Johnny Boy. Let's dance." And we danced and danced around the room, endlessly laughing our hearts out.

From that moment on, Doc lived a very active life for almost two decades, while traveling all over the world in his 727. He was eventually pardoned by President George Bush, years after Doc's supposedly good friend President Jimmy Carter failed to do so.

10

Misadventures

A SMALL PERSONAL DEBT OF $350 MILLION

Every man I ever worked with amused me, but close to the top of the list for amusement was Ed Carey, chairman of New England Petroleum Company. He was a small, thin man who barked orders and looked at you rather strangely out of the corner of his eye. Every time I came in his office, he was rocking away in a rocking chair.

Ed was the scion of the distinguished Carey family of New York. His younger brother was then governor of New York. Ed's company was the largest distributor of heating oil products on the East Coast, and he also owned one of the largest oil-transport facilities in the Atlantic located in the Bahamas.

I was called into Ed's life by George Williamson, who phoned one day from New York and said, "My friend Ed Carey has a few financial problems, and I think you might help him. When can you come to New York?"

"I'm coming there tomorrow," I answered. "Maybe we could have lunch together."

Ed had lunch every day at the same table in the same exclusive club in the Pan Am Building. I met them there, and after the usual get-acquainted conversation, I asked, "What are the problems of New England?"

George answered, "Ed bought some oil from Libya and is not in a position to pay for it."

"How much?" I asked.

"It's $350 million plus interest," he said.

"What happened to the money from the sale of the oil?" I asked.

"He doesn't know," replied George.

"You mean he didn't steal it or lose it gambling?" I asked suspiciously. "It just disappeared?"

"That's it. It just was lost in operations," said George.

He then told me the company had only $10 million in cash on hand, and every asset was mortgaged to the hilt. I suggested we speak to his accountants.

The accountants confirmed everything George had said. I told Ed we would see him the next morning.

Ed's office was on the eighth floor of a small building in back of the Waldorf-Astoria Hotel in New York. When we went in the next morning, there he was in his rocking chair, as unconcerned as a man could ever be. He told a funny story, and we all laughed.

Then I asked, "Ed, can you keep this company afloat if we take the Libyans off your back?"

"I think so, if I can find another source of oil," he replied.

"Well, it's too early to talk about negotiating with the Libyans," I said. "They will have you thrown into bankruptcy. Their lawyer is an old friend of mine, and that's his style. Do you have a good lawyer?"

"Yes," he said, laughing. "He's a character."

"Could we get him to come over here?" I asked.

"I'll call him," Ed responded.

The lawyer who joined us came in limping on a walking cane. He explained he didn't really need the cane, but he found women were so sympathetic that he couldn't stop carrying it. After we settled down to business, I asked, "Are you familiar with Ed's financial situation?"

"Fully," he said. "We are close friends."

"Then what we recommend is that you file suit in Federal Court against the Libyan Oil Company," I said. "With thousands of customers, you must have had some complaints. Use that as part of your suit contending that they gave you contaminated oil. They can never disprove it, for it came out of your storage tanks. Eventually, however, they will show from the loading sheets that it was typical Libyan Light they delivered. All you want to do is make a smoke screen to give Ed time to work out his situation. What is the federal docket here?"

"About two to three years."

"Okay. That will give him some time. If he can't make it then, Ed will have to sell New England. Delay the case as long as you can."

"Understood," he said. "What do you think we should sue for?"

"Probably $500 million, and use your imagination on any further damages. The objective is to confuse and delay. Be sure yours is the first lawsuit. Do it today if you can."

Ed just sat there rocking away, the fate of his company being negotiated by two people who in reality had little knowledge of his business. Finally, he asked, "Where am I going to get some more oil?"

Well," I said, "my good friend Reza Fallah, who runs the National Iranian Oil Company, is going to meet me here tomorrow. I'll ask him to see you, or maybe you can have lunch together. You can then approach him directly. He may have some new oil available because they have been doing a lot of drilling lately.

"But remember one thing, Ed. He is a close personal friend of mine, and I don't want the same thing that happened to the Libyans to happen to him. You're going to have to pay the Iranians and pay them on time."

"Of course," he said. "I'll be all right from now on."

George and I split a $100,000 fee for resolving the tangled situation. He went back to Texas, and I returned to London a few days later.

* * *

About a year later, I had another call in London from George Williamson on his friend Ed. He said simply, "Ed Carey is having some more problems, and I think maybe we had better meet him in New York and see if we can help him."

The next week, we met in Ed's office, where, once again, he was contentedly rocking away in his rocking chair. He greeted us cordially, then jovially told us a couple of new dirty jokes before I asked, "What's the problem this time, Ed?"

"Well," he said slowly, "with your help, we worked out a new oil supply from the Iranians and were able to negotiate 120-day payment terms. Somehow though, we let it get ahead of us, and now we are not in a position to pay them."

"Is the Libyan debt still in limbo?" I asked.

"Yes. We've had a few legal skirmishes, but nothing that's of any consequence."

"How much oil are you behind on with the Iranians?"

"I think with the two, the Libyans and Iranians, plus interest, we owe them somewhere around, oh, $700 million to $750 million."

I was shocked. Here was Ed Carey rocking along seemingly unworried about anything, at a moment when he was essentially bankrupt with debts of some $750 million. It was such a preposterous situation, I couldn't help but laugh. George and Ed joined me. The company was in such a hole, and the financial obligations so ridiculous, there was really nothing anyone could do but laugh.

Finally, I said, "Has anybody indicated any interest in buying New England Petroleum?"

"Not so far," said Ed.

I thought about my friend Orin Atkins, chairman of Ashland Oil, and decided to see if he might have any interest in purchasing Ed's company. As it turned out, Orin was in New York that day, so George and I went to talk with him about Ed's predicament. Orin agreed to gamble $50,000 to see if the Libyan and Iranian claims could be settled for stock or some nominal payment, on the grounds that he would continue to buy oil from them.

We were working on this idea when along came a man from Jacksonville, Florida, named Raymond Mason, who had the Charter Oil Company. Charter was an insurance complex and had a group of oil-related companies that included a small refinery.

Out of the blue, Mason offered to buy Ed Carey's bankrupt company and assume all liabilities, as I recall, for $10 million in cash and another $85 million in Charter stock (which was then selling at its all-time high price). George and I knew nothing of this offer until Ed told us it just dropped in his lap, so he grabbed the deal immediately.

Raymond Mason figured he could get a great source of oil from Libya and Iran by agreeing to pay off Ed's debt with a part of the profit from new oil they would supply his refinery.

I have never known a luckier soul than Ed Carey. Here was a man who was bankrupt one day for $750 million, and the next day had a $100 million fortune—without lifting a finger.

THE PATINO FAMILY

The Patinos were Red Indians from Bolivia. Their founder was a government clerk who saw that a fortune could be made from the country's tin mines. In time, he not only got control of the tin mines but also built 10 processing plants outside of Bolivia. His plan was that no matter what happened inside the country, he would always have control of the world's tin supply through his processing plants.

It was a remarkably successful idea, and his son Antenor succeeded him as head of the family. The other sons—a prince from Belgium, a strange Patino boy from Paris, one son living in England and another in Switzerland—were all independent Red Indians. All considered themselves leaders in a part of the European jet set and were as jealous of each other as it is possible to be.

In the mid-Seventies, Doc Hammer decided he wanted to get into the mining business by buying out the Patino operation. He called me in London and asked that I meet him in Paris to talk to the Patinos. At 10 o'clock on a Sunday morning, we sat down in Doc's room at the Plaza Athenee, and for the first time I saw the Patino statements.

They scared me because of the great variety of their business interests: 19 tin mills scattered all over the world, a highway development in Columbia, odds and ends of companies in the U.S. and Europe, ski resorts, hotels and a part interest in a brokerage business. Arthur Andersen, Doc's auditors, estimated the holdings were a "buy" at anything under $400 million.

We met the Patinos in a private dining room on the second floor of Fauchon's restaurant on the Champs Élysées. Antenor sat at the head of the table with Doc Hammer on his right. I was on his left. The others, except for the Belgium prince, looked to me like the European Mafia, each one willing to cut the other's throat with little or no inducement.

The usual social nothings proceeded through lunch, and just as dessert arrived, Doc said, "I apologize for having to leave you, but I have an important engagement in Washington tonight that I must make.

John Tigrett here will handle negotiations with you. He has my right of signature."

To say I was shocked is putting it mildly. To say the Patinos were mad is an understatement. But Doc was suddenly gone, and there we were. I apologized to them and said that I knew nothing of his plans but since we were there we might as well explore the possibilities. I had before me the papers Doc had given me, so I began reviewing with the Patinos the assets and the projections.

After about an hour, I made an offer of $325 million. Two hours later, we had finally agreed on a basic price of $360 million, with another $50 million contingent on certain factors.

They suggested we go to their company offices on the Avenue Foch, where I assumed they could get some secretarial help so we could draft a letter of intent, options and so forth. When we reached their offices, I found them to be the most beautiful in Paris, but they did not know how to reach a secretary, and had no idea how to locate anyone else who could use a typewriter. I was on my own.

I called the concierge at the Paris Hilton with my problem. He said he had the home number of a public stenographer he used occasionally on Sundays. I called the number and talked to the stenographer, who said she had a typewriter at home. In another 10 minutes, I was on my way. The Patinos did not lift a finger, not even to offer to drive me over or let me use one of the chauffeured limousines that each of them had waiting outside.

Before I left them all in the conference room, I said, "I'll be gone a couple of hours writing up an agreement of our understanding. None of you is to leave this office or to kill each other while I'm gone." No one laughed except Antenor.

The stenographer lived on the fourth floor of a building in a lower-middle-class area of Paris. It was a walk-up, and when she opened the door, I found a typical French family on Sunday. Everyone was in the kitchen, with food everywhere. The father was shirtless, and there were four other children besides the stenographer, Marie. She took me into her bedroom, which she shared with one of the other children. Her old Remington typewriter sat on the table there, and she typed as I dictated. There was no chance to edit or revise.

After a while, we had a four-page agreement typed—but only the original, and I needed seven copies. I called the Hilton, but their copy machine was locked away in an office no one could open on Sunday.

Then Marie said, "I know where there is a copy machine. It is in back of a candy store on the Champs Élysées."

"I'll drive you there," the father offered.

So off we went in a battered old Peugeot, with the hefty French father still shirtless. Sure enough, there was a coin-operated machine in the back of the open-area candy shop that required one franc per page. I reached in my pockets and discovered I had only enough change for 10 of the total 28 copies I needed to make.

I asked the candy-store clerk if she would make change for me, but being typically French, she replied curtly, "No."

So I calculated exactly how many candy purchases I had to make in order to end up with francs in change. The clerk grew more angry with every transaction, but finally I had enough coins to make all my copies. The shirtless father drove me back to the Patino offices, while I had a great laugh at having to scrape for a handful of francs in order to complete a $360 million deal.

My odd visit had taken two hours and 15 minutes, but I found the Patino clan was still at the offices arguing with each other. Each one read a copy of the sale, and one of them asked for a minor change. I wrote it in and initialed it, and the Patinos signed all seven copies. I kept the original, and one by one the Patinos departed. Only Antenor shook my hand and thanked me before leaving. No one offered me a ride.

I found myself on the Avenue Foch trying to hail a cab as the Patinos roared away in their chauffeured limousines.

GETTING QADDAFI TO PAY A DEBT

At one point, Muammar-al Qaddafi and his right-hand man, Major Jaloud, had a fight with the British Government that led to their requisitioning all the interests of the British, including 50 percent of the Hunt BP Petroleum oil operation. As a consequence, Bunker Hunt and Qaddafi became partners in the oil business, with Hunt as the operator.

The transition was initially rough, but things finally settled down and worked very well for some time. Because of a mix-up in the ever-changing Libyan bureaucracy, however, the Libyans later fell behind by 60 days in paying their share of the expenses for 40 oil workers. Bunker foolishly threatened Qaddafi, who simply responded by taking over the Hunt interests in Libya.

About a year later, I was in Miami when I had a call from Bunker asking me to come to Dallas to see him. I told him I was on my way to Europe, and if he wanted to see me before I left, he would have to come to Miami. He agreed.

My real reason for not going to Dallas was that I had found over the years that Bunker really didn't like to pay for anything. In all the time we were closely associated, to my knowledge he never picked up a single meal check. One night in a restaurant in Geneva, I decided to try to wait him out. But Bunker never made a move to ask for a check. Finally, when we were the only two people left, and the waiters were clearing the place, I broke down and asked for the check, which he let me pay.

After he arrived in Miami, we went to the racetrack for the afternoon, and one of his horses won the feature race. While there, he asked me if I thought I could get him money from the Libyans for the equipment he was forced to leave behind. I told him I didn't know and that I would have to see the figures and know the facts.

Then I advised him I would not spend any time on this matter unless I had a contract for expenses, a fee if successful, compensation for my time if unsuccessful, and an advance of $25,000. When we reached the hotel, I went to the manager's office and wrote up a short contract on his secretary's typewriter. Bunker finally signed it.

When I reached London, I called George Williamson, who was very friendly with both the Libyan chief accountant and the oil minister. Shortly thereafter, we headed for Tripoli.

Bunker's figures showed that the Libyans owed him about $40 million. However, when the Libyans were finished with their figures, including oil not paid for, they showed that Hunt owed them $35 million. We returned to London.

Bunker's people prepared some more figures and explained a portion of the Libyan ones, and we returned to Tripoli. After another three days, we began to make some progress and finally agreed on a figure of $23 million.

As usual, many people were involved. I decided that as risk insurance for these two difficult parties, it would be best to arrange for the Banque de Paribas in Geneva to physically handle the money in the transaction. I went to see Jean Jacques Michel, who was then running the bank. He agreed to handle it for a fee, and Bunker reluctantly agreed.

Bunker held up his decision on the settlement for a couple of weeks until finally a call came from the former governor of Texas, John Connally. John was head of a law firm in Houston and a former secretary of the Treasury. He was best known for having been shot while in the car with President Kennedy when he was assassinated. I knew John well, and he asked me just one question, "On Hunt's Libyan settlement, do you believe you've gone to the well for the last time?"

"Not only for the last time, my friend, but also that well is now dry as a bone. If another trip is made, it will have to be by someone else," I replied.

"I'll have Bunker call you right away with his agreement," he said.

After everything was finally settled, Bunker received more than $20 million.

There was an important sidelight to this Libyan–Hunt settlement. Since the Swiss Banking System was organized many years ago, there has always been a veil of secrecy regarding bank accounts there. No one—no government official, no foreign official—was ever able to obtain any information about a personal Swiss bank account unless they could prove criminal activity was involved. No one had ever pierced this bank veil of secrecy for the account of any Swiss or foreign citizen. But the winds of change were blowing.

Under tough pressure from the American Internal Revenue Service, the first lawsuit to break the Swiss banking secrecy veil was filed by the Swiss Justice Department on the Hunt-Libyan settlement. The suit lasted two years, and the Swiss banks defended it vigorously. Finally, however, in a historic ruling, the Swiss Supreme Court decreed that on proper petition by the U.S. Government, bank files must be opened.

With some ceremony, representatives of the U.S. Justice Department and the IRS, the Swiss authorities and the bank representatives went into the Banque de Paribas in Geneva to review the locked files on my Hunt-Libyan settlement.

They found, I am told, lots of papers and many calculations. But in the end, nowhere could they find any indication of how the Hunt-Libyan payoff money was distributed.

It remains a mystery to this day.

11

Jimmy Goldsmith

I'M NEVER GOING TO LOSE YOU!

When I first arrived in London in the early Sixties, Martin Condon gave me the name and address of a company called Illingsworth Tobacco, a snuff manufacturer. Martin asked me to see about buying the company, because under the breakup of the Tobacco Trust, Martin's snuff company in the U.S. could purchase other companies outside the country, but nothing inside the U.S.

I learned that a man named James Goldsmith owned Illingsworth as part of a food-and-distribution company called Cavenham. Two days later, I was on the fifth floor of a building on the M4 motorway, halfway in from Heathrow to London, which housed the Cavenham offices.

The doors didn't work very well, and the carpet was about worn out. I asked the young lady for Mr. Goldsmith, and from one of the offices came this very tall, thin young man of 29, who was both highly animated and most cordial. He ushered me into his office, a plainly furnished room with two chairs and a well-worn desk.

He immediately started talking business. I had two pages of questions about Illingsworth, and he gave me immediate answers to every one. He never had to refer to a single paper. Later on, when I checked some of the figures he had given me, they were 100 percent accurate.

I spent more time with Jimmy the next day and then made an inquiry for information on the young man by calling a U.S. banker friend who was running the London branch of First Chicago.

"From what I hear, he's a brilliant wildman," I was told. "He bought up some 19 old companies and tried to combine them into three or four plants. He's way out on a limb, and I hear this week he needs help badly. But we wouldn't loan him a dime."

Jimmy invited me for lunch at his house at 27 Chester Terrace. After lunch we took a walk in Regent's Park just across the street. As we walked along I said, "Jim, I'm going to buy that Illingsworth company from you for Conwood at your price. I'm not going to argue with you about the $6 million price you've set on it. But I'm only going to buy half of it for Conwood."

I saw his brow furrow and his face drop. "But why?" he said. "Why don't you take the whole thing? You know I need the entire $6 million."

"I do know that," I said. "But we're going to Switzerland tomorrow, and I'll borrow the other half for you there."

"But why work it out that way? It's too complex, and it doesn't make any sense."

"It makes a great deal of sense to me, Jimmy," I said. "You have the very finest financial mind I think I have ever seen, and I'm never going to lose you. This is just the beginning."

We successfully borrowed the $3 million at U.B.S. the next day, and Jimmy went on to refine his methods of buying undervalued companies and overhauling them to profitability—the art of the corporate takeover, it would come to be called.

And Jimmy and I happily made deals together for more than three decades. His fabulous achievements would see him knighted Sir James Goldsmith. But to me, he would always be my friend "Jimmy."

SAVED BY 7-ELEVEN

Some time after the Illingsworth Tobacco transaction, Jim's food-and-distribution company again reached the point where it was in desperate need of further expansion funds.

The answer developed out of a small acquisition Jimmy had made earlier of a chain of 18 CTNs, the British version of the convenience store. The CTNs were basically hole-in-the-wall operations that sold candy, tobacco and newspapers. Jimmy bought them out of bankruptcy for around £10,000.

Through a blind ad in the *Times* for a manager for the CTNs, Jim found an applicant who was a stock clerk in a co-op grocery. His name was Jim Wood, and as the new manager he shocked us by making the CTNs into a very profitable operation within the first 45 days—while running them out of his home!

During the next expansion, we bought a chain of about 250 CTNs from Cadbury that were losing money. Jim Wood turned these stores around too in a short period, and they also became worthwhile assets.

As our need for additional funds grew increasingly serious, I went to the U.S. to try to find money. After a number of calls in New York, Dallas and Chicago, I found nothing but dry holes. Discouraged, I decided to head back to London.

Before I left New York, I ran into John Rouscher of the Dallas investment bankers Rouscher-Pierce at the St. Regis Hotel. We walked across the street for lunch at Cote Basque, and afterward, as we were walking back, I asked him, "Johnny, do you know anyone in the U.S. who would like to have an interest in our CTNs in England?"

"As a matter of fact I do," he replied. "John Thompson, chairman of Southland told me at dinner the other night he thought they might be interested in making an acquisition in Europe."

"What is Southland?" I asked.

"They own the 7-Eleven stores. They have about 5,000 of them—convenience stores that are open from 7 a.m. until 11 p.m."

We had just crossed 55th Street, and I said, "Come with me, Johnny, I want you to do something." We walked inside the St. Regis and went down the stairs to the public telephones in the basement.

"Johnny, call your friend Thompson and let me talk to him," I said.

Johnny introduced me by phone, and I told Thompson about the CTNs, urging him to come look them over. Before we finished talking, he had agreed to come to England the next week with his principal officers.

We met in Jimmy's house at 27 Chester Terrace, and about 30 minutes later, they had agreed to buy a half interest in the CTNs for $11 million, with an additional $2 million to be paid if the profits came out as we expected. Jim Wood did bring in the profits, so our payment totaled $13 million.

We had been saved by 7-Eleven.

THE JIMMY I KNOW

In the years after that first deal, Jimmy, with some help from me, would build a $12 billion basically food business. It included control of five banks and two insurance companies as well. We were known as wild people—and we were.

I have never read even a line in the books written about Jimmy Goldsmith, or for that matter, any of those about Armand Hammer, Roy Thomson, Bunker Hunt or Paul Getty. Yet I was closely involved with all of them and with a number of other well-publicized people about whom many books have been written.

My reason for not reading any of those books is quite simple. Every man should have a right to tell his own story as he sees it, and ego always provides the grounds for altering the facts a bit.

Jimmy, a man of Jewish-English-French extraction, was the inheritor of some of those unique money genes that came out of the European ghettos of the 1700s. There were four prominent German-Jewish families that dominated the trading of gold in that era: the Rothchilds, the Warburgs, the Goldschmidts and the Schroeders. They were the business people, and though each German prince would lock them up in the ghettos every night, he always needed them. They were essential in making the world's commerce move.

Jimmy's heritage was the Goldschmidts. A branch of the family later simplified the surname to Goldsmith. They started the Commercz Bank, which is today one of Germany's largest. I first saw Jimmy when he was about 29, and already he was a big gambler in business as well as on the tables.

As one of the Rothschilds said about him, "He loves money. He loves luxury." And he has it, in the world's finest estates, his Boeing 757 and his endless corps of servants.

Jimmy surrounds himself with famous and highly intelligent friends. He is truly a billionaire. In my mind he has earned every penny of his fortune. He has what I believe to be the best financial mind in our world,

Sir James Goldsmith

and he uses it more productively than anyone I have ever known. Work to him is pure joy.

Jimmy is sometimes cruel about money to those he loves, but he has a conscience that at the last minute usually reappears. He is never overly generous, but often helpful. He is, in a strange way, the most devoted family man I know—a man of three wives, eight children, several mistresses and countless loves.

He spends time with each family. He adores the children, and he provides generously his time and money to all of them. If there is a current Godfather in the world today, it is Sir James Goldsmith.

For sheer charm, no one can match Jim. Women fall out over him for his smile (which goes all the way up his bald head), his sharp wit and his incredible mind. He plays women like violins, and they love it.

Jimmy enjoys nothing more than having good minds around the table, baiting them to take a position and then crushing them with sound argument. Jimmy is considered an ogre in many business circles—the very mention of his name in connection with a company will make any chairman shudder. He appears nerveless, but in truth he is a veritable bundle of nerves.

I admit I think of him as a small boy just coming into his own and fighting his way up. I recall his first important speech, which I edited. It was, I think, at a grocer's convention. We were just outside the hotel in Mayfair, and he had to go on in 10 minutes. He was so nervous he started vomiting. I held his head and cleaned him up with my handkerchief as best as I could. I then ran into the bar and brought out a double brandy, which he drank. After a bit more clean-up work, he went on. His speech that night was faultless.

Jim's temper is one of the worst. In the past, he could frighten anyone with it. In the last few years he has calmed down considerably. Yet, as far as my personal association with him is concerned over our three decades together, we have never had one cross word between us. It has been a most happy and wonderful association.

Jimmy's takeover technique is almost always the same. The takeover target may be a company, a board of directors, an officer or even one of his many employees. To begin with, Jimmy charms them with reason and common sense. If he finds resistance, he strengthens his arguments. If the resistance continues, he finally lowers the boom, and no one can lower it harder, or with more skill.

I had only been associated with him a few years when a very popular Sunday television show on finance was critical of Jimmy and his operation of Cavenham Foods. The hosts were two *London Times* editors.

Jimmy demanded return time, which was granted. For his appearance, he spent two days and nights with lawyers and others who took the other side asking critical questions. When he walked in the studio that Sunday night, he was perfectly prepared. Not only did he sweep the questioners off their feet with a torrent of words and make them look ridiculous in their lack of knowledge, but he also further embarrassed them in endless ways.

The next morning, the *Times* and several other newspapers reported what a cruel man Jimmy was to take these two fellows so completely apart. Cruel? By defending his company and his management?

What it really showed was that Jimmy Goldsmith always does his homework, regardless of the cost or effort involved. It was true of everything in business that I ever saw him do. Whenever Jimmy got interested in taking over a company, he quickly made sure he knew endlessly more about a company's books than did its chairman or president. Jimmy would spend weeks figuring out every possible maneuver the management could make, and he would find a countermove to match each one. He was an absolute master of the trade, and Wall Street recognized it. Even today, the Boone Pickenses and the Carl Icahns rank as amateurs in comparison to Jimmy Goldsmith.

Jimmy only failed twice, both times because of politics. One was in the Goodyear takeover, when the management was able to arrange a special meeting of the Ohio Legislature for the sole purpose of passing a law that would tie up any takeover for a period of five years before the new owners could assume control. Even then, the night before, Jim was able to force the Goodyear management to pay legal expenses of about $40 million dollars, as well as $95 million for his stock in the company.

The other time Jimmy failed was with the British American Tobacco Co., which a woman insurance commissioner in Washington State refused to let him acquire. She said he was not a suitable owner of the insurance company British American Tobacco owned. Jimmy had already sold it to France's largest insurance company, but she would not accept them.

It is also interesting to note that in the Goodyear case, the management did the four or five things after the settlement that Jimmy asked them to do to save the company.

After 30 years, I am more positive than ever that Jimmy Goldsmith had the best financial mind around, as well as more ability to prove it than anyone else alive.

And I still intend never to lose him.

T U R N I N G   P O I N T

The turning point in Jimmy Goldsmith's takeover career was the purchase of the Bovril Company. Bovril was the maker of three of the most famous products in Great Britain. In terms of image and stability, there was no more distinguished a company in the nation.

The product named Bovril was beef juice with a few added ingredients. A teaspoon added to hot water supposedly supplied added strength. Another product, Ambrosia, was rice pudding made from evaporated milk, and was the leading dessert for English families. Then there was Marmite, a product made from yeast that was supposed to be spread on toast every morning to give children added strength for the day.

I dutifully tried each one of these products, and I still believe they were the worst-tasting food products I have ever put in my mouth. However, you could not find a home in Great Britain that did not have all three of them in the cupboard. Both the English and the Scottish were raised on the taste of these concoctions.

The company chairman was Lord Luke, a well-known figure in the English Establishment. I called the main office outside London, and with some difficulty was put through to his secretary. I explained that I was with Conwood Corporation of America, which had investments in several English companies, and was interested in Bovril. I said I would like to meet the chairman, and an engagement was arranged for an afternoon about 10 days later.

On the appointed day I took a train out to their offices. I was well received, and after about 30 minutes was shown into Lord Luke's office. I asked if he minded a few questions about his balance sheet, and he said he would be delighted. I started by asking about an underutilized investment in Argentina, where they had large acreage and more than 100,000 head of cattle, and followed with several similar questions about Bovril's holdings.

For each specific question I asked, Lord Luke replied, "Well, let me see, I think we have a man that can answer that."

Moments later some other executive would show up and give me at least a partial answer. However, Lord Luke could not personally answer any specific questions about his balance sheet. It became abundantly clear that he had little or no knowledge of the business that he was supposed to be running.

After several questions, he interrupted me and asked "Do you like to play golf?"

"Yes," I said, "that's one of my favorites."

"Then you must let me have you meet us at Sunningdale for a game. By the way, I have a new putter that just came today."

With that, the putter was brought out, and for the next 15 minutes or so, we putted on his fine Oriental rug. Finally he said, "You must come down and see my new Rolls. It just arrived yesterday."

With that, we went down to the front of the office, where the new Rolls and chauffeur waited. Lord Luke had me test all the seats and was about to have the chauffeur drive me around the block when I told him I must be on my way back to London.

Jimmy met me at Claridge's on my return and asked, "How did it go? What do you think?"

"Jim, you can start buying up that stock tomorrow," I said. "Luke and that crew haven't the slightest idea about what they are doing, and they won't have a clue on how to fight a takeover."

We waited a few days until the next settlement period and then began buying stock.

From then on, a council of war was held at Claridge's every morning, mainly to brainstorm names of everyone we could possibly call to help finance the deal. Meanwhile, we proceeded to buy up Bovril stock as fast as we could, without regard to whether we had the financing or not. We ran out of money long before we reached about 40 percent of the common stock, and settlement day was rapidly approaching.

As had happened before a savior came to us out of the blue—a man named Steele who was a principal officer of Grand Metropolitan, one of England's largest conglomerates. He called Jim and said that he would be glad to take the dairies owned by Bovril off our hands if we should win our takeover fight. Jim asked Steele what they were worth, and he said around £9 million to £12 million.

From then on, we bought stock with complete abandon. A "white knight" was finally brought in by the Bovril management to fend us off, but it was too late. We reached control of 50 percent of the stock and celebrated for two days.

As I recall, we paid £36 million for Bovril, and within six months made about £50 to £60 million from asset sales. We still owned the company and the three, to me, strange but fast-selling products. We kept Bovril for many years before selling it off.

The Takeover Game

For three or four years, I tried to get Jimmy to venture into the United States, because I thought it was a fertile field for the takeover methods we were honing. Being a foreigner, however, he was afraid of the S.E.C. and all the other regulatory bodies of the U.S., which he did not have to deal with in Europe.

Finally, I think the one who really convinced Jimmy to take the plunge was Andre Meyer, a most tricky but famous Frenchman who ran the banking firm of Lazard Freres. Meyer suggested that we consider Grand Union Stores, a large chain of supermarkets operating from upper New York State down the Atlantic Coast through Puerto Rico. There were 1,100 stores, plus another 15 or 20 discount houses known as Grandways.

Grand Union was America's first supermarket chain, and its problem was simply that it had tired, noncompetitive management. With Meyer's help, we were finally able to buy control of the company and then shut down within 30 days all of the stores that had been losing money for more than 18 months. Then we gave Jim Wood the okay to expand the stores that were making money.

He made Grand Union the first chain of present supermarkets that were upscale in their design and appeal, based on Jimmy's concept of the "separate store" English system of years past. With wider aisles and separate areas for cheeses (directly imported from France) and meats, plus a bakery and fine produce, the changes we made in the stores were very popular with shoppers. The concept was based on creating a modern version of the old-fashioned European stores.

When we first reopened the redesigned New York store on 86th Street as a test, it did three times its previous sales volume in the first three weeks. And the formula proved just as remarkably successful in almost every store in which it was implemented.

In both Grand Union and our second U.S. venture, Diamond International, we had top-level advice in the corporate-takeover game from a young American lawyer named Joe Flom. He was a remarkably able lawyer who had foreseen the coming of the takeover game and had prepared himself for it. He saw that sleepy managements wouldn't have a chance during those aggressive times.

Jim and I had been interviewing law firms when we first came to New York and we were told twice, "The man you fellows need is Joe Flom."

After we found Joe and got him over to come talk with us, he slouched down on the sofa and started answering our questions with ease. His answers were uncomplicated and pure common sense. He understood us, and we understood him. I said to Jim. "He's our man."

He was and still is today. Without Joe Flom, I doubt we could ever have been as successful in the U.S.

Another lawyer who was a crucial player in those takeover confrontations was Marty Lipman. Either Joe or Marty usually represented the aggressors—while the other one was usually employed to defend the management! These two fellows made a remarkable business out of being on opposite sides in countless takeover battles.

I was at dinner one evening at Jimmy's New York home on East 86th Street, sitting between Joe and Marty. Jimmy always retained both of them for us, so that any management opposition had to go out in the wilderness to get defense lawyers.

Marty leaned over to me during the dinner and said, "John, I've about decided to go over to the other side. I think there's some money to be made there." Shortly thereafter, he brought out his "Poison Pill" formula—the proposed issuance of a large amount of new stock in order to prevent an attempted takeover.

It was a formula that proved successful time and again in the era of the takeover, and I think Marty sold it to every major company in America.

THE DEAL WITH NO DOWNSIDE

Diamond International, formerly the Diamond Match Company, was a very old and distinguished American company. It proved to be one of the most profitable deals in which Jimmy and I ever participated.

The key to the deal jumped out as I was reading the company's annual statement and noticed it had timber holdings of 1.7 million acres. The holdings were carried on the company's books at $24 million.

I assumed that for tax purposes Diamond was continuing to carry the holdings at their cost, but obviously this was a greatly undervalued asset. I speculated that the actual value of that land alone could make the takeover of Diamond a very profitable venture.

About the same time that Jim and I became interested, Solomon Brothers' Chicago office entered the picture through Ira Harris. One of the first things we did was have Solomon hire a timber-valuing company, Pickering, to give us a general estimate on Diamond's timber holdings.

After Pickering spent a few weeks making a survey of the property, Bowman Gray, the president of Cavenham's U.S. operations, and I sat in the Solomon offices in Chicago's Sears Tower listening to the report. After about five minutes, I interrupted the Pickering man to ask if he would give me the final total value figure on the timber and then go on with the details.

"Yes, Mr. Tigrett," he said, "We figure this timber has a total value in the current market of between $900 million and $1.3 billion."

The estimate was so much greater than even my most optimistic speculations that I excused myself for a moment, went to the nearest phone and called Jimmy immediately.

"My friend" I said to him, "we have finally found the deal for which we have been searching for the world over.

"It has no downside."

F A R E W E L L   T O   J I M M Y

Jim's philosophy was always different. He said, "John Burton, remember two things in life are important—where you marry and where you die."

He developed cancer of the pancreas and was in great pain for almost a year. We tried everything from Sloan-Kettering to Indian herbs. They all failed.

And so Jim, Jimmy, my Jimbo, Ruthless Raider, Maverick Midas, Financial Caesar, Godfather to many, Horseman of the Apocalypse, the Great Crusader, said goodbye to his family and eight children and left his French chateau. He was carried to his 757 and, with his lawyer, accountant and one mistress, flew to his house in Malaga, Spain. He died there only ten hours later in the same bed (in which he had been born), on July 19, 1997. His accountant called to tell me that by that final move, his estate had saved more than $500 million. His unique mind was sound to the very last moment.

I loved Jimbo as a son, brother, partner and friend. We had more than thirty years togther in the center of the most exciting times in the corporate world. In all that time, whether in defeat or success, we never had a cross word. Twenty years younger than I, he was my boy, and I will always hold him close to my heart.

PART FOUR:

Pat, Isaac and Kerr

Part Four

In Part Four, John meets the love of his life and sees his son Isaac take his place at center stage of the world business scene.

However, John's courtship of Pat Kerr gets off to a rather inauspicious start. When a colleague of his tells Pat of John's interest, she shows little interest in return, and John begins a determined pursuit of a woman who is equally determined to remain single.

"She had so many suitors, I couldn't keep track of them all," John writes. "I pursued her constantly, and she would see me occasionally."

Later, Pat demonstrates her own business savvy when she boldly lands $125,000 worth of orders from Neiman-Marcus—even though her Pat Kerr, Inc. fashion design firm does not exist when she calls on the great department store.

It will not be the first nor the last time that the belle from the little river town of Savannah, Tennessee, will amaze John. As he recalls, she becomes "a name to be reckoned with in New York's tough couture industry and number one in the design and production of the finest wedding dresses made in the world . . . without ever going down to Seventh Avenue."

And John sees his son Isaac enter the business that John considers the absolute worst in the world—the restaurant business—and make a dazzling worldwide success of it.

Discovering that Isaac has found perhaps the best single site available in all of London, John decides to back Isaac's new venture, the Hard Rock Cafe. John plays an important role in the story of the Hard Rock, but shares his absolute wonder at the ways Isaac blends spirituality with business to produce both profits and good works.

Also in Part Four, another son arrives when Pat gives birth to Harrison Kerr Tigrett. He grows up as a world traveler and keen reader and heads to college at the University of Virginia. His interests and ambitions, as well as his remarkable successes working summers in Washington, D.C., point him toward a career in politics.

The bond between father and both sons is strong. Just as John has been a player in so many international dramas throughout his life, so are his sons now beginning to play roles equally global and culture-changing in their impact.

— ROBERT KERR

12

The Incomparable Pat and Son, Kerr

A Russian Painting to Woo a Pretty Lady

One spring day in 1973, I was driving my American counsel, Don Pemberton, to Heathrow so he could fly back to Memphis. "Don," I said, "I'm on a most interesting and very serious search."

"What kind of a search?" he asked.

"A search for a P.A.—personal assistant," I said. "I have more work every day than anyone possibly can finish. I want the most competent and engaging person available. I want someone who has run or is running their own business. Someone totally secure but not overbearing. Someone who reads the *Wall Street Journal* and also *Rolling Stone*. Someone who is so well-informed yet discreet that you would never know it until they become your dinner partner. Someone who is just as much at home with a prime minister or a sultan as they are with a clerk at Harrod's.

"I want a person whose heritage is common sense and who is 'up' every day of the year. The right one can have any compensation they want."

"That's quite an undertaking," said Don.

Painting of Pat Kerr

"But I haven't told you the really difficult part. Now that I'm single again, it must be a woman between the ages of 25 and 35, outstandingly beautiful, with a 10-plus figure, and an ever-happy disposition."

"Boy, you have taken on a job. Have you had any prospects yet?" he asked.

"You'd be amazed. Once I put the word out, all my old friends, male and female, took it on as their personal obligation to find the right applicant. Cubby Broccoli sent over two of his James Bond girls from California. They were very pretty, but a little slow upstairs. An old partner from Rio sent up the most beautiful girl in the world, but unfortunately she spoke no English. My friend had misunderstood the mission."

I continued: "Then I received a beautiful letter from California that absolutely hit every requirement 100 percent. I became terribly excited waiting for her pictures to arrive a few days later. When they did, I tore open the package to find several poses of a smiling 410-pound beauty. Dana Broccoli had spent two days going through the United Artists files looking for this delicate creature."

"You know," said Don, "the only woman I have ever heard of that might even possibly fill those requirements is someone I have never seen or met. But, heaven knows I've heard enough about her from my friends. She's already a legend in Memphis. She has won most of the beauty titles, and I think now runs her own business, which is associated with the Miss Universe contest. Her name is Pat Kerr."

"Well, check her out, Don. Have her come in for an interview; then drop me a note on what you think."

Three weeks later, I returned to London from Saudi Arabia to find a letter from Pemberton. It read: *I think I may have found what you are looking for, but I doubt that you have even a chance of getting her. She has a good business, and the only impression she seemed to have of your offer was one of amusement. At the end, however, she did say, "Tell Mr. Tigrett I am not disinterested in his offer."*

Don included Pat's phone number, so I picked up the phone and dialed the number. A feminine voice answered, and I said simply, "What does 'not disinterested' mean?"

"It means," she replied, "what does your proposal involve?"

I laughed, "Why don't you come over to London at my expense and find out?"

"I couldn't possibly," she said. "I'm too busy, and besides, I have to be at the Miss Universe USA contest in New York this coming weekend."

"Well, that's a coincidence," I said. "I have to be in New York Saturday and Sunday as well [a trip I instantly planned at that moment]. Why don't you get us some rooms wherever you like to stay?"

"I'll be with the Universe people, but I'll be glad to make you a reservation somewhere."

"Where do you usually stay?" I asked.

"The Pierre."

"Okay. Get me a room at the Pierre. I'll get there about 4 o'clock

*Pat during the
Miss Universe Pageant,
the night John met her*

Saturday afternoon. Give me a call, and we'll plan to meet."

When I reached the Pierre, I found that Pat had reserved the largest suite in the hotel—four bedrooms. The maids were still dusting the place—evidently it had not been used for some time.

I then waited for the phone call, which finally came about 7:30 p.m.

"I'm so sorry not to be able to get by to say hello," Pat said, "but I've been terribly busy with Miss Universe, and the show starts at 8:30 tonight. Perhaps we can get together tomorrow," she said.

"Listen, young lady," I replied. "I've come 3,000 miles to get a look at you, and you can arrange to come by here at least for one drink."

"Well, I'll try, but I can only stay about five minutes. What's the room number?"

"You have me in 1105, 1106, 1107 and 1108. You can't miss it."

I rushed to change clothes for the third time, suddenly deciding a safari suit would be more debonair.

No Southern whirlwind ever came across a field creating more excitement and beauty than Pat Kerr when she entered the room in the Pierre Hotel that night. Dressed in advanced style, tanned, with beautiful long legs and a smile that never stopped, I knew in one minute I was a goner. She had it all, including exciting laughter and a confident voice that made you feel good all over.

She took three sips of champagne and said, "I'm so sorry to run, but they'll be waiting on me at the theater."

"I'll see you down," I said. These were the first words I had been able to squeeze in.

In the elevator, she offered a bit of hope.

"There's a party afterward, and if it gets dull, I'll give you a call and maybe we can get together."

"I'd love to," I said, as the limousine drove away.

I waited up that night until 3:30 a.m., but the phone never rang.

The next morning, I called the Hilton about 11 and asked Pat for lunch.

"I'll be glad to have lunch with you if I can bring a friend," she said.

"Male or female?" I asked.

"Female."

"I'll pick you up at 1 p.m. at the Hilton."

Her friend was Miss Massachusetts, and we went for lunch at Maxwell's Plum.

"I don't know whether you know it," said Miss Massachusetts, "but Pat is a marvelous painter. I think the beauty business is only a hobby. Her real profession is painting flowers, portraits—everything beautiful."

"How interesting," I said. "Perhaps you two would like to see the Russian exhibition that has just opened here."

"Are you kidding?" said Pat. "It's the first time the Hermitage has ever let out any of its treasures, and *Time* said the line is 10 blocks long. There never has been such interest in an exhibition. Besides that, I never stand in line for anything."

When we were in the car after lunch, I said to the driver, "Take us up to 72nd and Madison."

To Pat I said, "It's a cold rainy Sunday—maybe the line won't be so long today."

She just looked at me skeptically, especially when we saw people standing in line for five blocks under their umbrellas.

I said to the driver, "Go to the entrance of the Knoedler Gallery."

The girls said nothing.

When we pulled up, I stepped out and turned to the girls. "Come along," I said.

"You're not going to embarrass us," said Pat defiantly, remaining in the car.

"Listen, you two," I said. "Get out of there right now!"

Just as they climbed out of the car, they heard an official say, "Frank, hold back the line until Mr. Tigrett and his party can come in."

As we entered, the two girls on the door said, "Mr. Tigrett, how wonderful to see you. We didn't know you were in New York. Welcome to your Russian exhibition."

I could see the Cherokee Indian in Pat Kerr rapidly rising. As we reached the inside of the gallery, she asked, "Just what did you have to do with all this?"

"Not much really," I said. "Doc Hammer and I only handled the trading with Brezhnev and the Hermitage to bring the collection to America."

Her face became one wonderful smile.

"You S.O.B.," she said.

THE GREATEST FRAUD OF ALL

I asked Pat to marry me one week after we met. However, she had so many suitors, I couldn't keep track of them all.

Many of the suitors were famous and had great wealth, with their own private planes and pilots. I was, however, the only one old enough to be her father.

I pursued her constantly, and she would meet me occasionally. I don't think she ever really said she would marry me, but I kept making moves in that direction. All my friends helped, including Doc and Frances Hammer, Martha and Hal Wallis, Jimmy and Annabel Goldsmith, and Dana and Cubby Broccoli.

Everywhere Pat went, someone took up my case with her. I had nothing to do with it, but she must have been terribly bored with it all. And the most pressure of all came from Ruth and Doc Peale.

We went for lunch with them at their house in Pawling, New York, and before we left Doc Peale not only had agreed to perform the ceremony, but he had also all but set the date for us to marry in his great church at Fifth Avenue and 29th Street.

The date was finally set for November 24, 1973, just six months after we had first met.

* * *

This is a story Doc Hammer told to the wedding party at dinner at the "21" Club in New York the night before Pat and I were married:

"A year or so ago, John and I went to Zurich to sell a sulphur mine to an old art friend as an investment. I took with me a lawyer who was a Harvard graduate and also the president of Jefferson Lake Sulphur, one of our companies. When we finished the sale, we were all sitting in a TWA plane on our way back to New York. John and I were sitting together, and my associates were across the aisle.

"I sneezed, and John immediately got up, then came back in a moment with two pills and a glass of water. 'Take these, Doc,' he said. 'You may be catching a little cold, but if you take these two aspirins, let your seat back and relax and don't eat too much dinner, you can get over it.' I took the aspirin, let my seat back and began thinking:

"Here was my distinguished president of the Jefferson Lake Sulphur Company. We are selling the mine on a per-ton basis with certain credits. He was not able to get the correct per-ton price, so John finally goes and gets a calculator and figures it out. Obviously, this president of the sulphur company is a fraud. He doesn't even know the price of the product he's selling.

"And then this lawyer sitting across from me with the Harvard degree—we spent two hours listening to him dictate a contract in legalese that no one could understand. Then John says, 'I'll get another girl, and maybe we can simplify this agreement.' In 30 or 40 minutes, he brings in a three–page document on which we make two minor changes and then sign. So, obviously, this fine Harvard lawyer that I brought all the way from California can't even write an agreement—he, too, is certainly a fraud.

"And here I am, graduate doctor of Columbia Medical School. I've maintained my license to practice for more than 30 years and never practiced once—yet everybody calls me 'Doctor.' So obviously I am a fraud.

"Finally, there is John, who never graduated from anything. He figures out the correct price for the sulphur, takes over the contract from the Harvard lawyer and writes the agreement we signed. Then here he is practicing medicine without a license, diagnosing my illness, prescribing the medicine and telling me what I must do to get well. Here he is uneducated and unqualified in anything, practicing fearlessly every profession at every opportunity.

"Obviously, he is by far the greatest fraud of all!"

"I HATE BEING MARRIED!"

Before our wedding day, Pat decorated every inch of the vast Marble Collegiate Church in which we were to marry. But then she sent only a few invitations of her own, because as she explained, "No one expects me to really get married."

All my group came from Europe. Pat cried for the two solid days before the wedding. On the night of the big event, I waited in Doc Peale's chambers. He was moving around constantly.

"What are you so nervous about, Doc? You can't stay still," I said.

"I don't know, John. I'm just nervous about marrying the two of you. I never have felt this way before."

"Well, Doc, you probably don't even have to worry. Come here," I said. We went to the door looking into the church.

"You see that main aisle? Well, the chances of Pat walking down it are probably 70-30 against."

"Oh, no," said Doc. "I'll never get through this night."

Pat's father, Hubert, was to give her away. My son, Isaac, was my best man.

Finally, Pat and her father started down the aisle. I fully expected her to turn around at the last minute and go back, but she didn't. Doc Peale was so nervous, he couldn't remember some of the lines in the ceremony, and Pat and I had to prompt him.

On the way up the aisle, sweeping past the photographers, I kissed Pat as she cried, "I hate being married!"

HOW TO START A
BUSINESS FROM SCRATCH

A few years later, Pat was busy raising our son Kerr, painting and decorating our London house and doing many other things. We frequently commuted to Memphis, and one day while there, I told her I was going to Dallas the following day to visit with Bunker Hunt on some business.

Pat said she wanted to join me, with Kerr and his nanny. "For years now in Europe and here, people have come up to me and asked who designs the gowns I wear," she said.

"It's always difficult to tell them I designed them—instead of some famous designer. I think I'll go along and see if I can sell my designs at Neiman-Marcus."

"Great," I said. "I'll call Johnny Thompson or Bunker Hunt or one of our other friends and ask them to set up a meeting for you."

"No, sir! Don't you dare touch it, John Tigrett—I'll make my own arrangements," she warned me.

"Do you know anyone at Neiman-Marcus?" I asked.

"No, but I'll call the merchandising manager right now."

"Good luck."

Sure enough, within minutes she had called the operator at Neiman-Marcus and asked who was the head of merchandising. While she waited to be connected with him, she turned to me and said, "His name is Joel Rath."

To my amazement, she soon had Joel Rath on the line. Pat talked to him for about 15 minutes and described her designs in lace, then he called back to say he had five buyers lined up to receive her.

We went to Dallas and stayed at the Fairmont Hotel. The next morning, Bunker came by for me, while Pat and her eight bags went on to Neiman's.

About 5 p.m., Bunker and I were in the hotel room on the floor playing with Kerr when Pat came in.

"I'm exhausted," she said. "Get me a big glass of champagne. I'm going to take a shower."

"But how did you do?" I asked.

She tossed us a bunch of papers that went all over the floor. "You and Bunker figure it out," she said.

We picked up some of the papers on the floor and started looking.

"These look like orders to me," said Bunker.

Pat and John

When we added up everything, she had sold $125,000 worth of merchandise in an afternoon. The next week, they put her dresses in every Neiman-Marcus window and sold them out the same day—a store record. There was no turning back.

Pat Kerr, Inc.—which was not even in existence when we arrived in Dallas, and which had not a single employee—was now in business.

Kerr and John on a hunting trip

THE EDUCATION OF A GENTLEMAN: KERR TIGRETT

When Pat first learned we were expecting a child, I was only 64. We celebrated endlessly, then finally determined that our child would be born on American soil and in the South.

When our beautiful baby boy arrived in Memphis in 1977, our old friend Doc Peale came down and christened him Harrison Kerr Tigrett at 4 weeks of age. The next day, we took Kerr to our home in London.

Before long, he began his formal education at the Hyde Park Nursery.

A bit later, he began his informal education at Isaac's Hard Rock Cafe. However, the most invaluable phase of Kerr's education may well have come from traveling all over the world with us as he grew up.

At the age of 20, Kerr is a student at the University of Virginia and well on the road to a career—of his own choosing. He has some sound qualifications:

He is a reader of everything—good, bad and indifferent.

He is a worldly traveler who has already visited virtually every major country in the East and West several times.

He makes friends easily, and keeps them.

Always modest, he seems more secure at 20 than I do at 84.

In recent years, Kerr has spent each summer working in the political arena in Washington. One summer, he worked as Senate page to Senator George Mitchell, then majority leader of the Democratic Party in the U.S. Senate.

The very next summer—to our surprise—Kerr announced he would be working as head Senate page to Senator Bob Dole, who was then majority leader of the Republican Party in the U.S. Senate.

The next summer he interned with Tennessee Senator Bill Frist, a Republican. Most recently he worked in former Republican Senator Howard Baker's Washington, D.C., law office.

I asked Kerr how he managed to pull off such a dramatic leap from one political party to the other from one summer to the next. His response made me realize he was well on his way in his chosen field.

"Well, Dad," he said with a smile. "You have your sources, and I have mine."

O N E   R E M A R K A B L E   W O M A N

Every now and then, you see a pretty head that has poked its way out of the vast female sea and has risen well above it. You can recognize these rare and special individuals immediately, for it is like discovering a golden egg in an Easter egg hunt.

One of those shining, golden rarities is Pat Kerr.

Where the genes of great talent find themselves must be as much a mystery to them as to us. Only very rarely are they handed down in the same family. It is almost as though they were part of a unique flower swaying in the warm spring breeze—the pollen, or genes, falling aimlessly into strange areas to create our most remarkable humans.

How you move from being raised in a tiny farmhouse near the little river town of Savannah, Tennessee, to becoming a name to be reckoned with in New York's tough couture industry and number one in the design and production of the finest wedding dresses made in the world . . . no one knows. I can tell you this much, though—it takes not only drive, charm and genius ability but also a strong heart.

Much of her strength for being able to move across the world comes from Pat's personal security. It is a security bred from the strong roots of a stable, loving, religious family; from grooming blue-ribbon calves; and traveling 275 miles two times a week over bad roads to go to charm school. It also comes from making her debut through beauty contests and learning how to win, and lose, in a range of pageants from Miss Catfish to Miss Tennessee to the Miss Universe finals.

All of this and endless other small-town experiences can make one secure and fertilize ambition, yet they don't necessarily give you charm. Here is a woman who exudes charm and down-to-earth friendship endlessly. I have never seen anyone who has known Pat for more than a month ever just shake hands with her. There's nearly always the cry, "Pat!" with a big laugh as their arms go round each other.

She is the only person I have ever known whom hundreds of people consider their very best friend—and she is. She lifts every person she sees with her bright charm and her ever-warm smile, friendship and help.

One of the rarest and most elusive human qualities is style. I often wonder how one gets it. How do you come from Savannah, Tennessee, or Chicago or even Paris and have it? How does Pat Kerr walk in the Plaza Athenee in Paris, the Ritz in London, the Regent in Hong Kong or even the Holiday Inn in Dubuque and have every eye follow or steal a quick glance and wonder who she is?

I never enter a room with Pat on my arm—I walk just behind her. For without any apparent effort, she will make every head turn. I often wonder if it's the cut of her jeans or the long legs. Maybe it's the toss of her head or the air of seemingly casual indifference. Or is it that she simply has style and knows it?

In a lifetime of watching people all over the world, I've only known two women to have such style in abundance. One was my wartime love, Rosa Morley, the famous London actress. The other is my Pat.

I have never known a busier woman or one who accomplishes so much in a day's time, from her 6 a.m. wake-up calls to go to the health club, to her prayer groups, to her business, where she is the sole designer. There she cuts every piece of valuable antique lace—her trademark. She will design a $10,000 to $20,000 dress in less than 30 minutes, and often cut the lace for it freehand.

Then she can go on to the civic meetings or plan one of five major charity balls that she will put on annually. She was a success as the founder and chairman of the premier children's party in the nation—the Jingle Bell Ball—The Nutcracker Ball, and The Blues Ball, all annual events. Pat also organized the ceremony and raised the funds to light the main bridge across the Mississippi River at Memphis, providing entertainment for 200,000 people and a seated outdoor formal dinner for 2,500 guests.

For any event, she will design everything from the invitations to the entertainment and, with her assistants, account for every minute of every affair. They will all be fast moving and will start and end on time. Pat

Pat

Kerr is a master organizer who could easily be one of the highest paid women in America, but instead she gives away at least 70 percent of her time to charity or civic projects.

Here is a woman who has not even begun to reach her potential. Someday I hope she will turn her life around and begin to work for herself, with her sense of timeless, high-quality design unique in America. She has built up Pat Kerr wedding dresses to number one without ever knowing she was supposed to be on Seventh Avenue. Her designs in the tough fashion industry stand out like what they are—heirlooms. Her talents are endless, and she has only just begun to make use of them.

But she will never, ever forget that the little town of Savannah, Tennessee, is her home.

13

Isaac Tigrett –
One of a Kind

THE HARD ROCK CAFE:
A NEW WORLD CULTURE

There is one business in this world where 90 percent of the entrepreneurs want desperately to be involved and are absolutely confident they will succeed. The other 10 percent who are already in the business, with few exceptions, are trying desperately to get out.

The business is operating or owning a restaurant.

There is nothing that requires more management hours, that has as many problems (which change daily), or as many complaints from customers and produces less monetary return. Sixty-five percent of restaurants fail in the first three years.

Those were my thoughts concerning the restaurant industry when in January 1971, my son Isaac came to the London house we leased at 15 South Street, Mayfair, to tell me, "Dad, I've decided to start a restaurant."

I was so shocked I couldn't speak for a moment or two. In the last few years before that, Isaac had spent six months living in San Francisco's Haight-Ashbury district, at the peak of the hippie days. Then he spent six months living with Masai tribesmen in Africa. After that, he lived for six months with Indians up in the mountains of Jamaica.

Inside the original Hard Rock Cafe at 150 Piccadilly in London

When he arrived in London, he had very long hair, and he went around in sandals most of the time. Nobody in business at that time, except me, would really have anything much to do with him. And now he came to me telling me he not only wanted to go into business in London but also into the worst business I could imagine.

So I proceeded to lecture him on all the endless negatives of the restaurant business. Then I had Isaac call Jimmy Goldsmith, who told him the same thing, in even stronger terms.

"And there's no way I would invest anything in a restaurant," Jimmy said. "It's even worse than the chicken business."

But Isaac held on.

He said he had a new restaurant concept, and he kept after me until I finally agreed to at least visit the location where he wanted to open his restaurant and had obtained an option on the property.

We walked down to the place, at 150 Piccadilly, the last of the cars were being removed from what had been a Rolls-Royce showroom. I left Isaac and walked across Piccadilly, then looked back at the building from that side of the street.

I stopped thinking about the restaurant business for the moment and began thinking: How many generations does it take to have a chance to lease the only commercial place on Hyde Park Corner—the busiest spot in London?

I walked back to where Isaac was waiting for me and said, "Son, go sign that lease today. Don't argue with the man about the price, only the terms. Just be sure the length of the lease is for as far out into the future as he'll let you go. I'll talk to Jimmy, and we'll back you."

Isaac looked at me with a shocked expression. Had I lost my mind? All he could say was, "Dad, are you sure you are all right? I thought you and Jimmy both said you didn't want anything to do with this."

"Forget about that. I'll take care of Jimmy, and we'll borrow the money for you tomorrow."

Isaac signed the lease that same afternoon. The next day, Jimmy and I guaranteed a note for £40,000 to a small Dutch bank we controlled named Von Emden in Amsterdam.

I still had no interest in the restaurant business, just the location. I fully expected to have to write the loan off as a loss by the end of the year, and I told the puzzled banker exactly that.

But as Isaac explained his concept to me in more detail, I began to grasp the possibilities that he envisioned.

"You see, Dad, I'm not really going to be in the restaurant business," he said. "I'm going to be in the merchandise business."

He detailed a plan designed to set his restaurant apart from the rest of the business. "First, I'm going to sell the finest food that money can buy. It will be top quality. We will have a mixture of American and Scottish beef that I think makes the best hamburger in the world.

"Secondly, we are going to sell it out of a 'museum.' What I have in mind is to put memorabilia on every square inch of space available—rock and roll memorabilia, so the people will keep coming back to at least see and find things from artists they have loved through the years.

"And thirdly, and most importantly perhaps, will be the merchandise we offer. We'll start selling it out of the cloak room or by the cashier's counter, and then we'll eventually get a place close by for the clothing business. I think that will dramatically increase the profit margin of the restaurants."

I asked what kind of clothing he was going to sell.

"Well, first of all, I'm going to start off with what is known as a T-shirt. At the moment, that's considered just underwear, or something worn by mechanics and men working down on the docks. What I have in mind to do with the T-shirt is to make it socially acceptable," he said.

"I'll put the name 'Hard Rock' on it, and we'll only let them be sold wherever there is a Hard Rock. For now, that will be London. Someday, when we expand to Paris or New York, then you will only be able to buy a Hard Rock Paris T-shirt in Paris or a Hard Rock New York T-shirt in New York."

No element of Isaac's vision proved more insightful than his Hard Rock T-shirts. They became fashionable attire, and today you can see people wearing them all over the world.

While the former Rolls building was being painted and equipment installed, Isaac came to me one day and said, "Dad, my friend Peter Morton is having a lot of trouble. His Great American Disaster Restaurant is very popular but losing money. His father, who put up part of the starting costs, is being pretty mean to him. So Peter wants to try to sell the Disaster if he can. I told him if he did, I'd give him half of The Hard Rock."

"Sonny Boy," I warned him, "you never give anyone 50 percent of anything. It always leads to trouble. Of the five or six times I've been called in to arbitrate such a situation, I've never seen so much bitterness as over a 50-50 relationship. Either give him 51 percent or 49 percent, but never 50 percent."

A week later, I found Isaac had given Peter 50 percent of the Hard Rock for free. His explanation was, "But, Dad, I had already given him my word before I talked to you."

The night before the world's first Hard Rock Cafe was to open, I got a call from Isaac. He said, "Dad, if you can, I wish you would come down to the Hard Rock and help us beat up this place. We have the equipment necessary, but we need hands."

"What do you mean 'beat up' the restaurant?" I asked.

"It's too slick and shiny," he said. "I want it to look like it's been here for 50 years."

We went down immediately, and sure enough, there they were with chains, hammers, knives and all sorts of other things needed to work over the tables, the floor and anything else that was exposed, except for the memorabilia.

Along with the others, we spent six hours "beating up" the first Hard Rock Cafe. We even carved initials in the tables until our hands gave out. When we finished at 4 a.m. and toasted it with champagne, it indeed looked as if it had been there for at least 50 years.

At noon on May 2, 1971, the first Hard Rock Cafe opened at 150 Piccadilly in London. From that first day, it had long lines of people outside waiting to get in. It became the place where everyone who was hip—or wished they were—wanted to be seen.

Before long, Isaac had memorabilia from every rock musician you could think of—from the Beatles on down—displayed on the walls. They all wanted to contribute something that would be on display at the Hard Rock.

Isaac also started his first American-type soup kitchen. At 11 every morning, he fed the homeless who slept in St. James Park. In turn, they came up with the idea of stealing enough flowers from the park to be placed on the all the tables in the restaurant each day.

But despite all the business the Hard Rock was doing and all the attention it was getting, there was one ongoing problem in those early days: The place was losing money hand over fist.

I told Isaac to never, ever tell anyone that, because if people think a business is losing money, its image will change, and customers will stop coming. We all kept quiet, and the boys kept working to make the Hard Rock profitable.

However, the situation grew very serious. At that time, there was a

Isaac Burton Tigrett II

law in England that if you owed your suppliers for more than 30 days and you knew you could not pay them, you went to jail.

Isaac and Peter came to me one day and told me how bad things were. They were scared to death they were going to jail. I told them to let me see what I could do.

I thought about Uli Prager of Zurich, the largest and one of the most successful restaurant operators in Europe. As a favor, I had saved him once in a board fight, so I went to see him at his beautiful home on an island in Lake Moritz.

"I would like you to put $25,000 into the Hard Rock," I said. "I will be good for it, but the boys will realize more responsibility if someone else besides me is backing them."

"Of course," he said.

"And," I added, "I would also like you to send your best manager over there for five or six weeks to help them get their operation straightened out."

Uli agreed to that too. And from the minute his man walked in the door, the Hard Rock Cafe made money.

The first thing this fellow did was build a chicken-wire fence around the supply area and put a reliable man in charge of it. Anyone who took anything out had to sign for it and explain what it was to be used for.

He also checked out the kitchen and discovered that between the suppliers and the waitresses, they were shorting the restaurant a few dozen hamburgers a day.

By systematically straightening out all such matters, the Hard Rock became a consistently profitable operation. But the whole time, it was such a glamorous place, no one ever knew about any financial problems.

Before Uli's man left, he wrote a little handbook on how to run a Hard Rock Cafe. And my guess is that every Hard Rock Cafe in the world is probably using that handbook to this day.

* * *

In the years that followed, Isaac went on to open Hard Rock Cafes in New York and Dallas as well. When they opened the Hard Rock in New York, Pat persuaded Jack Soden to let them display a piece of Elvis memorabilia—the first time Graceland allowed anyone to do that.

At the New York Hard Rock, they placed one of Elvis' famous jeweled and embroidered jumpsuits on a golden throne all by itself high above the center of the main room. Then they put a spotlight on it. No one in the place could miss it.

When the New York Hard Rock had its grand opening, everybody—even Walter Cronkite and Doc Peale—came to see the place. By that time, the Hard Rocks were world famous, and everyone wanted to go to them.

The three sites—London, New York and Dallas—were selling more than $28 million dollars annually in clothing and $20 million in food and beverages, and they had leases for sites in two or three other cities.

Then one day, Isaac came to me and said, "I think I might want you to help me find something to do with the Hard Rocks."

"Do you mean you want to sell them? Why?" I asked.

"Well, I've thought about it a lot. Rock and roll is not out, and probably never will be. But it is on the way down."

As it happened, just a few days later, I was in Harry's Bar. A fellow I knew walked over to me and said he wanted to buy the Hard Rocks.

"I'll give you £50 million," he said.

I laughed. "I'm afraid we are not talking about the same thing. I thought you were talking about the Hard Rock Cafes. For that, you are going to have to pay around £100 million."

"That's ridiculous," he said, and went back to his table.

But 20 minutes later, he walked back over to where I was sitting, and said, "I will give you £60 million."

"Unless you can do a lot better than that, you are wasting my time and yours," I said, and he went and sat down again.

Then, just as I was leaving, he caught up with me and said, "I will give you £85 million ($140,000,000)."

"My friend," I said, putting out my hand, "you have just bought the Hard Rock Cafes."

Isaac and the other stockholders received for those three units and several franchises a price of $140 million cash when the deal was closed in 1988. Isaac's share came to about $65 million.

THE MAGNIFICENT HOSPITAL
FOR THE POOR

At the sale of the remarkably successful Hard Rock Cafes, I learned the corporate name of Isaac's company was Don't Let Your Meat Loaf, Baby. The sale was concluded at midnight at County Bank, the merchant arm of the National Westminster Bank in London.

It went on until that late hour because the lawyers spent hours in pointless arguments until finally I put my foot down. When we finished, I was exhausted.

As Isaac and I walked up the street looking for a taxi, I said, "Well, Sonny Boy, now that you have a few bucks, what are you going to do with it?"

"Well, Dad," he said, "tomorrow I am going to fly to Bangalore, India, and drive up to the town of Puttaparthi. There I will start laying plans for building the finest, most modern hospital in the world with my friend, Sai Baba."

Sathya Sai Baba is an Indian spiritual leader who has spent his entire life in a small town of 3,000. Yet from that unique stage, he has gained a reputed 50 million followers who believe in his philosophy for living. Isaac met Sai Baba in the mid-Seventies, and has looked to him for guidance ever since.

"It will be a free hospital for the poor," Isaac continued, to my amazement. "We will have the most inventive equipment and the best specialists the world can provide. The care will all be provided at no cost to the patients there."

"How much of your money are you going to spend?"

"All of it."

I stopped in my tracks.

"You're crazy, son," I sputtered. "Are you telling me that after working like a dog, selling hamburgers for 20 years, that now you're going to take your money and put it into a hospital for the poor in the most downtrodden part of India?"

"You've got it, Dad," Isaac replied.

"Well, just give me one good reason for doing such a foolish thing."

"There is just one reason, Dad. When I get as old as you are, I won't be able to remember selling hamburgers. But I will always remember having built a great hospital in India for the poor."

I stopped, thought for a moment, and tears came to my eyes. "Let's go to Tramps and get drunk, Sonny Boy," I told him. "I'll never mention the matter again."

* * *

The 225-bed hospital opened November 29, 1992. It was designed by the English royal architect, Keith Kritchlow, and built by 3,000 workers in nine months. Certainly it is unique in its beauty as a hospital. The *London Times* said it looked like "a heavenly apparition."

The American Hospital Association devised the hospital's magnificent program. The Indian Trust pays the daily costs of operation. It has seven white-marble operating rooms for specialized surgeries, and within the first six months of opening, more than 500 heart bypass operations were successfully performed.

At the opening ceremony, Isaac sat in the big gold chair on Sai Baba's right, with the prime minister of India on Sai Baba's left. Isaac passed a lighted candle to the prime minister, who cut the opening ribbon by burning it in two. More than 300,000 people attended from every part of the world.

Today, the hospital is known locally as "The Hard Rock Hospital."

MEMPHIS' PYRAMID—
ISAAC TO THE RESCUE

Politicians have been my nemeses for a very long time. They have caused me more trouble and cost me more money than all other types of humans put together. Memphis' Great American Pyramid, which eventually cost me $8 million, is a prime example.

Pat and I were on one of our frequent visits from London to Memphis—this time for her mother's birthday. A local banker called and asked me to see a friend of his who had an idea. The next day, two young men came to the apartment to show me a drawing of a small pyramid, which they proposed as the Memphis City Hall. The father of one of the boys had drawn the picture 25 years before. Their presentation was so confused that after 10 minutes I told them I had no interest and showed them to the elevator.

Two days later, we were on the Concorde heading home. I was quietly reading the *Financial Times*. While most individuals firmly believe they control their own minds, nothing could be further from the truth. The fact is that your mind controls you. My mind suddenly started thinking about pyramids. Not little ones, but a great one—almost as large as the one at Giza. One in which the ground floor area could contain six football fields. The first one to be built in 5,000 years and located on the banks of the Mississippi River in Memphis. After all, Andrew Jackson and his partner, John Overton, had named that high ground they bought from the Chickasaw Indians "Memphis on the Mississippi" for Memphis on the Nile in Egypt.

I thought of what a great trademark it would make for a sleepy Southern country town just awakening to the world. Before the Concorde touched ground at Heathrow Airport, my mind told me to get this great pyramid built and dedicate it to the one true heritage that Memphis owns—the home of American music.

On my next trip to the States, I visited seven recently constructed arenas to find out what mistakes had been made in design. All agreed that they were not large enough. The politicians had cut the budget at the last moment. The consultant on all of the arenas was Atlanta architect Henry Teague. I went to see Henry, and my friends and I agreed to pay him $300,000 for a preliminary plan of the arena he had always wanted to build. We wanted 22,500 seats, making it the largest in the South, and each seat would have the best view.

Meanwhile, my nemeses, the Memphis Politicians, were busy at work. They decided that the need for a new arena could be met by cutting off the top of the 30-year-old, 11,000-seat Coliseum and adding 5,000 seats. The cost would be $26 million, of which they had already spent $1 million on the plans.

By this time, my friends and I had already taken bids on Henry Teague's plans from three national contractors. The low bid was from an Indianapolis contractor, and we beat it down to $42 million, hoping to get it down to $40 million before we were done.

I then invited the city and county mayors (who were two very different individuals and hated each other) to lunch at my apartment to spring the Pyramid arena idea on them.

The local story was that after my presentation the two were on the elevator, and one said to the other, "You know Mr. Tigrett is a nice man, but he's getting rather old; I guess that somehow affects his mind." The response was, "Yes, I agree."

I leaked the Pyramid story to the media, which was just enough to put the Coliseum roof cutting on hold. From that time on, every time Pat and I visited Memphis for a few days, we presented the mayors and their councils with some novel approaches on the subject, which were turned down for one reason or another. A survey by the local newspaper showed that 65 percent of the citizens were against the idea. My only supporters of prominence were Fred Smith of Federal Express, Mike Rose of Promus Corporation, and the others who funded the preliminary study.

An offer to get Isaac to put a Hard Rock Cafe in the building drew surprising interest, except from one local religious group, which saw the restaurant as a "dope and sex den of iniquity."

Then Isaac came to town. "Dad, are you still fooling around with that Pyramid idea?" he asked.

"Well, what else is there for me to do in this dull town," I replied. "They turned me down about 25 times now, but they are weakening."

"If you really want to get it built," he said, "I'll show you how. I hear they say my cafes are dens of the devil, so get Mr. Smith to make two of his FedEx planes available. I'll invite both mayors and both councils to Dallas for a night at the Hard Rock and show them what a family place looks like."

I arranged the planes, and Isaac called everyone personally to invite them to Dallas for the next Saturday night.

When they returned, after all those months of argument, the next Tuesday both councils voted unanimously to build the Great American Pyramid in Memphis, Tennessee.

THE MOST BEAUTIFUL CAR
IN THE WORLD

When Gulf, Mobile & Ohio Car 50 rolled out of the American Car and Foundry in St. Louis in 1928, it was declared the largest, heaviest and most beautiful private railroad car in existence. My Uncle Isaac, who was chairman of the GM&O Railroad, used Car 50 as his traveling office.

I was 15 at the time, and my uncle often would take me with him. I loved the excitement of being on Car 50. However, after Uncle Isaac died, and as passing years took me all over the world, I lost track of that fantastic palace on wheels.

Then one day after Isaac had sold the Hard Rock Cafes, he called me and asked, "Whatever happened to Car 50?"

"I don't know, Son," I replied. "I expect it is on the scrap heap by now."

"Well, let's try to find it," he said.

Two weeks after that conversation, Isaac and I both had concluded that Car 50 must have indeed been scrapped. Then Isaac had dinner in New York with his friend Dan Aykroyd, the renowned comic actor of *Saturday Night Live* and Hollywood fame.

At one point in the evening, Isaac told Danny about our unsuccessful search for Car 50.

"I'll find it for you," Danny said.

He called his hairdresser, a man who coincidentally had made a hobby of studying private railroad cars for many years. And sure enough, he found Car 50 in a small town in Arkansas—where a family was living in it.

Pat with Dan Aykroyd

Isaac immediately went there and bought the car from them, then sent it to Dallas to be refurbished from the wheels up.

Today, Car 50 is restored to its former glory and beyond. Isaac has filled it with priceless antiques from India and around the world. He purchased the wooden carvings installed throughout the car from the palace of a maharaja after he died.

In its original incarnation, Car 50 was also used as a secret hideaway by Huey "Kingfish" Long, the audacious governor and senator from Louisiana. Huey would borrow Car 50 to make confidential political arrangements in the dining room.

Today, one room in Car 50 is dedicated to the Kingfish. A small brass plaque commemorates one of Huey's classic comments: *There may be smarter people than I am, but they ain't in Louisiana.*

ANOTHER NEW WORLD CULTURE:
THE HOUSE OF BLUES

Isaac Tigrett is not like any other person alive—male or female. I think he is truly a religious psychic. For the last 15 or 20 years, he has had a working partnership with Sai Baba.

This team of Isaac Tigrett and Sai Baba infuses business with spiritual vision, and the results are remarkable. I have no explanation for it. I only know what I have seen.

Isaac provides most of the ideas and the business acumen—but he says it is Sai Baba who opens the doors to make the ideas possible. The inspiration slogans used in Isaac's businesses—Love All, Serve All; Save the Planet; Help Ever, Hurt Never—come not from Jackson, Tennessee, but from Puttaparthi, India.

A few years ago, after he spent most of his Hard Rock Cafe money building Sai Baba probably the most beautiful hospital in the world, Isaac came to Memphis to talk about his next project to shake world culture: The House of Blues.

"As I see it, Dad, we'll have blues, rhythm and blues, some country and jazz, but basically blues every night in concert halls to hold from 1,200 to 2,500 people. We'll have the finest artists and the legends of American music," Isaac told me.

"Of equal importance is that in the House of Blues five days a week, we'll teach children in these halls—with real teachers and a tight curriculum—the origins of American music and its importance throughout the world.

"When we complete the eight units planned for the U.S. and the four in Europe, I expect to have from 2,000 to 3,000 children enrolled daily between the third and sixth grades. Beyond these basics, we will, of course, have restaurants, merchandise, et cetera, and some subsidiary companies—records, TV, et cetera—that will help build the brand name."

"And what, Sonny Boy, do you think these units will cost?" I asked.

"Ummm . . . I imagine they will average out at about $12 to $15 million."

"In other words; you're talking about $150 to $200 million to have some schoolrooms in the daytime and the blues at night."

"You got it, Dad," Isaac replied, laughing.

"Well, I had hoped establishing one new culture in the world would be enough for you. Your concept for the Hard Rock Cafe has already been copied by at least a dozen imitators."

"When I get the House of Blues basics complete and the franchises in place, I may develop even another new concept in the future," he said, laughing again. But I could tell he was completely serious.

"I don't think anyone really understands what I'm doing in creating a new world culture out of pure air and my mind," Isaac continued. "What I'm really doing, Dad, is bringing enjoyment—not for a few, but for everyone—and through it, bringing a lot of people together.

"My House of Blues will recognize and credit our debt to the African-Americans for giving us the basis of American music. And there's another side—we'll be creating a lot of jobs.

"I would estimate that with all the Hard Rocks and all the copies and all the suppliers, I created employment for a million people. There are not many folks around that can say that."

"Where is the money coming from for this new venture?" I asked.

"Oh, I'm not worried about that. Baba and I will figure out a way to get the money," he said with a shrug. "I'll find a good broker who likes the blues, and we'll put together a reasonable pro-forma statement. Then we'll roadshow in the U.S., Europe and the Pacific. I'll do the talking, and that should produce an initial $50 million."

I laughed out loud. "Sonny Boy, you're not dealing in the real world! I'll bet you 5,000 bucks you won't raise even $10 million on just a pro-forma statement with no actual operating figures."

"Okay, Dad. You're on."

"How much Hard Rock money do you have left after building the hospital?"

"About $5 million. But I'm going to use that to build a small trial unit in Cambridge, Massachusetts—the heart of American culture."

After that, Isaac and I talked every couple of weeks from wherever we were, but the $5,000 bet was never mentioned again. A couple of months had passed when I received a call from him from Singapore.

"Dad," he said. "Remember that $5,000 bet we made one night on House of Blues?"

"Yes, of course I do," I replied.

"Well I wish you'd wire me the five grand. I'm broke, and I need a little walking-around money."

"Haven't you forgotten the terms of the deal, Sport? You only win if you raise over $10 million."

"Oh, that. Well, we already have $45 million committed. We'll pick up the other $5 million tomorrow morning, and I'll be back in L.A. Sunday. We're rolling!"

I was speechless.

"Just one more thing, Dad," Isaac said.

"What's that, Son?"

"I love you."

THE WINDING ROAD TO AN EDUCATION

While he was growing up, Isaac was asked to leave a number of fine preparatory schools for failure to comply with their rules. Isaac had the same problem as Huckleberry Finn—neither could ever find any interest in discipline.

However, eventually, Isaac did manage to accumulate enough credits to complete by the narrowest of margins a high school degree. By that time though, he had determined that formal education was not suitable for him, and he gave up the idea entirely.

Nevertheless, through Isaac's work with the hospital for the poor in India and his promotion of two original music cultures around the world in his Hard Rock Cafes and House of Blues clubs, he has earned two honorary degrees from distinguished colleges: the Doctorate of Humane Letters from Centre College in Danville, Kentucky, and the Doctorate of Fine Arts from Rhodes College in Memphis.

President James Daughdrill, Jr. (right) of Rhodes College awarding Isaac an honorary doctorate of fine arts

Harrison Kerr Tigrett, age 17

*Kerr and U.S. Senate Majority Leader Bob Dole, for whom he was
the Head Page, 1995*

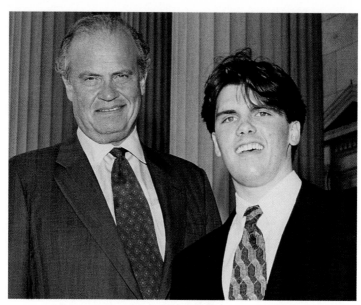

Kerr and the distinguished U.S. Senator from Tennessee,
Fred Thompson, 1996

Pat and Kerr at his graduation from Memphis University School,
1996, before attending the University of Virginia.

Former President Ronald Reagan with Pat and John at Jimmy Goldsmith's Mexican hideaway. One of the many memorable times Pat and John spent with Jimmy, on this occasion joined by Nancy and Ronald Reagan and Anna and Rupert Murdoch.

Jim Goldsmith and John in a planning session in Mexico. Will it be Goodyear or BAT?

Two old entrepreneurs . . . timeless friends

Isaac with his wife, Maureen Starkey Tigrett, and their daughter, Augusta King Tigrett, in 1991. Maureen died of cancer in 1994.

John looked on proudly as Isaac received a silver bowl at the opening of his magnificent hospital for the poor in Puttaparthi, India

Isaac Tigrett's private railway Car 50, his office on wheels.
It's reputed to be the most beautiful private car in America.
(Photo courtesy John Focht)

Pat, Isaac, John and Kerr on Isaac's honeymoon of his marriage to Maureen,
Cairo, Egypt, 1991

Diane and Fred Smith, Chairman of FedEx, in Washington where Fred received the most prestigious aviation award in the world, the Wright Brothers Trophy

Tennessee Governor Don Sundquist, Pat, and Dr. W.W. Herenton, Mayor of Memphis. Pat staged inaugural parties for both.

Pat relaxing in her favorite spot – Queen Mary's Rose Garden, London's Regent Park – with Kerr

Pat received many honors; this one is from the University of Memphis

*Pat at her favorite retreat, Acapulco,
1986*

*John, Pat and Kerr
"The Modern Day Three Musketeers,"
1989*

*Doyenne of fashion, Eleanor Lambert, visiting with
Pat and John in their penthouse in Memphis*

*Pat at one of her many
fashion shows staged annually*

*Kerr, Isaac and John Tigrett in Memphis, 1997. Isaac just received an Honorary Doctorate of
Fine Arts from the distinguished Rhodes College.*

PART FIVE:

An Incredible Cast of
Supporting Characters

Part Five

John continues to broker stunning deals of his own, highlighted by the $2 billion venture to find oil in the North Sea. He puts together an international consortium involving Armand Hammer, J. Paul Getty and Roy Thomson and waits out a nerve-wracking delay before striking one of the richest oil finds ever.

The deal brings John together with Thomson, the global media magnate and the character John calls the most intriguing in his life. On the day they meet, Thomson tells John, "When I die, I want to be worth a billion dollars." John ascertains that Thomson is "only" $384 million short of that goal and proceeds to help him meet it.

The secret? "It costs big money to go for big money," John explains.

However, as John also demonstrates, big money does not always mean big spenders. One day in London, he finds himself in a limousine with three billionaires—all of whom find an excuse to avoid picking up the check for lunch.

Back in Memphis, John meets an executive on the rise—Fred Smith—and they immediately strike up a close friendship. The encounter leads John to get involved with Smith's fledgling Federal Express operation and to play a role in taking it global. Memphis-based FedEx becomes one of the most successful businesses of the 20th century, and John calls Smith "the man who changed the pace of the world."

—ROBERT KERR

14

Fortunes Made and Lost

THE NORTH SEA CONSORTIUM

In the early Seventies, a time that saw the beginning of development of Europe's oil reserves, the British government announced it was going to award a number of blocks in the North Sea. Basically, this area ran from Aberdeen north to the Shetland Islands. Doc and I talked about it at length and finally determined to gamble on putting out two ships to go over the area and map out the highs.

Building a consortium was another matter, however. We thought the prospects in the North Sea were good, but the water was very deep, and drilling there was going to be an expensive gamble.

I went and talked to Paul Getty, and he agreed to put in Getty Oil for 20 percent. Allied Chemical was trying to get in this area with some group, and Doc Hammer finally decided to also take them in for 20 percent. Oxy was to be the operator and had 40 percent.

Under the British system at that time, you applied for specific blocks in the North Sea and then had to justify to the government why you wanted them. What we needed badly was some British participation, and I hit upon the idea of approaching Jim Slater of Slater-Walker.

At that time, Slater-Walker was considered the most successful banking house in London, with offices in all the principal markets in the world. I had never met Jim Slater, but I thought he knew me, so I called his office.

In the typical English fashion of the time, it took me three calls to get to his secretary, and two days for her to call back. Of course, she also said Jim was "so busy he could not see me for a week." I knew that in order to get his attention, I had to have a good proposition.

When we finally met, he let me know right off that he had only a few minutes of time available. I quickly outlined the proposal and agreed he could come in for 20 percent with £250,000, and that I would get the others to carry him up to £10 million before he would have to put up anything further.

He agreed to let me know in the next few days, and when he called, it was to say he had decided not to join the group. In his view, it was too big a gamble. I was very disappointed, for I badly needed a "local" in the consortium.

Several years later, when he had gone bankrupt, Jim Slater wrote his own story. In it, he said, "Every time I see my good friend John Tigrett, I have heart pains. What he offered me was the greatest bargain deal of my life. If I had just taken his proposition, I would not have lost my business, and I would have had an endless fortune."

* * *

In one of the many coincidences of my life, the next morning after being turned down by Jim Slater, I got a call from Lord Roy Thomson, the newspaper, magazine and television czar of the world.

I had never met him, but in one week I had him committed for the remaining 20 percent of the consortium. In Roy Thomson, I had also made a dear and fascinating friend.

THE BILLION DOLLAR MAN

Of all the great characters I have met in a long lifetime, I think the one who intrigued me the most was Roy Thomson. Roy was from the tiny town of Timmons in Ontario, Canada. His father was a barber, his mother a hotel maid.

Roy rose from that background with no financial help to become the press czar of the world, with newspapers from *The London Times* to *The Hong Kong Daily*, including more than 70 daily newspapers in the United States, the Scottish television system and more than 60 magazines in various industry fields.

Roy was a small, rotund man with glasses almost a half-inch thick that had a small hole in the center. I once had to speak about him in London before a large business group, and I pointed out how lucky he was to have had to wear those glasses from the time he was 13. For since that time, he could only see straight ahead to his objective. The sideline troubles and problems of getting there were not in his line of vision.

Many times when Roy and I were together, he would proposition me, saying, "Let's go to the States, Johnny Boy, just the two of us. We'll rent a car out in Missouri or Iowa or one of those states, and we'll just start driving. When we hit a town that has a newspaper, we'll find out who owns it and go see if we can't buy it."

I made a big mistake by not taking him up on that. With Roy, it would have been a fabulous trip.

When I began trying to put together the North Sea Consortium, I did not know him and had only seen him at two or three large charity dinners. His call to me came out of the blue.

"My friends Armand and Paul tell me I need you," he said.

"No one needs me, Lord Thomson," I replied.

"When can you come to see me?" he responded.

"When do you want me?" I asked.

"You can come right now," he said.

"Okay," I answered. "I'll be in your office within the hour."

J. Paul Getty with Lord Roy Thomson (right)

"It's at *The London Times* building on Grays End Road," he said.

When I arrived on his floor, I had to walk down a long hall filled with large modern paintings that Roy's son, Kenneth, owned. (Later I learned that Roy hated those pictures). As I reached his office, he greeted me at the door.

"Are you Lord Thomson?" I asked.

"Call me Roy," he said. "Come in my office."

His office was reasonably large, though not very expensively furnished, with a large map of the world on one wall.

I sat down by the side of his desk. "What can I do for you, Lord Thomson?"

"Call me Roy," he said.

"All right, Roy, what can I do for you?"

He looked at me through the little holes in those thick glasses and said, "When I die, I want to be worth a billion dollars."

That stopped me. I had never—and never have since—heard any opening statement even remotely like that. "What are you worth now?" I asked.

He pulled out a little drawer on the right-hand side of his desk, carefully looked at a statement and said, "Today, I was worth $616 million."

I laughed. "Well, you don't have very far to go," I said. "Only $384 million!"

From that moment until his death, I never saw Roy Thomson when he didn't know what he was worth—within a few million dollars.

"Roy," I said, "I think you might accomplish your objective in one of two ways—either property or oil."

"I know nothing about property and only a little about oil, but with the North Sea developing, I would look at oil."

When I explained the consortium deal for the North Sea to him, he said, "What will I have to gamble?"

"An unbelievable amount of money."

"I won't do that. I'll gamble $5 million."

I laughed. "Roy, it costs big money to go for big money, but I'll tell you what I'll do. From a political standpoint, we need a local in that consortium in order to get the right blocks. You would be a good one. I'll try to get the others to carry you through the first six or eight months. Then you'll have to pay up to protect your 20 percent interest, or it will be an interest of only $5 million as related to the total expenditures we've made."

"Make it a nine months carry."

"I'll try."

He finally put up $10 million at the outset. We struck what we named Piper Field, and he kept his 20 percent interest, but the total investment of the four partners eventually topped $2 billion.

Years later, the evening before Roy died at the Wellington Hospital just across the park from our home at One Cumberland Place, I slipped into his hospital room and sat by the side of his bed.

He slowly lifted his feeble hand out from under the sheet and put it on my knee.

"Well, Johnny Boy," he said weakly, "we made it, didn't we?"

That night, he was worth more than $1.3 billion.

MY CONSULTANT

The dining room of *The London Times* can only be described as "august." Portraits of all the former owners of *The Times* are hung in large gold frames around the room. The marvelous large, highly polished table could easily seat 30 people.

Every Tuesday, Roy would have an executive editor's lunch to which he invited a guest of honor, usually the most distinguished person in world government, business or science in visiting London at that time. The routine was that, as dessert was served, Roy began with his question for the guest of honor, and then everyone around the table, in turn, was allowed to ask one question.

Roy had been after me a number of times to come to one of these luncheons, and I finally accepted. When I reached the table, I found a beautifully engraved menu. On one side was the food and wine, and on the other side was the guest list. Headed with Lord Thomson as host, the guest list had each person listed along with a three-line description noting their accomplishments and honorary titles. This was true until the last name, which was mine. Beside my name was simply the word Consultant.

When my turn came to ask a question, I said, "First of all, I don't believe I'm qualified to ask a question, for I'm not even sure I belong in this group. I notice from the guest list that every person has a distinguished description of three or four lines of his accomplishments in life, mostly in initials, until you finally reach my name at the bottom with only a one-word description—'consultant'."

Everyone looked at their menu, and a ripple of laughter was heard around the table. Then Roy said, "I think your complaint is justified, John, and I'll take care of that." I then asked my question of the honored guest.

It was five or six weeks before I went to another Tuesday luncheon. When we reached the table, I picked up the menu and guest list and looked it over. All had the same type of descriptions until I reached my name.

Next to it were the words: *"My Consultant."*

Four for Lunch

Roy Thomson called one morning and asked, "Is Armand in town?"

"Yes, he's at Claridge's," I responded.

"Getty is coming in for lunch," he said. "See if we can't get you two as well."

I called Doc Hammer, and he was available, so Roy and Paul Getty picked us up at Claridge's. What Roy really wanted to do was to show us his new Rolls Royce. After we had properly admired his new car, the three of them got in the back seat, and I sat in front with the driver.

Before we left, I turned around and asked, "Where are we going for lunch? And my second question is: Who is going to pay?"

With the second question, they began scrambling.

"I didn't bring any money," said Getty. "I thought I was a guest."

"I left my money on the dresser," said Hammer. "If you go by Claridge's, I'll go upstairs and get it."

Roy fumbled in his pocket and finally said, "I have one of those dining cards, but I've never used it."

I turned to the driver, and sighed, "Go to Charles Street."

Then I began to think: Here I am with three of the most powerful and wealthiest men in the world. Of the four of us, I am the least able to pay—and I'm going to end up with the check!

Sure enough, all three had a big lunch on me at Marks Club. Not one offered anything but a "Thank you, John."

J. Paul Getty with Shell Oil chairman David Barran

P O W E R   P L A Y

After filing requests for the blocks sought, applicants were required to then meet with the staff of the Government Oil Bureau. In our case, we also presented a $6 million study of the ocean floor that the two ships had developed.

Our interview was set for September 10, 1970, and about a week before that, I had a worthwhile idea. I called Doc and said, "Why don't you get the Allied chairman and come here for the interview on September 10? I'll get Roy and Paul, and only the four of you will be there for the questions."

The interviews were conducted in a small, theater-style room with the bureaucrats on the stage and—usually—the companies' engineers lined up in the first row of seats anxiously waiting to answer the bureaucrats' questions.

So when the bureaucrats came out and saw that in this hearing, they were to question these four famous men, they were completely floored. They nervously asked only a few perfunctory questions and then thanked them for the ocean material.

Three weeks later, we were given the five blocks for which we had applied. All of these blocks were in water between 650 and 750 feet deep. The techniques of deep-water drilling had just progressed to this point, and we brought over from New Orleans a very fine rig with an 80–bedroom hotel, lounge, television room, gym, helicopter pad, and 24-hour-a-day gourmet dining room. It was named *Ocean Victory.*

The men worked two weeks on and two weeks off, and the 25-passenger helicopters went back and forth to Aberdeen twice a day. Six weeks from our fine grant day, we were in a position to drill, and the geologists had selected a beautiful high.

Five weeks from that auspicious start, however, we had a dry hole. A hole that is in 700 feet of water is a very dry hole in the oil business.

The rig moved to the second choice, and three weeks later we began drilling again. That hole was also dry, with not the slightest smell of oil.

By this time, Roy Thomson was in for a minimum of $15 million—$10 million of which he had just put in, and $5 million of which was carried for him by the other partners. He was calling me almost every night and had started to ask some very pointed questions. After the second dry well, even Paul Getty, the most veteran oilman in the consortium, began calling once or twice a week with questions and concerns.

We then moved the rig to the third site and started all over again in the deepest water yet, 720 feet from the surface to the drill head. We had been drilling about two weeks on Site No. 3 when I began having real doubts myself. Over and over, I asked myself if we should have gone outside Oxy's geologists or used Getty's people. Hundreds of different other questions and second thoughts came to me.

Things grew very tense. I decided to visit the rig. Women were not allowed, but I dressed Pat in bulky pants, a heavy mackinaw and a cap that could hide her hair, and we took off for Aberdeen. Our plane was met there, and we were taken to the helicopter. Soon we were on the *Ocean Victory*.

The rig was unbelievable, a vast mechanical city sitting in the North Sea with 15- to 40-foot waves bashing it on all sides. However, even though they were drilling in more than 700 feet of water, the design was so advanced that the drill stem never moved more than 1 1/2 degrees.

Odeco was the company doing the drilling, and after I talked to our two geologists at length, I visited with Bill Burns from Lafayette, Louisiana, who was head of the Odeco team.

"Bill, here are two telephone numbers," I said. "If you so much as smell oil in this well you are drilling, I want to be called immediately. It makes no difference what hour it is or what the conditions, but I want you to tell me what you found. From now on, that is your number-one priority."

Two weeks and two days later, the phone rang at 3 a.m. When I sleepily answered, I heard the words: "Mr. Tigrett, this is Bill Burns on the *Ocean Victory*. We have just passed through 150 feet of oil sands, and how much more there is, we don't know. But I do know that we have hit a monster—there could be a billion barrels of oil!"

"Congratulations, Bill!" I screamed. "At last, we've made it."

My excitement awoke Pat, who mumbled, "What's wrong with you?"

"Nothing, darling. I just have to phone a couple of fellows."

I dialed Roy's number, and the German woman who looked after him answered.

"This is Mr. Tigrett. Get Lord Thomson to the telephone, please," I said.

"But Mr. Tigrett, he's asleep," she protested.

"Get him to the phone right now!" I said. "It's an emergency."

"What are you doing waking me up at this hour, John?" Roy asked in a groggy voice when he got to the phone.

"For a damn good reason, you old rascal. You have struck oil in the North Sea, and it's a monster! Good night!" I said, and hung up.

Next I called Getty, who always had three or four female "secretaries" you had to go through to get to him. I finally bluffed them into getting him on the phone.

"John, I was asleep. What is the hour?" he asked when he came on the line.

"It's the witching hour for you, Paul," I said. "You have just struck oil. They have already been through 150 feet of oil sands and haven't stopped yet. Our first indications are that it will be the largest field in the North Sea. Now you can go back to sleep. Good night, you lucky old bastard."

And with that, I hung up on J. Paul Getty and went back to sleep.

The years ahead would confirm that we had indeed struck a monster oil field, and everyone involved in the consortium would make a fortune off it in the years to come.

THE GAMBLE TO SAVE
JIMMY GOLDSMITH

There are many strange minds in this world. I've often thought of them as having a little dial in the back of the brain that has been turned to "off-center", so the mind concentrates on envy, jealousy, viciousness and often serious criminal intent.

Jimmy Goldsmith, because of his lifestyle and the vast amount of publicity he has received most of his life, attracted a number of these "off-center" minds. He was in fear of his life and his children's on several occasions. In a number of instances, he ended up in the courts over such matters, and he won every time.

There were many crazy accusations against Jimmy over the years. Once he was accused of heading a Jewish conspiracy whose goal was to gain control of Great Britain's food supply and force starvation on every Gentile. Another held that he was responsible for a suicide and was connected with Lord Lucan in an unfortunate murder.

I was closely associated with Jimmy at the time, and nothing could be further from the truth than those stories. However, one nut attracted both a writer and an editor for *The London Sunday Times*. I think the editor perhaps took up the cudgel against Jimmy because of me, as I was once told that every executive on *The Times* and *The Sunday Times* resented my close association with Roy Thomson and was out to get me if they could.

This was not an unusual situation in a large organization. I understood it very well and I faced it in several other places. I was the outsider, with no title, to whom the boss was listening on matters that oftentimes affected the lives of those within the organization.

At that time, Jimmy and I were right in the midst of a very rough fight to take over Bovril, the turning point of Jimmy's career. Roy had been in Toronto for a month, when I had a secret call from his secretary in London telling me that a highly damaging article on Jimmy was going to run in *The Sunday Times*.

We arranged to have an advance copy slipped to us, and sure enough, the business about the "Jewish conspiracy" was augmented with column after column of derogatory statements, rumors and so forth. It filled a full page and a half and would be the lead story that Sunday.

If it appeared in that form, we would unquestionably lose the Bovril fight, and Jimmy would suffer for a very long time before he could get any justice in court.

Roy Thomson had one firm policy in running his newspapers. He never, ever interfered with the editorial content of any paper. His interest was only in how many lines of advertising the paper carried. I have seen him carefully measure ad-linage of newspapers from everywhere on the globe and hardly ever pay any attention to the news.

As soon as I read the piece on Jim, however, I called Roy in Toronto and explained the whole situation in detail. I also told him we needed some help. He said, "John, you know very well my policy. I've never stopped or altered a story in my lifetime. I simply can't do it now."

I pointed out the injustice and the embarrassment the lawsuit would produce, and the fact that Roy was a fair man printing a bunch of lies and unfounded rumors. All he said was, "I'm sorry."

I hung up. It was Friday afternoon.

That night, I couldn't sleep. At about 3 a.m., I put in another call for Roy. I said, "Roy, I called to plead with you one more time. You just can't run that story on Jimmy. It's nothing but a pack of lies, and it is not representative of you and your remarkable career. You know me and trust me, and you know I am telling you the truth."

There was a long silence. Then I added, "While it may be of no importance to you, if you run that piece, you will also lose me and our friendship."

"I'll think about it, John," he said.

That Saturday night, Jimmy and I were on a platform at Euston Station as the 9 p.m. train carried *The Sunday Times* north for distribution. As the trucks came pouring in, we caught one of the drivers and bought two papers from him. We rushed through looking at every page for the story. It was not to be found.

"Let's go get drunk," Jimmy said.

"I'm with you," I replied.

The next Monday, Roy's secretary called me and said, "The staff has not yet recovered from the shock, Mr. Tigrett. But I wanted to tell you that *The Sunday Times* editor received a telefax Saturday morning which read, 'Do not print the story on James Goldsmith until you have my personal approval.' It was signed by Lord Thomson."

The day Roy died, he also told me that his actions then marked the only time in his entire career that he had ever stopped a story in any of his newspapers.

15

Oil Tales

MISSING A FORTUNE BY 200 YARDS

There is no business like the oil business. It has been the source of more fortunes in the 20th century than perhaps any other commodity. It has also been the source of countless dealings that have kept my life interesting and my heart both amused and touched. There have been great friendships and remarkable stories that have come out of the fascinating business of drilling for oil.

In 1966, I went with Doc Hammer to see the largest oil well ever found in Africa—75,000 barrels of high-quality light crude per day, deep in the Libyan desert. It was on concession No. 202, which had been held first by Mobil Oil for five years before Occidental took it over. Mobil had drilled 17 dry holes and finally turned it back to the government.

We landed on a metal strip laid over the desert sand. As we were walking toward the drilling area, we passed a pile of rocks about 200 yards from the well. I asked the geologist, "What was there?"

"That was the last well Mobil drilled on this concession," he said. "Where Oxy drilled and found this unbelievable well is where they had their field office. Mobil sat on the oil and never knew it."

Oxy found a fortune less than 200 yards from where Mobil had drilled a dry hole!

CHECK UP, CHECK UP, CHECK UP

Following their remarkable discovery in the Libyan desert, Occidental determined to build a 36-inch pipeline running 600 miles from there to the Mediterranean. Doc finally selected Bechtel of San Francisco as the contractor, a company that was probably the most qualified of a small group of worldwide contractors. He specified to Bechtel that the pipeline must be completed with oil flowing through it, six months from the effective starting date.

About a month after the start, I received one of Doc's typical 3 a.m. calls. "John," he said, "I wish you would hire an engineering group for us, please. Also, lease them an airplane and get some rooms for them with your friend at his hotel in Tripoli."

"Okay, Doc," I said. "It will take a couple of days."

A few days later, I called him again and said, "All right, I have the engineering group ready, Doc. What do you want them to do?"

"I want you to have them fly that pipeline every day and check up on our people that you already have checking up on Bechtel. If they see any holdup or any delays for any reason, they are to call me night or day, and I'll give Bechtel in San Francisco hell. Be sure the chief engineer has my private numbers for the direct lines at the office and at the house by my bedside. Instruct him firmly to call me regardless of the hour, day or night, if he sees a holdup for any reason. He is to call me every Sunday to report on the progress made."

Two weeks later, another 3 a.m. call came from Doc: "John, I wish you would find another one of those engineering groups, lease a similar type airplane for them, and get some more rooms at the Waddan in Tripoli from your buddy. Give them my direct office and bedside numbers where they can reach me at any time, day or night. I want them to check up on that group you hired last week to check up on the people you have who are also checking up on Bechtel. They are also to call me once a week about the progress made."

The first oil flowed through that pipeline exactly six months from the day it was planned. It was a massive undertaking completed right on time—with the help of a slave driver cracking the whip by telephone from his Los Angeles home. He trusted no one and never stopped checking up on everyone—in triplicate.

OPENING A SWISS BANK ACCOUNT

The Hunt family built one of the world's great fortunes in oil. However, Bunker Hunt knew little of the world when we first met. Even after he struck a vast pool of oil in Libya, he was basically still a country boy from Texas.

He reached me by phone in New York one day and asked me if I knew how to set up a Swiss bank account.

"Yes," I replied. "When do you want to do it?"

"Right away," he replied.

"I was going to London tomorrow night," I said. "But let me see if I can change my plans. If I can, we'll go to Zurich on Swiss Air instead."

He arrived the following day at Kennedy with a lawyer whose sole ability was telling one old joke after another. When Bunker found we all had first-class tickets, I thought that he would have a heart attack. Despite his vast fortune at the time, I am reasonably sure it was the only trip in his life that he ever traveled first class on an airline.

As we took off our coats, I noticed that about 4 inches of Bunker's pants had been gathered in the back with a large safety pin. After we had finished in Zurich, I had him return via London so I could take him to a London tailor and have him measured for a suit at my expense. Bunker was so proud of that suit; I never saw him for the next year or two that he didn't have it on.

On the flight to Zurich, Bunker brought along three bundles of cattle magazines. As soon as we took off, he proceeded to read each one and then throw it on the floor.

Bruno Saager was a close banking friend of mine in Zurich. He ran Union Bank, the largest bank in Switzerland. I had called him from New York to arrange an engagement for the next morning, and I told him the purpose was to open a bank account for a friend.

"What's his name?" he asked.

"N. B. 'Bunker' Hunt of Dallas, Texas," I said.

"What does he do?" asked Bruno.

J. Paul Getty with Bunker Hunt (right)

"Bruno, you Swiss are supposed to know everything," I said, laughing. "I'll give you the rest of the day to find out who Bunker is."

The next morning in Zurich when I called, Bruno said, "Why don't you come over about 11:30 a.m., John? We'd like for you and Mr. Hunt to have lunch with us in the bank dining room."

I knew then that they had found out who Bunker Hunt was in detail.

We arrived in Bruno's office promptly at 11:30, and I said, "Bunker, tell Bruno what you want to do."

"Well, Mr. Bruno," he said, "I have a letter here from the chairman of the First National Bank in Dallas."

He gave the letter to Bruno, who read it and put it on the table. It read simply: *This will introduce our good customer, Mr. N. B. Hunt. We believe he is in a position to carry through whatever he undertakes.*

Then Bunker said, "I want to set up a bank account with you, Mr. Bruno." With that he pulled out an old envelope from his pocket and studied it for a minute.

Finally, Bunker continued. "It's for either $17 million or $37 million," he said. "The figures have gotten smudged on this envelope. Anyway, whatever it is, you should have it by now. I told the bank in Dallas it had to be here today."

The thought of opening that account started the blood pumping in Bruno's neck, and his face quickly resembled the color of a beet. I laughed at his obvious excitement.

"Bruno, why don't you call and see if the money has arrived," I said.

I didn't have to ask twice. He quickly checked on the matter and learned that Bunker's deposit had indeed reached Union Bank.

It turned out to be $37 million.

LIBYAN PACKAGE STORE

No drink containing alcohol is supposedly permitted in the Muslim world. There are to be no exceptions. But I have not been in a single prince's palace in Saudi Arabia that they did not have fully stocked bars hidden behind false walls.

When King Idris was in charge of Libya, he was very generous in his interpretation of Muslim laws. Mohammed Nga, the owner, had an open bar in the Waddan palace and a gambling casino for foreigners. He also had a luxurious apartment and club room across the street, which the oilmen used as a private club to entertain guests and girlfriends.

To meet the needs of the men working in the desert on Concession 202 and those building the pipeline, Occidental built a metal building next to the drilling area with a fully stocked liquor store that sold all brands at wholesale.

In the late summer of 1969, Colonel Muammar al-Qaddafi led a revolution and ran King Idris out of Libya. Within the first 10 days of his rule, he closed down the gambling and completely destroyed every bar. The Oxy liquor store was closed down and triple locks put on the two doors with a guard at each end 24 hours a day.

A week later, the oil boys from Texas and Louisiana had a "high-level" meeting to discuss a solution to the problem. They made arrangements to borrow one of the large cranes that Bechtel used for handling pipe. They also moved their lunch area to the shadow of the liquor store, where every day they would discreetly loosen the large turnbows that held the building to its concrete ground posts. Once loosened, they could be easily removed.

Two nights later, when the guards changed, strong sleeping pills were put in their coffee and the turnbows quickly removed. Then the big crane was hooked to the roof, and the metal building was lifted up 10 feet. Three trucks were backed up and every bottle of alcohol carefully removed. The building was then lowered, and the turnbows replaced. When the guards awoke, nothing looked altered.

The trucks delivered their cargo about 25 miles north where Bechtel kept a storage yard for its 36-inch pipe. At the far end of the yard, behind the stacks of pipe, the liquor store quietly reopened with the same manager and operated until well after the pipeline was finished. Stock was replenished when necessary by airplanes that had to be sent outside Libya for "special heavy maintenance."

As for the old empty liquor store in the desert, I had an Oxy employee check on it some two years later. It was still being carefully guarded 24 hours a day.

C A U G H T !

In the Sixties and early Seventies, as the director of the National Iranian Oil Company, Dr. Reza Fallah was a very powerful figure in the oil world. He and his counterpart, Sheik Yamani of Saudi Arabia, more or less set the pace for the world oil industry. When either one was scheduled to give his views on oil prices and supplies, you could count on a full house of reporters, bankers, analysts and speculators.

From the time I first sat down in his office and we looked across the desk at one another, Dr. Fallah and I were warm friends. That friendship lasted until his death. He was a small man of absolute integrity, with a great sense of humor and endless knowledge of the oil industry. I never faulted him the fact that he built a considerable fortune—most of which he later lost in the Iranian Revolution—from participating in Iran's oil deals that he controlled. It was and is their way of life.

In Western nations, we live by choice under a set of rules and so-called moral laws. But that does not apply to people with a different heritage who live under other sets of standards. They are entitled to their standards as much as we are to ours. They have had their pattern of life for hundreds of years, and I have always believed it is their right in those countries to have their own moral patterns. It is also their land and their oil.

My first arrangement with Reza was to arrange a trade with him for 18,000 tons of phosphate monthly in return for Iranian oil. Occidental had a large phosphate development in Florida, and the trade was ideal for both Iran and Oxy.

When my negotiations started, I found that once details and prices had been agreed upon, the prime minister had to put his stamp of approval on the agreement. While we were working out the details, Reza had Prime Minister Hovida for cocktails at his marvelous house. The three of us found much common ground, and the negotiations proceeded smoothly.

At the time, the market price for oil was posted. However, the price of phosphate was flexible. So I was able to make a trade roughly 15 cents better for Occidental than the minimum per-unit price Doc Hammer had instructed me beforehand that he could accept.

So when Doc called that evening and I outlined the agreement, it put him in a very elated mood. Over and over, he kept telling me how wonderful it was that we had a deal for 15 cents better than expected.

The next morning, I called on Prime Minister Hovida to have him initial the document. I thought at the time that he received me with an unusual show of cordiality, constantly laughing and telling me joke after joke.

When I gave him the final draft of the agreement, he read it with interest. Then he said, "Oh, by the way, John, I thought you would enjoy seeing my new desk recorder. It's an electronic wonder."

He opened the side drawer of his desk and said, "It's a remarkable and ingenious machine. You should get yourself one. Just listen to it."

With that, he turned on the recorder. On the playback, you could hear quite clearly every word that Doc and I had exchanged the night before about the great deal we were getting on the phosphate.

When the recording concluded, I simply said, "By the way, Mr. Prime Minister, do you have a pen handy?"

With a great smile on his face, he handed me a pen. I used it to lower the price to be paid for the phosphate by 15 cents. He had me.

"Just kindly initial the change, my friend," I said, returning his smile, "so everything will be official."

You Take the Beads

I first met John Whitehead, the chairman of Gulf Oil, at a dinner when he came to Memphis to see Kemmons Wilson. Later, Gulf bought a substantial interest in Holiday Inns with the idea of building Gulf Stations on property adjoining the motels.

John and I kept in touch, and one day he called in London and asked if I would buy an oil-distribution company for them in Lebanon called Hypoc. They did not want it bought under the Gulf Oil name, but wanted to use a small European subsidiary.

I met with John's London associates the next day. They explained that Lebanon had a semi-monopoly on gas and oil, and because the company was controlled by the government, I would first have to have the approval of the president of Lebanon before I could trade for it.

Beirut, Lebanon, at that time was everyone's favorite city of the Middle East. It was the crossroads, the Switzerland of the Arab world. It had a marvelous climate with great hotels, exceptional food, wonderful beaches, a Vegas-style night club with gambling in the hills and the friendliest people anywhere. In addition, it had the great Gold Street, a small street with about 25 jewelry shops, where you could buy fine antique or new jewelry for less money than anywhere else in the entire world.

Two weeks after the London meeting, I found myself in Beirut, where I was met by a Gulf executive. He had arranged for me to have lunch with President Thomas the next day. That night he took me up to the nightclub in the hills, where we watched the first show and gambled a bit at blackjack.

The Gulf man and his associate met me for breakfast the next day, and I told them not to bother with me any further that morning because I wanted to do some shopping and see some of my friends on Gold Street. I would get to the president's quarters at the appointed time on my own. They took me outside and showed me where the president's quarters were, on the top of a hill overlooking Beirut.

I was to meet them there at 12:45 that afternoon. I did my trading and came out of my favorite shop at the far end of Gold Street at about 12:20 p.m. to discover the streets were jammed beyond belief. I could not find an available taxi anywhere.

I ran up and down the streets looking for any kind of a carrier and saw that traffic was hardly moving. By that time, my watch showed it was already 1:10 p.m. Then finally I saw a fellow leaning against an old beat-up car, flipping his keys. I offered him $5 to take me to the president's house on top of the hill.

Being Lebanese, he said, "No, thank you." We finally settled on a price of $30—for a $2 taxi ride. When we reached our destination, it was 1:35 p.m. I was almost an hour late. After I paid the driver his extortionist fee, I saw that the Gulf people were anxiously waiting in front for me. They were nervous wrecks.

They took me immediately to see President Thomas. As soon as I saw the man, however, I realized I would have no problem. He was a big, horse-faced man with blue eyes and a great smile sitting behind a long, shiny desk. In one hand he held a beautiful set of worry beads.

I was introduced by the Gulf executives, who fell all over themselves offering excuses, then left. But I decided to attack rather than apologize.

"Mr. President," I said, "you must do something about these Beirut streets. At noon, they become so crowded no one can move—and all your traffic policemen suddenly disappear. I have spent more than an hour traveling a distance of less than a mile."

He laughed and said, "Is that your alibi?"

"Yes, and it's a good one," I said. "While we are talking about your problems, I see you are working those worry beads pretty hard. What else do you have to worry about?"

"Well," he said, "the thing that has been worrying me the most is our recent Hypo Bank failure, with its branches throughout the world. I wanted us to become the Switzerland of the Middle East as far as banking was concerned, so we could have some stability in our mixed population. We cannot, as I see it, unless we make good the deposits involved in this bank failure. It is obvious, but I cannot get our Senate to see the light. I also can't get them to see that our schools have to have more money and better equipment. Instead of helping me out on that, however, it looks as though they are going to cut the school budget."

I thought for a moment, then I said, "You don't know how lucky you are. All your problems are right here in your hands. You either solve them or forget them. In a small country like this, 35 miles wide and 120 miles long, you can deal directly with the problem and get back home at night."

I paused briefly, then continued. "Look at my problems," I said. "I have just agreed to put in 19 hotels in 14 countries for Holiday Inn. I don't speak the language, except in one. I know nothing about the real estate in the countries, and I have no experience in contracting. How would you like to be faced with that?"

This terrific man, a troubled leader of his people, looked at me with his gentle blue eyes for just a moment. Then he smiled and threw the beautiful worry beads across the big desk.

"You take the beads," he said. "You've got more problems than I have."

* * *

As it turned out, the negotiations in Lebanon went well, and we bought Hypoc for Gulf. Subsequently, one of the larger and more beautiful Holiday Inns was constructed in Beirut.

Sadly, that Holiday Inn was also the first building to be completely destroyed in the fighting of the Lebanese civil war that began a few years later.

ONE NARROW ESCAPE

In great episodes of political upheaval—riots, revolutions, revolts, rebellions and turmoil—generally the last people to know the true situation are those in charge of the government. Their reaction is usually two days too late. They simply refuse to believe what is happening.

Certainly that was true in the Iranian Revolution. Watching the scene develop on television—with 300,000 religious marchers taking to the streets, then 500,000, then perhaps as many as a million—the shah always believed things would cool down. He remained certain the U.S. would support him and the people would come to their senses.

As the tumult escalated, I had two great friends that I thought were vulnerable. One was Dr. Reza Fallah, who had the largest house in Teheran, a beautiful work of architecture in the Frank Lloyd Wright style on top of the highest hill at the end of a beautiful drive named for Reza— Avenue Fallah. It had the finest Persian rugs and a safe filled with jewels. The other was the former Prime Minister Hovida.

When the first mob hit the streets, I called Reza and urged him and Hovida to get out. He said, as I expected, "We have no serious trouble. That's just a group of religious fanatics. The police will take care of them."

Pat and I jointly called Reza once or twice a day from that moment on through the next 10 days, urging him to come out. Finally I made arrangements for a helicopter from Turkey to fly to a spot on the Caspian Sea where Reza and I once spent a weekend together.

On my daily call that evening, I said, "I'm coming over to get you tomorrow. I'll meet you at our rendezvous on the Caspian."

"Oh, no, don't do that," he said. "We are bound to have U.S. support and are in no real danger."

But I kept insisting, and finally he agreed to come to London for two nights and explain the situation to me. The next day he had a military plane take him to Istanbul, and he flew commercial from there to London. Pat and I met him at Heathrow and took him to our home at One Cumberland Place.

When we arrived, there were two or three urgent phone calls waiting for Reza. We left him alone to return the calls and sat in the adjoining dining room. About 30 minutes later, when Reza opened the double doors, he was in tears. He threw his arm around me and cried deeply, so deeply that he could not talk for some time.

Finally, he said, "A mob went to my house tonight, tortured my servants to make them tell them where I was, then killed each one of them and burned my lovely house to the ground."

* * *

Reza had a terrifyingly close call, but thank goodness he got out. However, one of the deepest regrets of my life is that I was unable to save the life of my dear friend Hovida, the former prime minister. After the shah left Iran and the revolutionists took charge, Hovida was put in jail and then 10 days later suddenly released.

As soon as this was known, Reza spent two days on the telephone trying to locate Hovida. When we finally found him, I told him that I would come to meet him immediately and get him out.

"No, John. They have just released me. They know I am no danger to them, and perhaps in some way I may be able to help my country."

We called him five more times over the next three weeks. During our last conversation, I begged Hovida again and again to meet me at our Caspian rendezvous. Reza had arranged a car to get him there, and I had the planes lined up. He absolutely refused, yet I am sure that if he knew I was waiting at the Caspian he would have come out.

Three days later, in the middle of the night, a religious group seized him, took him before a kangaroo court, and immediately executed him by firing squad.

Prime Minister Hovida was an exceptional man of great character and truly loyal to his country. I will always wish I had gone after him.

I should have taken the gamble!

16

Unforgettable Individuals

VICHYSSOISE—KEMMONS WILSON STYLE

Over the years, I have had the good fortune to rub shoulders with many of the world's most successful people. They have moved about the world, making deals worth millions and billions of dollars, headed great corporations and nations, and influenced the course of history.

However, each and every one was also a human being, with all the foibles and eccentricities that endear them to me as individuals.

* * *

Kemmons Wilson, who reinvented the world of hotels and motels with his Holiday Inns, is one of the few people time has left unaltered. We have been close friends for 50 years, and he has yet to change a thing about himself.

He still looks the same, trades the same, eats the same food, has the same parlor tricks that he tries on every stranger, hands out the same fake currency with his picture on it, and leads his wonderful family in the same way he always has—with him insisting they all do exactly what he says.

Dorothy and Kemmons Wilson

Kem first asked me to help him get his Holiday Inns into Europe in the early Sixties, after I represented him in Morocco in the joint deal between Holiday Inn and Occidental. In 1965, after I moved to London, I took pleasure in introducing him to the Europe I knew and in trading for Holiday Inn. However, no matter how marvelous the restaurant or club I took him to, Kemmons rarely ate anything but hamburgers or hot dogs.

One of the first dinners I gave for him in London included about 20 of London's leading socialites and bankers. We began with drinks at my home in Regent Park. Kemmons loves Jack Daniels and Coca-Cola, but as soon as I saw him pull out his disappearing-rabbit parlor trick, I thought we had better move on.

Dinner was served at Parkes, a restaurant on Beauchamp Place where I had an alcove reserved. I seated Kemmons between Lady Londonderry and a lovely actress. After some small talk, the first course was served.

The next thing I heard was Kemmons' booming voice announcing, "My soup is cold!" Then I heard the softer and proper voice of Lady Londonderry trying to explain to him that vichyssoise was supposed to be served cold.

"No," Kemmons replied. "All soup is supposed to be served hot.

Here, waiter! Take this soup and heat it up."

To try to avoid further problems, I slipped out of my chair and went back to see my friend Mike, the head chef.

"Mr. Tigrett, I can't heat vichyssoise," he said. "It will just curdle into little balls."

"Mike, I don't give a damn how much it curdles," I said. "Please heat it up quickly and bring it in so I can stop this embarrassing scene."

I slipped back into my chair, and a few moments later saw a waiter pass with the heated vichyssoise. The next thing I heard was Kemmons boom out, "Now that's how soup ought to be served—hot! This is delicious."

On another occasion, Jimmy Goldsmith and I gave Kemmons a dinner at which we entertained the city's leading bankers and investment advisors at an exclusive London club. At the time, the Holiday Inn chain had just topped 1,500 motels and had the largest restaurant operation in the world, with some 1,650 restaurants.

When the main course was served, Kemmons asked, in his always booming voice, "What is that?"

"It's young Welsh lamb, sir," replied the waiter. "Our very best."

"I've never eaten lamb, and never expect to," said Kemmons, loud enough for practically everyone in the room to hear. "Haven't you got a hamburger or some hot dogs back there in the kitchen?"

The conversation stopped, but Jimmy saved the day. "Of course they do," he said. "Waiter, get Mr. Wilson a good American hamburger."

Ross Perot's New Chevrolet

Jimmy Goldsmith and I were looking around for a new deal when we came up with the idea of combining some assets with Bunker Hunt's family and taking the company public.

At that time, the Hunts had a remarkable worldwide reputation—one not necessarily based on fact, for hardly anyone knew any facts about the Hunts. However, almost anybody everywhere would have been happy to have a small piece of the Hunts' fortune then.

Their image and power were based on rumor (that they were the richest people in America), on mysterious associations (it was whispered that they were in business with shadowy foreigners), and on psychology (they were reputed to be fearless gamblers who would put any fortune on the line).

I called Bunker, and he thought our proposition sounded like a good idea. So Jim and I went to Dallas, and in three days we had an agreement. We celebrated with a champagne luncheon in the Dallas Petroleum Club atop the First National Bank Building.

A small man with a crewcut came over to our table, pulled up a chair and talked with Bunker. Neither Jimmy nor I caught his name.

When he left, I asked Bunker, "Who was that fellow?"

"His name is 'Pee-ro.' He used to come in my office to repair the computers. He was the repairman for, I think, IBM."

"What does he do now?" Jim asked.

"Well, I don't really understand it, but he found some way to connect computers, or he makes them do something. Anyway, they say he's done right well."

"What exactly does 'right well' mean, Bunker?"

"They say he's worth over a billion dollars."

"Has it changed his lifestyle much?" Jimmy asked.

Bunker thought for a moment, then finally said, "Well, he bought a new Chevrolet."

MEMPHIS SLIM, "YOU SHO DONE RIZ"

Pat and I have many friends in the music and entertainment world. Some were and are great stars, some just entertainers. However, all had their feet on the ground. One I always felt close to was the late Peter Chatman, an enormous, 6-foot 8-inch black man, who realized fame under the name of "Memphis Slim."

Slim came out of the cotton fields near Ruleville, Mississippi. He was a natural piano talent without ever taking a lesson. He taught himself to play, with those enormous hands, in a little church on the Brown Plantation, after picking cotton all day.

He started playing in a "colored house" on Memphis' famed Beale Street, where he was an immediate hit. His blues were the blues of the South, and his piano playing was the very best around.

Josephine Baker, Billie Holliday and other black artists were having great success abroad in those days. Slim decided to try Europe, and particularly Paris, where blacks were more accepted by society at large.

From the time he first appeared in Paris, there was never any doubt that "Memphis Slim" had found a true home for his remarkable talent. He never left Paris until a year or two before he died. By that time, there was no city in Europe that did not pay "Slim" homage.

We were friends for many years, and I never failed to see him when we were in the same town. He never changed, and his philosophy of "jus' floatin' through life" is one I have long tried to follow.

At the height of Slim's fame, I came into Paris on a cold and snowy night. On my way to my hotel room, I asked the concierge to find out where Slim was appearing. He told me Slim was at the famous Apollo on the Left Bank. I took a taxi and reached the club just before midnight.

As I was paying the driver, a long white Rolls-Royce pulled up a few yards ahead of my taxi. I was standing in the snow when out of the Rolls emerged this giant of a man wearing a long white mink coat that almost touched the ground.

I let him get to the entrance before shouting, "Hey, Slim!"

When he turned around, I cried, "My, my—boy you sho done riz."

When he saw who it was, he fell over in the snow, rolling with laughter, and said to me, "Ain't it so, brother John. Ain't it so."

I loved Memphis Slim.

Johnny Aspinall: A Unique Man

When Jimmy Goldsmith and I became friends and business associates, we each brought to the table our own group of friends. Of all the people who were close to Jimmy, the one who intrigued me the most was John Aspinall. He is without a doubt the most unusual personality I have ever encountered and the most interesting.

When I first heard of John, he was running a floating crap game in London. Unlicensed, it moved to a different hotel every night. He and Jimmy had naturally become friends while in school at Eton, where they both were gamblers. They cut their gambling teeth together, betting on horses and kiting checks regularly between three or four small branch banks.

Eventually, John secured a license under the English Gambling Act and started the Clermont Club on Berkeley Square. He leased the basement to his friend Mark Birley, who started what has become the only continuously successful private nightclub in the world, Annabel's.

The Clermont became known as the high-stakes club of Europe, where the best of the English establishment and the wealthy of Europe came to gamble in this beautiful house with exquisite decorations and the best chef in Great Britain.

From a very young age, John had been fascinated by wild animals, and he studied them at every opportunity. He even kept several just outside London.

One night at the gaming tables, he won a fabulous country place named Howletts, which he used as the location to start a private wildlife preserve for the wild animals he had been keeping.

Later, when he had more wild animals than he could keep at Howletts, he acquired Port Lympe, the former house of the Sassoon family, as a second wild animal preserve.

I read the Sassoon guest book one night at Port Lympe. The Sassoons had been hosts to almost every famous European of the period. I was particularly intrigued by one page in the book, on which an entry had

John Aspinall and Jara

been written the night after Winston Churchill was elected to the House of Commons.

The entry read simply: *A Pullman car has now joined the Big Train.* It was signed by Churchill.

John has spent his life with wild animals, whether on the gambling tables or in the jungle. From his teens to the present day, he has given every single penny he has made in gambling, above his living, to the care of wild animals. He has devoted his entire life to protecting and raising them, only to put them back in their natural habitat with protection.

Some years ago when he fell on hard times, he sold his family's priceless antiques in order to feed his animals. He has been the only person in the world to successfully breed and raise eight giant gorillas. Today, his daughter runs the only gorilla "orphans home" in Africa for young gorillas whose parents have been killed by hunters and poachers. At last count, his daughter was looking after 60 young gorillas.

John walks with gorillas, lions, tigers and elephants. He puts his arm around them, and they return his love. *National Geographic* magazine has said he knows more about wild animals, their habits, their needs and how to handle and protect them than any other human alive. He now operates the two largest private wild animal preserves in the world.

I am grateful to Johnny Aspinall, not only for being my friend but also for introducing me to this unique life.

David Frost —
The Ultimate Interviewer

Another friend I made from among Jimmy Goldsmith's entourage of friends was David Frost, a most talented fellow. To progress from the English comedy show *This Is the Week That Was* to interviewing presidents and other heads of state is quite a jump.

I think David was able to accomplish this because he is such a nice man. Though he is a truly great interviewer, he never asks "mean" questions. He gives his interview subjects a chance to answer the hard questions, but he is so adroit that he leaves the choice to them. This is what has built his remarkable reputation and makes anyone in the world accessible to his telephone call.

David was instrumentally involved when Jimmy and I became interested in trying to buy the other half of the James Bond partnership with our great friend "Cubby" Broccoli, who produced the fabulously successful series of Bond films. Control of the rights we sought to purchase was held in a trust at the Union Bank of Switzerland, which had also financed Cubby's partner in his attempt to buy Technicolor.

Typical of almost every movie deal, our efforts to buy into James Bond were screwed up very badly. To make things worse, Cubby's partner was, without any question, the most objectionable man I have ever met. Naturally, I was the one they volunteered to deal with this impossible fellow. It was a great test of my tolerance and patience.

Every time we thought we were ready to close the purchase, this fellow would bring in a rather questionable "white knight" to make a bid on the Bond partnership, and we would have to start all over again. However, David was a great help, and somehow we finally worked out a deal that seemed to satisfy everyone.

Then just two days before our scheduled closing, a story appeared in the *London Evening Standard* revealing our negotiations, which until then had been kept private and confidential. As a result, United Artists—the studio that financed the Bond movies—suddenly entered the bidding.

The next day, UA made an offer of $28 million in cash, which was $5 million more than our offer, and closed the deal.

To this day, whenever David and I see each other, we commiserate over our misfortune in having been outbid for the James Bond partnership. What fun we would have had helping Cubby (who needed no help) film the further adventures of Agent 007. Cubby's family has continued to produce the Bond films after Cubby's passing.

David's able assistance in that deal, however, was probably one of the factors that led Jimmy to put up $200,000 for David's project to interview Richard Nixon on television about the Watergate tapes. David also raised funds from other sources, I think possibly a total of $700,000, and then took a BBC film crew with him to film the interview at Nixon's home in San Clemente, California.

Jimmy and I arrived in Los Angeles to see how things were going. We went to the Beverly Hills Hilton, where David had his headquarters, and met him just as he was coming in from the first day's filming.

We learned several things that caused us concern. First of all, David's people had been unable to sell a single national television spot for the broadcasting of the interview. Every big corporation was still afraid to touch Nixon at that time. Second, the scripts were so mild, and David was so nice about his questions, that the interview thus far was dry and dull. Nixon, as we all know, did not have the personality to provide any excitement himself. And third, David was saving for the final day's filming the question the world wanted Nixon to answer most of all: *Why didn't you burn the tapes?*

The most important thing Jimmy and I did that evening was to get David to agree to include Nixon's response to the big question in the first segment of the broadcast. When that answer was aired, it provided a remarkable answer for all of us, forever altered the structure of political values under which the United States was born and had grown.

In essence, Nixon answered, "I never thought any Congress, any political party, or any group of individuals could ever, ever bring down the President of the United States, the single most powerful position in the world."

The day before the first Nixon interview was to air, *The New York Times* ran a story that heightened interest in the broadcast and led Nissan Automobile Company to buy a few advertising spots in it. That broke the logjam, and other commercial sponsors came along after that.

Still, little if any money was made on the project, but none was lost. And David's reputation has soared ever since.

The President Tells a Story

Jimmy Goldsmith called me from Paris two years ago and said, "I wish you and Pat would come down to Mexico next week and help me entertain some interesting guests."

"Sorry, Jimmy," I said. "I can't."

However, Pat took the phone, and a few minutes later I heard her say, "Of course! We'll be delighted."

When we arrived at Jimmy's unbelievable compound at Carreres and walked down for dinner, there seated to my right were Nancy and former President Ronald Reagan, and on Pat's left were Rupert Murdoch and his delightful wife, Anna.

With Jim and his mistress, Laure, we all spent a week together—one of those rare moments in life filled with ease, comfort, friendship, great wine, good food and marvelous stories.

I soon understood why President Reagan had captured the hearts and minds of America during his time in office. He was a gentle man of great principles who taught us by example to put aside our doubts and believe again that America could be the source of our own courage. And he did it so easily by taking a few simple positions on the needs and understanding of his people, and by having the character to stand firmly for them. His presence on the American and international scene will always be deeply missed.

One evening on the beach, watching the fire, I was between the president and Rupert when President Reagan said, "Johnny, let me tell you all a Washington story."

He told it, and we all laughed. It was a good story.

We had hardly stopped laughing when he said, "Let me tell you all a story." He proceeded to repeat word for word the story he had just told us. We all laughed again.

Five or 10 minutes went by. Then the president said once more, "Johnny, let me tell you a story."

He began the same story, but after a minute or two of talking he stopped and said, "Oh, I told you that story before, didn't I?"

"Yes," I said reluctantly. "You did, Mr. President. It's a good story."

"You must forgive me," he said. "I left part of my brain in Washington and part of it in California."

Neither Rupert nor I answered. We just watched the fire flicker, through our misty eyes.

THE TREASURES OF LIFE

Life's real treasures always seem to come when you least expect them. The sun breaking through the clouds and producing a memorable sunset of pink-and-purple shafts that go up to the unknown. The happy smile of a young child that lights up a whole face—and also lights up yours. A host of great white clouds that somehow forms itself into an armada of wonderful chariots, floating across the sky making dreams.

One night at dinner in Laurel, Mississippi, on my uncle's private Car 50, I sat next to a Mrs. Chisholm, who was the wife of the town's leading banker. During dinner she told me of a exceptional young man who had just married their daughter and moved to Laurel. "This town is so small," she said, "even with my husband's help he can't find a decent job—and we're desperate. Have you any ideas?"

A week before, Sears had given me a contract to produce a large number of toddler rockers, which we had developed; they were going to feature them in their Christmas catalog.

"Mrs. Chisholm, send your boy to see me, and I'll see what I can do," I said. I found a place for the son-in-law, working on the rockers. He performed an excellent job and made a worthwhile living for his new wife.

Some months later I came up from New Orleans to check on production. I was met at the train and en route to the plant informed that Mrs. Chisholm wanted me to stop by for lunch.

At noontime, I appeared at Mrs. Chisholm's house. During lunch, we talked about the usual, everything from weather to politics. As coffee was served, Mrs. Chisholm said, "Mr. Tigrett, you did our family a great favor when we needed it—and we continue to be indebted to you. Today, we would like to repay you, in part, by having our Leontyne Price give you a private musical concert. Leontyne is the daughter of our wash woman, who's been with us for years.

"Since I was a former teacher of music, her mother asked me to come hear her sing one Sunday in their little church. The result was that my husband, Alex, and I sent her to New York, and she graduated with the highest honors at the Julliard School of Music. She was in training for a year with the best operatic teachers in New York and last week was selected to play the lead in the new George Gershwin musical on Broadway."

With that, Mrs. Chisholm put me in a chair next to the piano, opened the door to the kitchen, and said, "Come in, Leontyne; we're ready."

Through that kitchen door came the most magnificent black woman I have ever seen. She was well over 6 feet tall, big boned in structure and had a commanding presence that was beautiful to see. "Mr. Tigrett," she said, "I'm going to sing parts from some operas, then some musical numbers and finally the hymns I grew up on. If there is anything special you'd like, don't hesitate to ask for it."

For the next two hours, I sat in Laurel, Mississippi, in silent awe. I was mesmerized listening to the most powerful, most remarkable voice of our time with a natural range that was endless. When she came to the church hymns, Leontyne sang with such feeling that I cried. For a long time afterwards, I could still hear that unbelievable voice.

After Broadway, she went on to become the great star of the Metropolitan Opera and had endless acclaim in Milano, Paris, London, Stockholm, Rio, etc., always billed as "the most magnificent voice of our century."

While I often read about her, I never saw her again until I was having dinner one night in San Francisco at the Fairmont Hotel. There was a sudden hush in that great room, and I looked up to see Leontyne coming in with a distinguished-looking group. I doubted that she would remember me, but I finally got up my nerve and started across the room. She saw me immediately and pushed her chair back to stand up. As I reached her, I said hesitantly, "Miss Price, for 30 minutes I've been sitting over there wanting to come and speak but wondering if you would even remember who in the hell I was," I said.

"Forget you, Mr. Tigrett—I'll never forget you!" she said as she grabbed my hand. "Outside of my momma, you are the only person in the world to whom I've ever given a private concert." Then she leaned over and kissed me.

17

Fred Smith and
A Product Like No Other

"MAYBE I CAN FIND SOME COMPENSATION"

While we were living in London, Pat and I kept an apartment in Memphis because our roots remained in the nearby Tennessee towns of Jackson and Savannah. We returned occasionally to see our folks and friends, while we considered whether our young son, Kerr, should have an English or American education.

On one of those visits to Memphis, we were attending the symphony when I met a remarkable young man for the first time.

"I'm John Tigrett," I said to him. "What's your name?"

"Fred Smith," he replied. "This is my wife, Diane."

"What do you do?" I asked.

"I run a company called Federal Express," he answered.

"What does Federal Express do?" I inquired further.

"We carry packages and documents," he explained

"Sounds interesting. Let's have dinner soon," I suggested, and promised to call him.

This was my introduction to Frederick Wallace Smith, my warm, wonderful friend whom I consider to be the most competent executive in the world today. He is a man to whom grand strategy is second nature to his operational mind.

We had lunch or dinner several times during that visit, and before Pat and I returned to London, he asked if I would join his board of directors.

I said, "Fred, you're most kind, and I'll help you every way I can overseas. But I don't want to go on your board. I just resigned from a number of boards in Europe."

"Well," he said, "maybe I can find some compensation that will intrigue you."

"I'm always interested in compensation," I said.

Several months later, when we were in Memphis again, I called Fred. We met later that afternoon for a couple of beers at the bar in the Butcher Shop Restaurant on Front Street.

"How did you come over?" he asked.

"Pan American coach, and it sure was crowded," I replied.

"How would you and Pat and Kerr like to have first-class, worldwide passes on Pan American?"

I hesitated, then said, "When do you want me to go on your board?"

"Next week," he said.

I did.

This episode showed me that Fred Smith, in addition to being a world-class executive and strategist, is also a confidence man par excellence and one without a conscience.

We never did receive those passes.

Fred Smith and John

CHANGING THE PACE OF THE WORLD

To call Fred Smith simply an entrepreneur hardly does him justice, for no entrepreneur in my lifetime ever developed a product for the world market that faced—and overcame—as many major overwhelming problems as did Federal Express.

The first was money. After going under twice, he finally raised $65 million—more venture capital than had ever been raised for a new product anywhere at that time. Along the way, there were endless other searches for money.

The story about Fred once making his payroll on a Las Vegas blackjack table is true. He was so discouraged when Henry Crown in Chicago first turned him down that he went to O'Hare Airport and took the first plane out. It was to Las Vegas. Fred played blackjack all night and won $27,000 in time to meet the FedEx payroll due the next day.

Second, FedEx was a new product unlike any other. Almost any new product an entrepreneur offers may be put on the market in one small area and duplicated as the business expands. However, here was a product where everything—planes, trucks, offices, personnel, et cetera—had to be in place across the entire country before you could even open for business.

Third, he had enormous and strong competition throughout the world. If any one of his competitors—Emory, UPS, etc.—had seen his vision, they could have copied his idea overnight and taken the market away from him at the outset. Not one of them saw the light until it was too late.

Fred Smith was, and is today, a driven man who works constantly to devise new and more efficient ways of carrying out his dream. He always manages somehow to keep ahead of his competition by at least three to five years.

THE WORLD ON TIME

Fred Smith's idea with FedEx was to bring the world together, to join the cities on the globe so that they were never more than two days apart for mail, packages and cargo. That may seem like a simple idea, but it proved to be quite an undertaking.

It requires more than 220 large aircraft—727s, DC10s, MD11s and 747s, as well as 250 smaller aircraft, such as Fokker F27s and Cessna 208s. Further, it called for 140,000 employees and 44,000 trucks in more than 230 countries.

For communication and tracking, it means putting together the largest bank of computers in one business in the world, plus a satellite television system with more than 2,500 "drops" in the U.S. alone.

No matter what the weather, you have to be prepared to pick up every night and deliver the next morning or second morning an average of 2.5 million packages. And during particularly busy seasons, that number will soar to more than 4 million packages a night.

Most importantly, you have to be able to tell the customer, usually within one minute, where his package is or who signed for it—whether he gave it to FedEx in Panang, Malaysia, or Dubuque, Iowa.

Fred Smith is a Memphis boy who volunteered as a foot soldier in the Vietnam War, who escaped with his life several times by the narrowest of margins and then volunteered again for a second two years as a front-line helicopter pilot.

He came home and set about fighting for an idea that has since changed the world. He has put together the finest, most dependable communication system in history—absolutely, positively. It is exactly as the FedEx slogan promises: *The World on Time.*

PUSHING FEDEX OUT INTO THE WORLD

As soon as I joined the FedEx board, having spent so many years in Europe, I began to hammer on the fact that they must build a worldwide system. The company's 55 percent of the U.S. market would not be enough to ensure its continued success over the long run.

I am sure a number of my fellow directors, many of them conservative bankers, became annoyed at my driving that point home at every opportunity. However, they finally gave in—I think to get me to shut up—and decided to try taking FedEx to Europe.

A year or so later, at the annual meeting, the employees presented me with a stunning Waterford cut-glass globe of the world engraved: *Thank you for pushing us out into the world, Mr. Tigrett.*

Recently, Fred and I were having a private dinner at "21" in New York with George Mitchell, the former Senate majority leader, and five other prominent senators. Fred introduced me by saying, "This is my good friend, John Tigrett. He is the man responsible for pushing FedEx out into the world."

I sat up a little straighter in my chair and began preening myself with little modesty as I basked in the glow of that grand accolade.

However, Fred then added, "And it only cost us $350 million to get it straightened out."

18

Looking Back

A CONTRIBUTION TO THE WORLD

L ooking back over so many years and so many memories, there is one
  story that stands out as having the most significant consequences for
the course of world history. My role in it unfolded the same week in the
spring of 1974 that I met Pat Kerr in New York.

After having lunch with her and then touring the Russian exhibition
together that Sunday afternoon, I was hoping to see her again on
Monday. Then early Monday morning, I got a call at the Carlyle from Doc
Hammer.

"John, I want you to come to the Orion Club for lunch with some of
our Russian friends," he said. "I'll have Maury Leibovitz with me."

"Sorry, Doc, I have a luncheon appointment," I answered. I didn't
really have an engagement at that point, but I was hopeful that I would
be getting a call from Pat.

"Then come by after lunch. We'll wait for you."

That afternoon, I went by the Orion and spoke briefly to the Russians.
As I left, Doc and Maury followed me outside. Doc looked worried.

"John, you must help me out," he insisted.

"All of Occidental and the whole oil world could be at stake. Qaddafi

has finally persuaded several other Arab producers to take over our interests there—and all the other oil companies. If he does, the world will be
thrown into a never-ending fight. You must go with me to Malta tonight
and help me lay out a strategy. George Williamson, the local manager and
his staff, are meeting us there at noon tomorrow."

"I'm sorry, Doc, I just can't," I replied. "I'm in the process of getting
a divorce from Rita, and I have to be on the witness stand in Humboldt,
Tennessee, Friday morning."

"You can have the Gulfstream to get you back in time. I'll go
on commercial."

Trying to think quickly of any excuse, I said, "Doc, I also have the
complication of having a principal witness with me here. I just can't leave
the country."

"Well, bring him with you."

"It's not a him—it's a her," I said with a smile.

"So much the better," said Doc. "Come inside and we'll telephone
her. Give me the number."

I handed him a slip of paper with Pat's name, hotel and room number, feeling absolutely confident she would say, "No."

Doc had her on the line a moment later. "Pat, this is Dr. Armand
Hammer," he said with the practiced warmth he could turn on at will. "I
need John to help me on a matter, and I want you to go along to Malta
with us. We'll have dinner there and then come back."

"I've never been to Malta," Pat said. "I'd love to go with you."

"Great. Do you have your passport?"

"No, Dr. Hammer, I don't usually carry my passport between
Memphis and New York. It's in my apartment in Memphis," Pat replied.

"Do you have a friend who can get your passport to the airport?"

"Yes, I think so."

"Then I'll send the Gulfstream down to pick it up. Have your
friend take your passport to the private-plane operator at the Memphis Airport."

"Are you serious?" asked Pat.

Pat and John with Armand Hammer and his wife

"Of course I am. And John and I will pick you up at 8:30 tonight. We'll take off from Newark at 9:30 p.m."

As we walked into Butler Aviation in Newark, New Jersey, that evening, the Gulfstream was just landing with Pat's passport. The time was 9:30 p.m.

Once we had settled down on the plane, I began asking Doc a number of questions about the latest news from Libya. How firm did Williamson say Qaddafi and Major Jaloud were? Was it another bluff? What other oil-producing countries did they have with them?

The more questions I asked, the madder Doc grew. He said, "No matter what they do, we will fight them every way in this world before selling. I'll have Louis Nizer take them up to the World Court, and they'll never sell a drop of our oil for a hundred years!"

I let him rage on for five or 10 minutes, then I shocked him with my observation on the situation.

"You're crazy, Doc," I began. "You'll end up losing everything Oxy has in Libya. These countries are now emerging from the Dark Ages, and neither you nor anyone else can stop them. You don't have to be a psychic to see that—just read the daily papers. Oil has propelled them into another world, and they are now on their way to taking back their land and their oil.

"You can probably hang on for another 10 or 15 years by working with them. But eventually they will have it all. The oil world as you know it has changed. The power of the emerging countries is in a new phase, and as much as you hate it, you are going to have to recognize it."

Doc was livid. "I am 75 years old tonight, and I'll not let those cutthroats take me over until I'm in the grave!" he huffed.

Fortunately, Pat took over at that point. She saw things were getting out of hand.

"Stop arguing, you two," she said. "It's time for the Doctor's birthday party."

With that, she opened a large tin of Russian golden caviar and stuck five matches in it for Doc. He calmed down some and joined in the spirit of the moment by bringing out a wooden case Brezhnev had given him as a birthday gift.

The box contained the most beautiful cut-glass bottle we had ever seen. More importantly, it was filled with the most marvelous vodka we had ever tasted.

Pat lit the "candles," and we all sang "Happy Birthday" to Doc. He made a wish, blew out the matches and cried like a baby. He was genuinely touched by our simple celebration.

When we reached the Hilton at Malta, however, Doc was still as hard-headed as ever on selling Occidental's Libyan interests. I knew I had to talk to George Williamson as soon as he arrived—before he saw the Doc.

I waited by the desk, and when I saw George coming, I stopped him even before he could register. I hurried him outside by the swimming pool and asked, "How serious is Qaddafi?"

"Major Jaloud tells me Qaddafi has made up his mind that he is going to control Libyan oil," George replied. "They have also lined up four or five other countries to join them."

"Will he settle for 51 percent, with Oxy continuing to be the operator?" I asked.

"I think he would jump at it. It gives him what he wants, and he has no way of operating the properties."

"Okay, George, that's what we'll try here today," I said. "If we do it, we're going to catch unbelievable hell from the other oil companies for being the first to give up control of our interests there. But it will be the groundbreaking for what is surely destined to come before much longer.

"One last thing. We've got to persuade Doc, and much will depend on your being very, very firm with him. No matter what he says, remember there is no alternative. They are going to take over Occidental first, then all the other oil operators in Libya. And the other countries will join them.

"Never change that line. I will offer the 51-49 compromise at the last minute and see if he won't agree. Let's go."

When we all met, Doc argued with us for several hours. As it neared time for George to return to Libya, I finally said, "Doc, let's offer them a compromise. They may not take it, but if they do, we will be partners for a number of years. Let's sell them 51 percent—only for cash—and contract to operate the field for a minimum of 10 years with further options."

It was a torturous moment for the Doctor. No one said anything.

Finally, he asked, "George, do you think you can get them to accept that?"

"I don't know, Doc," George answered. "I'll try."

"Well, good luck," said Doc.

"Remember, George—all cash, no payouts," I said in my last words to him. "Stand like a rock on that."

Qaddafi and Jaloud accepted the proposal the next day, and a week later it was announced in headlines all over the world. We received more criticism and threats from the other oil companies than I ever anticipated. But the die was cast.

From that day on, every oil company on foreign soil was in negotiation. Ultimately, they all sold. But so far as I know, every one of them ended up accepting payment for their interests in oil. Occidental was the only one to be paid in cash.

* * *

As I look back on a long life, if there is any one thing I did of importance for our world, it was in seeing that the ownership of our major sources of energy was bound to change hands and doing my small part to smooth the transfer of power.

I do not overexaggerate when I say that changing Occidental's arrangement with Libya that day also, in its way, changed the course of the world and saved it from endless turmoil.

In reporting on those changes, *Forbes* magazine concluded: *"In retrospect, the Occidental-Libya settlement by sale of 51 percent of the production may well have been the most important single event since the end of World War II—and one that marked a turning point for the modern world."*

In Gratitude

This book of stories was written with deep gratitude to my four exceptional sons—John, Isaac, Hewitt and Kerr—for the endless joy they have given me over the course of a long life. John and Hewitt, in our brief time together, gave my life great happiness, and at their passing, the deepest, never-ending heartaches anyone could ever know.

Isaac and Kerr, born 28 years apart, enhance my life every day I live with their contrasting worlds—worlds that keep my mind alive and waiting anxiously for their next chapter. Isaac has already made his fame by giving some of the world's greatest cities his two original cultures—the Hard Rock Cafe and House of Blues—and by building his magnificent hospital for the poor in India. In a few years, Kerr will be at the threshold, ready to make his try. If he can find in some of my life's experiences a single bit of help and guidance, that alone will give this book the status—for me—of a sensational best seller.

Memphis, Tennessee
July 4, 1997
John Burton Tigrett Sr.